Race, Time, and Utopia

PHILOSOPHY OF RACE

Series Editors
Linda Martín Alcoff, Hunter College and the Graduate Center CUNY
Chike Jeffers, Dalhousie University

Socially Undocumented: Identity and Immigration Justice
Amy Reed-Sandoval

Unruly Women: Race, Neocolonialism, and the Hajib
Falguni A. Sheth

Reconsidering Reparations
Olúfẹ́mi O. Táíwò

A Realistic Blacktopia: Why We Must Unite to Fight
Derrick Darby

Critical Philosophy of Race: Essays
Robert Bernasconi

Beauvoir and Belle: A Black Feminist Critique of The Second Sex
Kathryn Sophia Belle

Race, Time, and Utopia: Critical Theory and the Process of Emancipation
William M. Paris

Race, Time, and Utopia

Critical Theory and the Process of Emancipation

WILLIAM M. PARIS

OXFORD
UNIVERSITY PRESS

Oxford University Press is a department of the University of Oxford.
It furthers the University's objective of excellence in research, scholarship,
and education by publishing worldwide. Oxford is a registered trade mark of
Oxford University Press in the UK and certain other countries.

Published in the United States of America by Oxford University Press
198 Madison Avenue, New York, NY 10016, United States of America.

© Oxford University Press 2025

All rights reserved. No part of this publication may be reproduced, stored in a retrieval system, transmitted, used for text and data mining, or used for training artificial intelligence, in any form or by any means, without the prior permission in writing of Oxford University Press, or as expressly permitted by law, by license or under terms agreed with the appropriate reprographics rights organization. Inquiries concerning reproduction outside the scope of the above should be sent to the Rights Department, Oxford University Press, at the address above.

You must not circulate this work in any other form
and you must impose this same condition on any acquirer

Library of Congress Cataloging-in-Publication Data
Names: Paris, William M., author.
Title: Race, time, and utopia : critical theory and the process of
emancipation / William M. Paris.
Description: New York : Oxford University Press, 2025. |
Series: Philosophy of race |
Includes bibliographical references and index.
Identifiers: LCCN 2024033186 (print) | LCCN 2024033187 (ebook) |
ISBN 9780197698877 (paperback) | ISBN 9780197698860 (hardback) |
ISBN 9780197698884 (epub) | ISBN 9780197698907 (ebook) |
ISBN 9780197698891 (updf)
Subjects: LCSH: Free will and determinism. | Time management. |
Choice (Psychology) | Teleology.
Classification: LCC BJ1461 .P345 2024 (print) | LCC BJ1461 (ebook) |
DDC 123/.5—dc23/eng/20240905
LC record available at https://lccn.loc.gov/2024033186
LC ebook record available at https://lccn.loc.gov/2024033187

DOI: 10.1093/oso/9780197698860.001.0001

The manufacturer's authorised representative in the EU for product safety is
Oxford University Press España S.A. of El Parque Empresarial San Fernando
de Henares, Avenida de Castilla, 2 – 28830 Madrid (www.oup.es/en or
product.safety@oup.com). OUP España S.A. also acts as importer into Spain
of products made by the manufacturer.

To my father, whose life was an example of having one foot in this world and the other in the next.

Contents

Acknowledgments   ix

    Introduction   1

1. Racial Justice and the Problem of Consciousness   23
2. Race and the Fragmentation of Time: Critical Theory and the Utopian Hermeneutics of *The Souls of Black Folk*   57
3. Contesting the Polity: Black Nationalism, Utopia, and the Reconstruction of Racial Life   98
4. Racial Fetishism and the Alienation of Time: A Fanonian Critical Theory of Utopia   145
5. Justifying Freedom: James Boggs and the Utopia of Black Power   176

    Conclusion   219

Bibliography   229
Index   249

Acknowledgments

This book is the end (and beginning) of a long journey in search of my understanding of "utopia" that began at Northwestern University in 2018. I would like to, firstly, thank José Medina for the postdoctoral fellowship at Northwestern University as well as his incredible mentorship and support over the years. I truly do not think this book would have emerged without his counsel and intellectual engagement. Secondly, a special thanks to Megan Hyska for her friendship and willingness to read my work in various stages of completion. Her curiosity and generous spirit have been invaluable. Finally, I would like to thank the entire Northwestern University community—Barnor Hesse, Jennifer C. Nash, Mark Alznauer, Cristina Lafont, Penelope Deutscher, Axel Meuller, and Rachel Zuckert—for both their one-on-one conversations and their invitations to present my work in their classes.

My philosophical career would not have been possible without the faith and support of my dissertation advisors Robert Bernasconi and Nancy Tuana. Their professional and personal advice over the decade-plus that we have known each other has indelibly shaped my work, my teaching, and the mentorship I provide to others. They have been models of support and encouragement that I can only hope to emulate closely in the years ahead. My graduate work at Penn State remains formative and so I would like to thank Leonard Lawlor, Eduardo Mendieta, Amy Allen, Sarah Clark Miller, John Christman, Nicolas de Warren, AnneMarie Mingo, Gabeba Baderoon, Mariana Ortega, Melissa W. Wright, and Lori Ginzberg.

I would also like to thank the friends I have made from my time at Penn State: Desiree Valentine, Kaity Newman, Daniel Smith, Lindsey Stewart, Jameliah Shorter-Bourhanou, Aminah Hasan-Birdwell, and Kimberly Harris. Special thanks to Nicole Yokum for her years of friendship and her amazing work as my postdoctoral fellow at the University of Toronto. Her insightful work on Frantz Fanon and psychoanalysis always remains a generative resource for my own thinking and I return to it often. I would also like to thank Kris McLain. Your willingness to engage in long conversations about both philosophy and family life in person and over the phone have remained real sources of joy and inspiration. Finally, I would like to give my special thanks to Ursula Roessiger for her care, support, and immense philosophical wisdom. Your ingenuity has shaped my thinking on race and utopia in innumerable ways.

Special thanks to my colleagues at the University of Toronto. My cotaught seminar on myth and utopia with Owen Ware was incredibly inspiring. Conversations with Rebecca Comay have sparked insights concerning pessimism and race. Long coffees with Robert Gibbs on utopia and Jewish thought were of immeasurable value. I would also like to thank Sergio Tenenbaum, Jennifer Nagel, Rachel Barney, Donald C. Ainslie, Imogen Dickie, Tarek R. Dika, Joseph Heath, James John, Michael Miller, Amy Mullin, Avia Pasternak, Christian Pfeiffer, Michael A. Rosenthal, Gurpreet Rattan, Arthur Ripstein, Marleen Rosemond, and my department head Martin Pickavé for making me feel welcome and supporting my work on this book.

I would also like to thank Kwesi Thomas for his absolutely stellar work as my research assistant in the Summer of 2023. Your comments, critiques, and editorial work were absolutely essential to the completion of this book. Thank you. I would also like to thank the graduate students at University of Toronto who have engaged with my ideas on utopia, critical theory, and W. E. B. Du Bois: Leena Abdelrahim, Matthew Delhey, Spencer Albert, Carlos Anaya, Alexander Drusda, and Caitlin Hamblin-Yule.

Although my time at Wesleyan University was short, I want to thank the faculty and students for making me feel most welcome and engaging with my ideas. In particular, I would like to thank Lori Gruen, Stephen W. Horst, Joseph T. Rouse, and Elise Springer. Our conversations over coffee, meals, and hikes were invaluable during the difficult year of 2020.

Furthermore, I would like to thank the institutions over the years that have invited me to present some of the ideas in this book to their departments and communities: Loyola University Chicago, Marquette University, Pomona College, Elon University, University of Sheffield, University of Western Ontario, Queen's University, Siena College, UC

ACKNOWLEDGMENTS xi

Berkeley, the Black Research Network at the University of Toronto, Western University, St. Louis University, University of Guelph, McMaster University, University of Waterloo, Boston University, Carelton University, and Penn State University.

I would like to thank the editors at *Puncta: Journal of Critical Phenomenology* for their comments on an earlier version of chapter 1, published as "Crisis Consciousness, Utopian Consciousness, and the Struggle for Racial Justice," *Puncta: Journal of Critical Phenomenology* 5, no. 4 (2022): 144–166. Their insights and feedback undoubtedly made the work stronger.

The support for this book extends beyond the universities at which I have taken up residence. I would like to take a moment and thank these individuals: Maria del Rosario Acosta Lopez, Lauren Guilmette, Ryan Johnson, Lewis Gordon, Tommy J. Curry, Joel Reynolds, Olúfemi O. Táíwò, Melissa Rees, and Ashley J. Bohrer.

In particular, I would like to thank Liam Kofi Bright for his comments on an early version of chapter 2 and all of his other philosophical help and encouragement. I would also like to thank Laura Specker Sullivan for our summer workshop groups. Exchanging chapters was immensely helpful as I worked to finish the book. I would like to thank Jeta Mulaj and Jacob Singer for their in-depth feedback on earlier version of chapter 5.

I would like to thank Peter Ohlin and series editor Chike Jeffers for their vote of confidence in the project. I would also like to think the anonymous reviewers for Oxford University Press and their helpful suggestions on how to refocus and sharpen the book.

Special thanks also goes out to Margy MacMillan for all the copyediting work on the entire manuscript and the words of encouragement. I am deeply grateful.

I would be remiss if I did not give special thanks to Sadie Evans for listening to my struggles, keeping me on task, being a sounding board for my ideas, and, of course, making sure I took care of myself during the final months of this project. I could not have asked for a better partner in all senses of the word.

Finally, I would like to thank my mother. I cannot imagine that any of this would have been possible without her. And to answer her constant question over the years, "Is the book done yet?," I can finally answer "Yes." I hope it makes you proud.

Introduction

Utopia as Historical Tendency, Not Ideal Model

Race, Time, and Utopia is a reconstruction of what I take to be the utopian tendencies that have been immanent in historical processes of emancipation from racial domination. It is a social theory of how domination has been contested and how our present social relations frustrate the ongoing task of full self-emancipation. In other words, it does not have as its foundation an account of *racial justice* per se as developed in the ideal/non-ideal literature of political philosophy.[1] Indeed, my critical theoretical paradigm of utopia departs markedly from contemporary approaches to utopia in political philosophy.[2] Both defenses and criticisms of utopia in contemporary political philosophy take utopia to be a model that the theorist *applies to* social reality in the interest of generating ideas concerning the just society. This usage of utopia, as an abstract conceptual device, is consonant with what Charles Mills has described as the "ideal-as-idealized-model."[3] What I take to be the defining element of utopia in this tradition is the implicit concession that utopia is not a historical tendency that has

---

[1] See Charles W. Mills, *The Racial Contract* (Ithaca, NY: Cornell University Press, 1997); Charles W. Mills, *Black Rights/White Wrongs: The Critique of Racial Liberalism* (New York: Oxford University Press, 2017); Bernard Boxill, *Blacks and Social Justice*, revised ed. (Lanham, MD: Rowman & Littlefield, 1992); Howard McGary, *Race and Social Justice* (Malden, MA: Blackwell, 1999); Tommie Shelby, "Racial Realities and Corrective Justice: A Reply to Charles Mills," *Critical Philosophy of Race* 1, no. 2 (2013): 145–162; Tommie Shelby, *Dark Ghettos: Injustice, Dissent, and Reform* (Cambridge, MA: The Belknap Press of Harvard University Press, 2016).

[2] "We view political philosophy as realistically utopian: that is, as probing the limits of practicable political possibility." John Rawls, *Justice as Fairness: A Restatement*, ed. Erin Kelly (Cambridge, MA: The Belknap Press of Harvard University Press, 2001), 4. See also Ben Laurence, *Agents of Change: Political Philosophy in Practice* (Cambridge, MA: Harvard University Press, 2021), esp. 34–36, and David Estlund, "Utopophobia," *Philosophy & Public Affairs* 42, no. 2 (Spring 2014): 113–134.

[3] Mills, *Black Rights/White Wrongs*, 74.

shaped the world, but is an ideal that the philosopher introduces to social affairs.

The dominance of this mode of theorizing has eclipsed an alternative conception of utopia as embodied by the work of the Marxist philosopher Ernst Bloch.[4] Bloch conceptualized utopia as a historical "surplus" whose genesis was to be located in past struggles for emancipation. This surplus, often captured by prescient works of art, contains explosive and as yet unfulfilled expectations of a classless society. He notes that "great art and great philosophy is not only its time manifested in images and ideas, but it is also *the journey of its time and the concerns of its time if it is anything at all*, manifested in images and ideas. From this vantage point, it is new for its time. From the vantage point of all times, it is that which is not yet fulfilled."[5] Unlike Bloch, I will not constrain my analysis to works of art. Instead, I will look at different historical contexts of struggles against racial domination.

Nevertheless, Bloch introduces a compelling alternative to conceptual accounts of utopia. He does so by developing a social ontology of historical struggles for emancipation that suggests utopia is both immanent to the conduct of agents in the world and tends to exceed the historical contexts of its emergence so long as the conditions of emancipation have not been fulfilled. It is this surplus from "failed" struggles for emancipation, Bloch supposes, that provides the resources for new struggles of emancipation freed from ideologies that tend to naturalize our present form of life. Utopia is a non-synchronous *tendency* that runs up against our established patterns of life. As opposed to ideology which "justifies its time" the utopian surplus that is bound up in the real histories of emancipatory struggles "rips open the times" and not only explodes our common sense, but raises our expectations for what society needs to become.[6]

---

[4] Ernst Bloch, *The Principle of Hope*, vol. I, trans. Neville Plaice, Stephen Plaice, and Paul Knight (Cambridge, MA: MIT Press, 1986); Ernst Bloch, *The Utopian Function of Art and Literature: Selected Essays*, trans. Jack Zipes and Frank Mecklenburg (Cambridge, MA: MIT Press, 1988); Ernst Bloch, *Heritage of Our Times*, trans. Neville Plaice and Stephen Plaice (Cambridge, UK: Polity, 1991); Ernst Bloch, *Traces*, trans. Anthony A. Nassar (Stanford: Stanford University Press, 2006).

[5] Bloch, *Utopian Function*, 38.

[6] Bloch, *Utopian Function*, 39. I am influenced by Daniel Bensaïd's distinction between necessity as "what will happen" and necessity as the delineation of "the horizon of struggle" that establishes what must be confronted for the accomplishment of social

I will have much more to say about Bloch in the chapters that follow. But it is worth noting that on this account utopia is not an ideal model that the philosopher imposes upon society. It is a conceptual analysis of real historical movements and a reconstruction of the principles that animated them. Naturally, the problem is that many of these struggles did not succeed, did not slough off the conditions that make domination possible, and thus we must ask how it is possible to grasp a tendency that has not yet been fully actualized. What follows should be understood as an archaeology of utopian tendencies as understood by Ruth Levitas. The archaeological approach attempts to piece "together the images of the good society that are embedded in political programmes and social and economic policies."[7] My amendment to Levitas's formulation is that I will not attempt to put together an image of the *finished* good society, but instead I aim to illuminate a real historical *process* that has been blocked, covered over, and distorted by our present social relations. It is a process that remains unfinished and whose completion cannot be accomplished in theory, but through the self-emancipation of actually existing agents. No doubt the risk of this approach, as Dan Swain has observed, is that I must presume "that there has to be something to excavate and reconstruct."[8] I leave to the reader's final judgment whether this is so. My intuition has been to begin from the indignities of racial domination and develop a more comprehensive account of how domination is sustained and what emancipation entailed by attending to the arguments of historical figures like W. E. B. Du Bois, Martin Delany, Marcus Garvey, Frantz Fanon, and James Boggs.

I am aware that by positioning this book so closely to the tradition of critical theory as developed through Marxism the centrality of "utopia" must appear puzzling. After all, was it not Friedrich Engels who

---

emancipation even though it is always possible that the utopian tendency will fail. Daniel Bensaïd, *Marx for Our Times: Adventures and Misadventures of a Critique*, trans. Gregory Elliott (New York: Verso, 2002), 57.

[7] Ruth Levitas, *Utopia as Method: The Imaginary Reconstruction of Society* (New York: Palgrave Macmillan, 2013), 153.

[8] Dan Swain, *None So Fit to Break the Chains: Marx's Ethics of Self-Emancipation* (Boston: Brill, 2019), 116.

castigated the "Utopians" of his time for thinking that "[t]he solution of social problems . . . [will] evolve out of the human brain. . . . It was necessary, then, to discover a new and more perfect system of social order and to impose this upon society *from without by propaganda*."[9] The argumentative sweep and context of Engels's analysis depends on the idea that utopia is merely a theoretical blueprint that utopians arbitrarily force onto the dominated proletariat. His concern was that this approach neither understood the sources of domination nor grasped that emancipation must also be a process of self-emancipation. The account of utopia that I reconstruct shares neither of these disqualifying qualities. In fact, I think his critique hits closer to home for ideal theory in much political philosophy.

Which is not to say that only because Engels thinks these are disqualifying criteria one must assent that it is so. Instead, the normative spine of my argument in what follows is that a free society must emerge from the transparent process of self-emancipation. Insofar as self-emancipation is taken to be a utopian process it can neither neglect developing a social theory of how a given society blocks self-emancipation nor can it presume to dictate what an emancipated society will look like in the day to day. The social theory of what blocks the actualization of utopian tendencies, I think, must begin with an analysis of the domination of time and history by a given form of life.

Utopias and the Indignities of Social Domination

I aim to develop the hypothesis that racial domination is at bottom the domination of time by one group over another and thus emancipation must entail delivering the control of time out of the hands of one set of agents and into another's. I admit this hypothesis will seem obscure at first given that most analyses of racial injustice focus on workplace discrimination, residential segregation, police violence, or wealth inequality, to name a few. What I hope to show is that a society cannot be racially unjust without fragmenting the social time of the dominated.

---

[9] Friedrich Engels, "Socialism: Utopian and Scientific," in *The Marx-Engels Reader*, 2nd ed., ed. Robert C. Tucker (New York: W. W. Norton, 1978), 687.

In fact, on closer inspection, when talking about racism it is hard not to notice how thoroughly the motif of time underwrites the feelings of indignation that attend the experiences of racial injustice. For instance, Toni Morrison claims "the very serious function of racism ... is distraction. *It keeps you from doing your work.* It keeps you explaining over and over again, your reason for being. Somebody says you have no language and so you spend 20 years proving that you do."[10] Notice the invocation of time being *wasted* by the implication that one's history does not exist. Or we could look at the common invocation of imprisonment as "doing time" when we think of the unjust imprisonment rates in many poor black and brown communities. We need not only focus on the months and years that the incarcerated individual loses, but also the lost time that is felt by the families and community of the individual.[11] Finally, we may look at Ruth Wilson Gilmore's famous definition of racism as "the state-sanctioned and/or extralegal production and exploitation of group differentiated vulnerabilities to *premature* death."[12] Lives and livelihoods cut short by unjustified and arbitrary powers cannot but appear as the unjust interruption of social time.

These are only three examples of distinct forms of racial injustice, but all involve some form of curtailing or shaping the course of time for an individual or social group. How we arrange our time is the fundamental basis of all social life. In his examination of the relationship between slavery, time, and freedom, Mark H. Smith observes how "former slaves tended to interpret their freedom in terms of having the right to regulate and define their own work and rest hours, in other words, to lay incontrovertible claim to their own nonnegotiable

---

[10] Toni Morrison, "A Humanist View," Portland State University's Oregon Public Speakers Collection, May 30, 1975, https://www.mackenzian.com/wp-content/uploads/2014/07/Transcript_PortlandState_TMorrison.pdf.
[11] See Tommie Shelby, *The Idea of Prison Abolition* (Princeton, NJ: Princeton University Press, 2022), 75–76.
[12] Ruth Wilson Gilmore, "Race and Globalization," in *Abolition Geography: Essays toward Liberation*, ed. Brenna Bhandar and Alberto Toscano (New York: Verso, 2022), 107; emphasis added. See also Latoya Hill and Samantha Artiga, "What Is Driving Widening Racial Disparities in Life Expectancy?," KFF, May 23, 2023, https://www.kff.org/racial-equity-and-health-policy/issue-brief/what-is-driving-widening-racial-disparities-in-life-expectancy/.

time."[13] The struggle for emancipation from racial domination, I think, will tend to have as its foundation the struggle for control over one's time; it will tend to be the concomitant struggle against the indignity of having one's time constrained by the arbitrary and uncontestable whims of others. If I am right on this score, then critical theory can aid the project of racial justice by elucidating the mechanisms for disciplining time in a given form of life.[14] Where one works, how one's time is directed on the job, how long one has to work, how much time one has to save and spend, in what ways one's time is deemed valuable are all important questions to answer if we are to envision a racially just society.

The sociologist Rudolf Rezsoházy argues, "Each society, with its corresponding culture, works out a certain conception of time which is accepted as natural by the majority of its members and used as a criterion for regulating their activities." He continues, "Within each society, significant groups such as social classes, town and country dwellers, or different generations, may diverge considerably in the way they conceptualize time and behave in relation to it, and in their manner of using it."[15] A society may be comprised of distinct *forms* of life that organize time according to different rhythms and values. For instance, how time is organized when one goes to work (what speed one must work at, which habits are considered most productive, what ends are to be accomplished in a given day) will most likely differ from how time is organized at home with one's family. However, one's job and one's family are embedded in a wider form of life that must manage

---

[13] Mark H. Smith, *Mastered by the Clock: Time, Slavery, and Freedom in the American South* (Chapel Hill: University of North Carolina Press, 1997), 150.

[14] In chapter 3 I will describe these mechanism as "anchoring practices."

[15] Rudolf Rezsoházy, "The Concept of Social Time: Its Role in Development," *International Social Science Journal* 24, no. 1 (1972): 26. Rezsoházy further breaks down social time into five dimensions (timing, the handling of time, forecasting, historical time, time as a value): "time as a value is part of the actor's whole system of values, and plays its part in the choice of the purpose of the action and the rational devising of ways and means; time conceive[d] as progress, or the spirit of progress, also contributes towards the choice of the aims of the action, acting as a vocation and a driving force, the will-power which propels; forecasting intervenes in strategy, as an element of the plan; and the best possible spacing out of time plays a decisive part in implementation and in the everyday conditions of a behavioural model which is essential to the success of any project whose execution depends on the solution in detail of problems involving synchronization and organization of sequences" (34).

and organize time around producing and distributing the essentials of social life. In most contemporary societies, our wider form of life is anchored in the time required for capital accumulation.[16] There is no guarantee that how one wishes to arrange one's time when it comes to family life, work, or even leisure will synchronize with the demands of one's wider form of life. Losing time with one's family, losing one's job, losing time for rest are burdens and indignities that racially dominated peoples face regularly. These "non-synchronicities," as I will call them in chapter 2, ought to be a fundamental concern for racial justice since they strike at the heart of how our social life is organized.

It might seem surprising that a book which promises to provide a critical theory of utopia begins with an account of unfreedom rather than detailed descriptions of "an (as yet) unrealized ideal society."[17] On this model, utopias are vivid accounts of substantially better societies where citizens live in presumed harmony with one another. The foundation of utopias would appear to be something closer to *perfect justice*. From Plato's *Republic* to Thomas More's *Utopia* the image of the just society has been the foremost attribute of these works.[18] As I noted above, I think this common conception of utopia gets things the wrong

---

[16] See Georg Lukács, *History and Class Consciousness*, trans Rodney Livingston (Cambridge, MA: MIT Press, 1971), 88–92; Moishe Postone, *Time, Labor, and Social Domination: A Reinterpretation of Marx's Critical Theory* (Cambridge: Cambridge University Press, 1993), 286–307; E. P. Thompson, "Time, Work-Discipline, and Industrial Capitalism," in *Class: The Anthology*, ed. Stanley Aronowitz and Michael J. Roberts (Hoboken, NJ: John Wiley & Sons, 2018), 27–41; Stavros Tombazos, *Time in Marx: The Categories of Time in Marx's Capital* (Chicago: Haymarket Books, 2014).

[17] David Leopold, "On Marxian Utopophobia," *Journal of the History of Philosophy* 54, no. 1 (January 2016): 113. See also Ben Laurence, *Agents of Change: Political Philosophy in Practice* (Cambridge, MA: Harvard University Press, 2021), 32–35, and Ben Laurence, "Justice in Theory and Practice: Debates about Utopianism and Political Action," *Philosophy Compass* 18, no. 11 (2023): 1–12, https://doi.org/10.1111/phc3.12945. For a contrary view, see Gregory Claeys and Lyman Tower Sargent's claim that "no fixed definition as such is possible" for utopia, in "Preface," in *The Utopia Reader*, ed. Gregory Claeys and Lyman Tower Sargent (New York: New York University Press, 2017), 2.

[18] Plato, *The Republic*, ed. G. R. F. Ferrari, trans. Tom Griffith (Cambridge: Cambridge University Press, 2019) and Thomas More, *Utopia*, 3rd ed., ed. George M. Logan, trans. Robert M. Adams (Cambridge: Cambridge University Press, 2016). Indeed, Hannah Arendt suggests that "Plato, who was the first to design a blueprint for the making of political bodies, has remained the inspiration of all later utopias." Hannah Arendt, *The Human Condition*, 2nd ed., intro. Margaret Canovan (Chicago: University of Chicago Press, 1998), 227.

way round. Utopias are always *responses* to existing problems in social life, and it is the aim of critical theory to reconstruct these problems as injustices that block social freedom.

Whoever reads utopia knows that politics cannot be far behind, and politics, whatever else it may be, is the site of *struggle*.[19] Politics, as many of us are patently aware, is the place of imperfection, fallibility, and disharmony. More to the point, it is precisely because the conflicts of social life can never be fully resolved once and for all that politics will always remain *necessary*. Whether due to bad luck, ordinary human vice, or the "reasonable plurality of conflicting and incommensurable doctrines" such as religious beliefs politics can never dream of achieving a state of uniform perfection.[20] And yet, this is exactly what utopian thinking is often taken to be aiming at: the end of human politics and division. It is this characteristic that has made it an object of derision and fear.

Karl Popper insists that "the Utopian attempt to realize an ideal state, using a blueprint of society as a whole, is one which demands a strong centralized rule of a few, and which is therefore likely to lead to a dictatorship."[21] Judith Shklar, for her part, claims that utopia is "an expression of the craftsman's desire for perfection and permanence. . . . [It] is of necessity a changeless harmonious whole, in which the shared recognition of truth unites all citizens. . . . In utopia, there cannot, by definition, be any room for eccentricity."[22] Against the "utopianism" of socialism, F. A. Hayek insists, "According to our modern planners . . . it is not sufficient to design the most rational permanent framework within which the various activities would be conducted by different persons according to their individual plans. . . . What our planners demand is central direction of

---

[19] "Utopia begins with politics. Utopia might not end with politics, but the nature of political life, the distribution of power among individuals and in society, and the legitimacy of authority over the community lie at the heart of the utopian thought." Mark Stephen Jendrysik, *Utopia* (Cambridge, UK: Polity, 2020), 1–2.
[20] John Rawls, *Political Liberalism* (New York: Columbia University Press, 1993), 135.
[21] Karl Popper, *The Open Society and Its Enemies*, intro. Alan Ryan (Princeton, NJ: Princeton University Press, 2013), 149.
[22] Judith Shklar, "The Political Theory of Utopia: From Melancholy to Nostalgia," in *Utopias and Utopian Thought*, ed. Frank E. Manuel (Boston: Beacon Press, 1967), 105. See also Judith Shklar, *After Utopia: The Decline of Political Faith* (Princeton, NJ: Princeton University Press, 2020).

all economic activity according to a single plan, laying down how the resources of society should be 'consciously directed' to serve particular ends in a definite way."[23] Here we can see a pattern of critique emerging from mid-20th-century liberals that condemn utopianism as driven by a fervor for absolute "justice" that can only end in control and the elimination of individual initiative. Utopias begin by dreaming up an abstract ideal and then seek to impose it on the messiness of social life.[24]

These are damning critiques of utopia. But are they right? After all, we should not be too hasty to dismiss a concept that has been central to struggles against racial injustice and domination.[25] My contention is that criticisms of utopia too often reduce utopian thought and practice to the "blueprint" of the ideal society rather than addressing the injustice that utopia attempts to name. Paul Ricœur helpfully identifies in the phenomenology of utopia the primary experience of *estrangement* from the seemingly natural conditions of one's social life.[26] I think this experience of estrangement, or more precisely separation, is integral to struggles for racial justice. To live in a racially unjust society, I will claim, is to live in society that is patterned on the supposedly natural subordination of one social group to the imposition of arbitrary norms of life by another social group. These norms—whether explicitly racist à la Jim Crow segregation or implicitly so around wealth accumulation that leads to the disadvantage of racially subordinated groups—are

---

[23] F. A. Hayek, *The Road to Serfdom: Texts and Documents*, ed. Bruce Caldwell (Chicago: University of Chicago Press, 2007), 85. See also Chris Matthew Sciabarra, *Marx, Hayek, and Utopia* (Albany: State University of New York Press, 1995).

[24] James C. Scott makes a similar observation as it concerns the tendencies of modern statecraft: "The utopian, immanent, and continually frustrated goal of the modern state is to reduce the chaotic, disorderly, constantly changing social reality beneath it to something more closely resembling the administrative grid of its observations.... The builders of the modern nation-state do not merely describe, observe, and map; they strive to shape a people and landscape that will fit their techniques of observation." James C. Scott, *Seeing Like a State: How Certain Schemes to Improve the Human Condition Have Failed* (New Haven, CT: Yale University Press, 2020), 82.

[25] See Robin D. G. Kelley, *Freedom Dreams: The Black Radical Imagination* (Boston: Beacon Press, 2022); Alex Zamalin, *Black Utopia: The History of an Idea from Black Nationalism to Afrofuturism* (New York: Columbia University Press, 2019); Jayna Brown, *Black Utopias: Speculative Life and the Music of Other Worlds* (Durham, NC: Duke University Press, 2021).

[26] Paul Ricœur, *Lectures of Ideology and Utopia*, ed. George H. Taylor (New York: Columbia University Press, 1995).

interwoven with *justification narratives* that naturalize dominative social relations as either just or, at the very least, unchangeable.[27] Justification narratives include claims about the biological inferiority of the racially dominated or the supposedly regressive culture of the racially dominated. Whatever the content of the narrative, the effect is to bind the racially dominated to norms of social practices and regard that they themselves are not empowered to script or contest. Utopia, then, is the effort to break the grip of these justification narratives by developing freer forms of life that reveal the contingency and lack of justification for domination.

What is potentially emancipatory in utopia is the exercise of renarrating the norms a social group finds legitimate and just. For instance, as I will cover extensively in chapter 3 through the work of Martin Delany and Marcus Garvey, black nationalism should be understood as the critical denunciation of a racial polity that systematically holds black people as underserving of equal regard.[28] The practice of drawing up justifications for why black people should have their own nation is itself a demonstration of the self-activity of black people that also names the injustice of civic exclusion. To say that the dream of an autonomous black nation is infeasible wholly misses the point of the exercise. By taking themselves to be justified in promulgating norms of regard that acknowledge their agency, black people denaturalize the assumption that they are fated to live in a form of life that includes them only to condemn them. More to the point, black nationalism draws a conceptual limit around the racial polity and postulates that there *is* a future beyond it. One need not endorse black nationalism as a political project to appreciate how it reveals racial injustice.

I think the emphasis on implausible perfection and enforced harmony that liberal critics of utopia so disdain reflects their misunderstanding of utopia as the vain yet dangerous wish for a life of unending happiness. But when one observes what the dominated in racially

---

[27] I adapt the concept of justification narratives from the work of critical theorist Rainer Forst. See chapter 3 for an in-depth engagement with this concept.
[28] Throughout this book I have made the decision to not capitalize "black" or "white" when referring to races.

unjust societies say and do, one will find that the spur of utopia is rarely unhappiness at one's lot in life, but rather outrage at the indignity of being subordinated to conditions of domination. Douglas Mao insightfully relates utopia to indignation rather than unhappiness when he notes that "[u]nhappiness, even in the form of immiseration on a large scale, may be something to lament, but people will rarely describe themselves as indignant *at* unhappiness itself.... Rather, the indignation at play here must be directed against whoever or whatever is responsible for the unhappiness... that render[s] the totality in need of righting.... Utopias ... tend to train their attention at least as strongly on the *whatever*—on the systems, institutions, customs, and practices that seem most implicated in the going awry of the world."[29] Utopias seek to disclose how a form of life—its institutions, customs, and practices—reproduces unfree social relations through their indignity. To foreclose utopias as dangerous wishes for happiness risks foreclosing a form of social critique that attempts to point toward the possibility of social transformation.

Race, Time, and Utopia anchors utopian critical theory in the analysis of forms of life that systematically impose indignities on the racially dominated. I develop a social theory for why racial injustice will remain a necessary part of political life so long as we remain mired in our current form of life. Far from engaging in the literary work of writing blueprints for the future I will show how utopia emerges from immanent and historical social dynamics of domination. My aim will be to show that understanding utopia is important for any emancipatory theory because utopias are essentially about isolating the mechanisms of domination conceptually so that they can be uprooted practically. Without the critical analysis of how present forms of domination are recursively generated, utopias become what liberal critics lament: vain wishes for the impossible. What we should want from a critical theory of utopia are criteria that will allow us to delimit conceptually the principles that would make possible the achievement of an emancipated form of life.

---

[29] Douglas Mao, *Inventions of Nemesis: Utopia, Indignation, and Justice* (Princeton, NJ: Princeton University Press, 2020), 28.

Racial Injustice, Forms of Life, and the Domination of Social Time

Any given society will be comprised of multiple forms of life. That is to say, people will adhere to diverse patterns of organizing and justifying how they make use of their time. One might think that for all of us, time is divided by seconds, minutes, and hours and thus we all live in the same form of life. We are all given 24 hours in a day, and it is up to us all, individually, to decide how best to maximize the value we can squeeze out of the time that we are given. In this view, abstract and homogeneous time is the "natural" state of the world.[30] Some people may want to spend their time by focusing on their careers, families, or volunteering, for example. What matters is that we are all free to choose what we will do with the finite seconds, minutes, and hours that we have. The assumed naturalness of "clock time," as Lewis Mumford describes it, allows us to develop a sense of injustice as the unjustified control or evaluation of another's time.[31] To impose one form of life onto another is to violate their dignity as a self-determining agent who has their own reasons for shaping the pattern of their life in light of their own values and goals. So, preliminarily, we might distinguish between forms of life by examining how a bundle of social practices normatively shapes the use of time.

For instance, we might look at the normative criteria that comprise childhood education. Students are often evaluated according to how well they perform vis-à-vis the generic student at their grade level. Teachers may report that an individual student in the sixth grade is reading at a "fourth-grade level" and thus has fallen "behind." Similarly, an employee will find themselves evaluated according to the average output of their fellow employees. Now what distinguishes the school from the workplace are not only the standards of measuring "progress," but the putative aims of these practices. The development of a child is not the same as the training of an employee. If a middle manager

---

[30] See Byron Ellsworth Hamann, "How to Chronologize with a Hammer, or, The Myth of Homogenous, Empty Time," *HAU: Journal of Ethnographic Theory* 6, no. 1 (2016): 261–292.

[31] Lewis Mumford, *Technics and Civilization* (Chicago: University of Chicago Press, 2010), 14–25.

at Amazon went to an elementary school art class and "graded" the students according to their speed and efficiency in order to determine what their wages would be, we would think that not only has a category mistake been made about what is appropriate to the form of life that is elementary school, but the introduction of these practices threaten to dissolve the ethical significance of the educational form of life. To reduce the time of childhood to the time of employment seems to us, now, an injustice insofar as we think that the compulsion to work would erode the dignity of what it means to be a child.

It is important to recognize that this limit between childhood and employment is not a historically invariant fact, but the product of political struggle. Karl Marx describes the long struggle between capital and the working class over the appropriate length of the working day for working-class children. In a particularly vivid passage, Marx describes capital's agitation over laws that sought to limit the employment of children: "This turned on the age-limit of the category of human beings who, under the name 'children,' were restricted to 8 hours of work and were subject to a certain amount of compulsory education. *According to the anthropology of the capitalists, the age of childhood ended at 10, or, at the outside, 11.*"[32] We can glean three important insights from this brief examination of the separation of childhood and employment. First, forms of life, as Rahel Jaeggi notes, always have a normative character or make some claim about the appropriate evaluation of time organization.[33] Second, these forms of life can and do conflict with other forms of life over how time should be organized. Third, political struggles often concern whether a particular form of time discipline will have the power to shape a particular form of life.

I take these three insights as offering a different grammar for evaluating the persistence of racial injustice that departs from the focus on "the distribution of benefits and burdens" in a given society.[34]

---

[32] Karl Marx, *Capital: A Critique of Political Economy*, vol. 1, trans. Ben Fowkes, intro. Ernest Mandel (New York: Penguin Classics, 1990), 392, emphasis added.
[33] Rahel Jaeggi, *Critique of Forms of Life*, trans. Ciaran Cronin (Cambridge, MA: Harvard University Press, 2018), 41–42.
[34] Tommie Shelby, *Dark Ghettos: Injustice, Dissent, and Reform* (Cambridge, MA: Harvard University Press, 2016), 20. See also Bernard Boxhill, *Blacks and Social Justice*, revised ed. (Lanham, MD: Rowman & Littlefield, 1992); McGary, *Race and Social Justice*; and Mills *Black Rights/White Wrongs*.

Instead we might understand racial injustice as the domination of one form of time discipline over other forms of life. Charles Mills points in this direction in his critique of the colonial "Euro-story" that relegated non-white peoples to the status of uncivilized "savages or barbarians." He goes on to claim, "The temporality of the Marxist narrative likewise privileges the West, with its stadial progression of primitive communism, ancient slavery, feudalism, capitalism, and then socialism. The times of the non-West are awkwardly articulated to this historical materialist calendar. If capitalism is a progressive social formation, its onrushing time to be valorized as dissolving the time-encrusted links of the past, so that all that is solid melts into air, then the alternative times of, say, Amerindia, Asia, pre-colonial Africa, Native Australia, become devalued."[35] Now Mills is mostly focused on how the dominant *narrate* the time of the dominated in order to justify either regimes of oppression or, at the very least, condescension toward racial others. He thinks that "[i]n revising the accepted narrative of the relations between colonialism, African slavery, and European Enlightenment liberalism and egalitarianism . . . a new temporal order [can] be created for all of us, rendering obsolete the 'racial' time of human groups in relations of domination and subordination and signaling the advent of a new and united egalitarian time for the human race as a whole."[36] Mills, rightly, in my view, emphasizes the centrality of narratives for justifying how we organize our time. His argument ends on what one may see as a "utopian" note that calls for a new narrative of our form of life that includes all people.

Narratives, however, are only one component of the racial domination of time. Racial injustice also includes the practical subsumption of the dominated to orders of time that erode forms of life with alternative temporal organizations. In his description of the antebellum American South, Mark Smith argues that the rise of the Industrial Revolution imposed a form of life defined by mechanical clock time

---

[35] Charles W. Mills, "The Chronopolitics of Racial Time," *Time & Society* 29, no. 2 (2020): 312–313. For a contrary view of Marx's own understanding of progress and capitalism, see Harry Harootunian, *Marx after Marx: History and Time in the Expansion of Capitalism* (New York: Columbia University Press, 2017), ch. 1.
[36] Mills, "Chronopolitics," 314.

onto forms of life that were committed to "natural time" that oriented work around the rhythms of seasonal agriculture.[37] The organization of time through endlessly competitive global markets compelled slave owners to develop new techniques for efficient production or risk being wiped out.[38] The irony of this shift is that once slaveholders adopted clock time as a "legitimate arbiter of social and economic organization" they altogether seemed to increase their dominative power over the time and labor of the enslaved, while they themselves became ever more dominated by the implacable demand to squeeze ever more value out of every minute and hour.[39]

Now the injustice of chattel slavery might seem rather obvious. There is one group of people who are forced to submit to the will of another group. What I want to analyze is the implicitly temporal character of the domination here. The slaveholders had to subsume the enslaved to the organizational norms of clock time where one's time has calculable value (in terms of a wage) without incorporating them as agents who have the standing to contest and negotiate the constraints of clock time. After all, in principle, the time of the enslaved belonged to the slaveholders and thus they had no need to justify to the enslaved how they would use their time. One might think that in the long term, having the enslaved be *in* but not *of* a form of life that equated value and freedom with how the individual uses their time is inefficient, but that is beside the point. What is important is to grasp how racial injustice is underwritten by domination over time. Mark Smith insists that the enslaved did not internalize clock time until they were free and had to accept "the logic of timed labor [where] they effectively joined the ranks of the burgeoning international proletariat" and they, thus, came to understand "the value and nature of time, its marriage to money, its insidious, ubiquitous tyranny, and that its ownership stood at the fulcrum of class relations."[40] The wrong I aim to diagnose in this book is

---

[37] Smith, *Mastered*, 11–14.
[38] On the relationship between plantations and market dependence, see John Clegg, "A Theory of Capitalist Slavery," *Journal of Historical Sociology* 33, no. 1 (2020): 74–98 and John Clegg, "Capitalism and Slavery," *Critical Historical Studies* 2, no. 2 (2015): 281–304.
[39] Smith, *Mastered*, 14.
[40] Smith, *Mastered*, 174.

not reducible to either inclusion or exclusion. Rather I want to show that the terms of inclusion are what matter.[41]

Binding a form of life to the normative time-discipline of another form of life that cannot be contested is an inhibition of freedom. Martin Hägglund argues, "To be free is not to be free *from* normative constraints, but to be free *to* negotiate, transform, and challenge the constraints of the practical identities in light of which we lead our lives. The question is not *if* our freedom will be formed by social institutions—there can be no freedom that does not have institutional form—but *how* and *by which* social institutions our freedom will be formed."[42] Forms of life are the condition of freedom insofar as we are practically free to interrogate and transform how they organize our time and toward what ends. But insofar as these norms and justifications are outside of our power to modify or control, then our time is dominated. As I will show in chapter 4, in the work of Frantz Fanon we can find the resources for a critical theory that examines how social institutions of the past can come to deprive freedom of access to the temporality of novelty and creativity. I will argue that racially unjust societies tend to reproduce what I call *racial fetishism* where the time of racialization appears to control our social conduct. Indeed, I will argue that an important facet of racial justice should be the emancipation from a form of life that disconnects social practices from the freedom of self-determination.

The problem is that we really do live in societies where diverse forms of life are increasingly disciplined by a form of life that appears to be outside the control of ordinary agents. Societies organized around the accumulation of capital radically shape the time organizations and

---

[41] Keeanga-Yamahtta Taylor, in her examination of unfair housing policies in black communities, argues, "The reality of a racialized political economy challenged the idea that inclusion in the financial and public services that for so long had excluded African Americans was enough to overcome the physical and economic devastation of Black urban communities ... inclusion in those processes while ignoring the larger dynamics created by residential segregation laid the basis for even greater exploitative and predatory practices—or predatory inclusion—in transactions involving the urban unhousing market." Keeanga-Yamahtta Taylor, *Race for Profit: How Banks and the Real Estate Industry Undermined Black Homeownership* (Chapel Hill: University of North Carolina Press, 2019), 254.

[42] Martin Hägglund, *This Life: Secular Faith and Spiritual Freedom* (New York: Anchor Books, 2019), 274.

expectations of other forms of life. The sociologists Pitirim A. Sorokin and Robert K. Merton noted in 1937, "With the spread of interaction between groups, a common or extended time system must be evolved to supersede or at least to augment the local time systems. Since the rhythm of social activities differ[s] in different groups or within highly differentiated society, local systems of time reckoning are no longer adequate."[43] Insofar as any form of life must have some relationship to labor and production in order to persist over time, we should inquire into how the time of labor and production are organized. If it is true that capitalist societies have radically changed how we organize our time, then it would be implausible to think that the problems of racial injustice are not also substantially modified by this form of life. Indeed, if we take the emergence and reproduction of a capitalist form of time as a historically specific problem for racial injustice then our critical theory of utopia should reflect this problematic. I will suggest that contemporary forms of racial injustice, unlike in the time of slavery, are not primarily a problem of direct coercion through the threat of violence (though violence obviously remains) but the internalization of a time-discipline that one must assume but cannot contest.[44]

Barbara Adam describes the reification of time where "time is controlled and where it is used as a medium for the translation of labour power into a monetary value" that circumscribes much of contemporary life.[45] The task that I set myself in this book is the analysis of the tension between racial injustice that seems concrete and particular and the domination by the abstract time of the market throughout social life. What I aim to show is that this tension does change the terrain of racial injustice, but also makes clear that an ongoing motif of struggles for emancipation is the struggle for control over the value and normative constraints of one's time.

---

[43] Pitirim A. Sorokin and Robert K. Merton, "Social Time: A Methodological and Functional Analysis," *American Journal of Sociology* 42, no. 5 (March 1937): 627.

[44] David S. Landes, for instance, distinguished between mere "time obedience" and "time discipline": "One can ... use public clocks to summon people for one purpose or another, but that is not punctuality. Punctuality comes from within, not from without." David S. Landes, *Revolution in Time: Clocks and the Making of the Modern World*, revised and enlarged ed. (Cambridge, MA: Harvard University Press, 2000), 6.

[45] Barabra Adam, *Timewatch: The Social Analysis of Time* (Cambridge, UK: Polity Press, 1995), 28.

Thus, two questions orient the arc of this book. First, how should we diagnose and conceptualize the temporal domination of racial injustice? Second, if we have internalized this form of life then with what resources can we develop principles for a transformed and free form of life that we have never experienced? These two questions bind together "critical theory" and "utopia" to develop both a novel account of injustice and the principles of a not yet experienced freedom.

Plan of the Book

In what follows, I develop an account of racial injustice that centers the relationship between freedom and time. I analyze the writings of W. E. B. Du Bois, Martin Delany, Marcus Garvey, Frantz Fanon, and James Boggs in conjunction with critical theorists and contemporary political philosophers of race. My hope is that I demonstrate the critical resources that can be found in the ideas of past thinkers of racial injustice as well as generate a coherent paradigm for analyzing contemporary forms of racial domination in capitalist societies.

Chapter 1 provides an overview of what I take to be the central problematic of contemporary accounts of racial injustice: why does it remain so difficult to build durable constituencies that can struggle for racial justice? I contest accounts that foreground either ignorance or insensitivity on the part of the majority. Instead, I argue that we should develop a social theory that explains the potential relationship between consciousness and social relations. Through the concepts *crisis consciousness* and *utopian consciousness* I claim that struggles for social transformation will often emerge when background expectations for social practices no longer reliably establish the conditions for success. For instance, during the COVID-19 pandemic millions of people found their habits and expectations for their work life radically disrupted and thus were forced to question how they were to continue on successfully. This was a key element in the emergence of the George Floyd protests. I describe this as a moment of crisis consciousness. However, crisis is not enough to sustain the transformation of a dominating form of life. What is needed is the transformation of collective expectations for how society should be organized that pushes people to move beyond their present form of life. I call this utopian consciousness. The problem, as I will elaborate, is that crisis consciousness and utopian consciousness are rarely synchronized; they are often temporally out of joint. The crisis conditions that make social transformation appear necessary rarely accord with practices necessary for envisioning a more just form of life and vice versa.

Chapter 2 picks up this thread concerning the out-of-joint temporality of racially dominating societies with an examination of the early works of W. E. B. Du Bois. In Du Bois, we find a rich social ontology of the political and cultural dislocations that attend the economic transformations at the turn of the 20th century. Du Bois attempts to cope with these transformations by training a cadre of African-American leaders—the Talented Tenth—who will mediate between the black proletariat and the wider society. What Du Bois discovers, despite himself, is that the Talented Tenth are out of sync with the social practices of the black working-classes they are meant to lead and the form of life they seek to reform. What he shows is that racial injustice more often disintegrates rather than integrates any sense of sharing a form of life insofar as it curtails some futures in favor of others. There will always be members of the racially dominated who live in relative freedom and security and thus have a different sense of the past, present, and future than other members. My hypothesis is that the internal differentiation and fragmentation of social temporality is not an accidental feature of racially unjust societies, but that such societies are necessarily *temporally out of joint* or what Ernst Bloch calls *Ungleichzeitigkeit* (non-synchronous).[46]

In chapter 3, I attempt to explain the source of non-synchronicity in racially unjust societies by explicating how racial domination entails foreclosing the ability of the dominated to critique and transform the normative justifications that organize their time. I claim that the black nationalism of Martin Delany and Marcus Garvey expressed a utopian yearning for creating a space of reasons where black citizens have the sovereign power to organize and discipline social time how they see fit. I take Delany and Garvey as espousing the position that the nation

---

[46] Ernst Bloch, *Heritage of Our Times*, trans. Neville Plaice and Stephen Plaice (Cambridge, UK: Polity Press, 1991).

is the form of life that anchors other social practices, and thus to be in but not of a nation is to lack control and dignity. The utopian insight of black nationalism is that social transformation requires uprooting the more fundamental practices that anchor the expectations and justifications of a form of life. However, I will argue that the tendency to conflate nation and race risks reifying race as if it has a life of its own independent of our social practices rather than following from the organization of our social practices. Racial justice does indeed require changing our anchoring practices so that new forms of life may be developed. However, struggles for racial justice must accomplish these transformations without fetishizing race as an alien force that controls our conduct.

Chapter 4 expands on what I call *racial fetishism* through a close reading of the work of Frantz Fanon. Here I argue that racial fetishism, which I take to be analogous to commodity fetishism as described by Marx, blocks struggles for racial justice in two interrelated ways.[47] First, racial fetishism introduces cognitive distortions into the experience of all agents living in racially unjust societies that make it *appear* as if race operates independently of our social practices. Second, race can appear this way because the organization and effects of our social practices really are not under our control. Fanon articulates a concern that racially unjust societies mire agency in the "dead" social practices of the past and thus foreclose the creative and future-oriented element of human action. What he calls the "zone of non-being," I argue, is the utopian capacity of agents to transgress the limits of past experience and introduce novel expectations into social life.[48] Racial fetishism, as I interpret it through Fanon, is a symptom of unjust economic relations that gives the racially dominant power over the racially dominated. Thus, racial fetishism is a *secondary* phenomenon to the *primary* conflict of the capitalist form of life. However, what is important in Fanon

---

[47] For insightful accounts of what Marx meant by "commodity fetishism," see Arthur Ripstein, "Commodity Fetishism," *Canadian Journal of Philosophy* 17, no. 4 (December 1987): 733–748 and Norman Geras, "Essence and Appearance: Aspects of Fetishism in Marx's *Capital*," *New Left Review* 65 (1971): 69–85.

[48] Frantz Fanon, *Black Skin, White Masks*, trans. Richard Philcox (1952; New York: Grove Press, 2008), xii; Frantz Fanon, *Œuvres*, ed. Jean Khalfa and Robert Young (Paris: La Découverte, 2011), 64.

is that the secondary nature of racial fetishism does not mean that it is less important or without its own complexity. Instead, it shows that racial fetishism is anchored in a broader form of life and thus can help explain the ongoing reproduction of racial injustice.

Chapter 5 concludes these investigations by examining what I take to be the connection between black power and utopia in the work of James Boggs. A Detroit autoworker who analyzed the impact of automation and deindustrialization on black working-class communities, Boggs offers crucial resources for a social theory that relates the objective temporal dynamics of capitalist societies to regressive habits and social practices. Boggs insists that capitalist societies are forms of life where technological production rules over political capacities and decision-making. Boggs offers a theory of black power that aims at critiquing and displacing the power of capitalist social relations over black forms of life. Bringing Boggs into conversation with the work of Rainer Forst, I argue that we should understand black power as a framework for envisioning a society where social relations are transparent and open to critique from the racially dominated. This would necessitate the creation of society where the justifications for how we organize our social time are brought under the control of contestable political institutions rather than political institutions being constrained and enabled by the "silent compulsion of economic relations."[49] It is only by moving beyond the *conflictual form of social time* that typifies the capitalist form of life that we can reach the "egalitarian time" of which Mills speaks.[50]

A critical theory should endeavor to present an account of social life that diagnoses and evaluates how its subjective and objective aspects condition and mediate one another. By focusing on the out-of-joint temporality of horizons, their anchoring practices, and the conflictual form of time in which they are situated I show that racial justice requires more than the equal distribution of goods. What we should theorize is the possibility of overcoming the conflictual form of time that uproots and destabilizes the coherence of our social practices. This is the *utopian* aspect of my analyses that has less to do with

[49] Marx, *Capital*, 899
[50] Mills, "Chronopolitics," 314.

imagining a wholly different way of life than drawing the insight from our social conditions that our present form of life wreaks havoc on our *forms of life*. Racial justice will require a focus that goes beyond the state, to the transformation of the social form of time in which the state is itself embedded.

1
Racial Justice and the Problem of Consciousness

Introduction

Consciousness seems to have a central, if ambiguous, status in theorizations of social transformation. After all, in the context of hermeneutical injustice we speak of the importance of "consciousness-raising."[1] We point to young people and activists as evidence of a radical consciousness that is aware of injustices to which previous generations are assumed to have been insensitive. We even highlight the importance of changing social consciousness in order to produce more just norms of recognition as it concerns differences in race, gender, sexuality, and ability. In one view, consciousness appears as a site of agency in theories of historical freedom and thus should be the central object of critical attention.

Nevertheless, consciousness just as often appears to be an obstacle to social transformation. In the Marxist tradition, "false consciousness" prevents agents from understanding the influence of noncognitive motives such as economic constraints in their belief formations.[2] Alternatively, agents may not know or understand the "implicit" beliefs that they hold in reference to other social groups and thus might not

---

[1] See also Miranda Fricker, *Epistemic Injustice: Power and the Ethics of Knowing* (New York: Oxford University Press, 2007) and José Medina, *The Epistemology of Resistance: Gender and Racial Oppression, Epistemic Injustice, and Resistant Imaginations* (New York: Oxford University Press, 2013) on the epistemically liberatory effects of the oppressed collectively cognizing unjust social structures.

[2] Tommie Shelby, "Ideology, Racism, and Critical Social Theory," *Philosophical Forum* 34, no. 2 (Summer 2003): 170–172. Michael Rosen offers a compelling genealogy and critique of the concept of false consciousness in *On Voluntary Servitude: False Consciousness and the Theory of Ideology* (Cambridge, UK: Polity Press, 1996).

grasp essential features of their subject formation.[3] Furthermore, certain strains of Marxist and psychoanalytic theorizing would object to an overemphasis on the capacity of consciousness to alter its social environment or autonomously form itself, respectively.[4] These theories instead urge us to focus on the role of social forces (of the market or the unconscious) that are external to agents and will determine the shape of consciousness.

Unless one subscribes to a strictly functional-determinist view of social reality, consciousness then, however ambivalent, will have some role to play in theories of social transformation and justice. When we refer to consciousness in the context of theories of social transformation, we might mean the minimal capacity for agents to cognize and become aware of what is around them. However, I think this is too thin for a plausible theory of social transformation (as I will argue at length). According to what I will call the *awareness model of consciousness*, consciousness tends to be figured as mostly passive or reactive and therefore cannot adequately explain why agents attempt to reshape the form of life in which they live. After all, we can assume many agents are aware of the injustices they face within a form of life, but rebellion and protest are the exception, not the rule. If one subscribes to a version of the awareness model of consciousness, then the explanation for the lack of apparent struggle to change our form of life will rest

---

[3] See Charles Mills, *Black Rights/White Wrongs: The Critique of Racial Liberalism* (New York: Oxford University Press, 2017), 49–72, and George Yancy, *Black Bodies, White Gazes: The Continuing Significance of Race in America* (New York: Rowman & Littlefield, 2017), 17–51. It is not the focus of my project in this book, but it is important to note that serious questions have been raised about the efficacy of scientifically tracking "implicit" biases as opposed to "explicit" biases. For instance, Samuel Reis-Dennis and Vida Yao, in their article "I *Love* Women: An Explicit Explanation of Implicit Bias Test Results" (*Synthese* 199, nos. 5–6 [2021]: 13861–13882) contend that the IAT (Implicit Association Test) does not sufficiently control for the hypothesis that it captures explicit beliefs agents hold rather than implicit. This means that our approach to belief formations such as racism need not presume that these beliefs are hidden or unthematized by agents. If this holds then the contemporary focus on agents needing to excavate beliefs that have hitherto remained beyond the reach of their consciousness may be counterproductive.

[4] See Louis Althusser, "Ideology and Ideological State Apparatuses," in *Lenin and Philosophy and Other Essays*, trans. Ben Brewster (New York: Monthly Review Press, 2001), 85–127 and especially Étienne Balibar, *The Philosophy of Marx*, trans. Chris Turner (New York: Verso, 2007), 46–77 on "commodity fetishism" in Marx.

on some idea that agents have been duped by ideology.[5] Critical theory should resist an overemphasis on ignorance as a social explanation and instead, as Robin Celikates argues, "tie in with everyday practices of justification and critique, rather than . . . take the historically rare and empirically implausible extreme of total ideological blindness as a starting point."[6]

In place of the awareness model of consciousness, I argue theories of social transformation should describe consciousness as the agential capacity to establish *horizons of normative expectations*.[7] Agents actively construct justifications for what ought to happen in the course of their interactions with social environments and delimit what they take to be possible or impossible given what they know of their environment. A normative expectation can range from "If I keep my head down the police should not bother me" to "Assuming society will always be arranged in this manner I should do *x* if I am going to bring some stability to my life." Horizons of normative expectation allow agents to

---

[5] What I mean by the "awareness model of consciousness" indicates what I take to be the commonsense orientation toward how social problems are conceptualized. For instance, Jacob Blumenfeld makes the following observation in the context of climate change: "There is the common belief that genuine awareness and acceptance of the existence of anthropogenic climate change (as opposed to either ignorance or denial) automatically leads one to develop political and moral positions which advocate for collective human action toward minimizing suffering for all and adapting human societies toward a fossil-free future. This is a mistake. Against the idea that scientific awareness of the facts of climate change is enough to motivate a common ethical project toward a unifying good, I argue that climate change awareness can just as well equally motivate heightened divisions of humanity into anti-egalitarian, xenophobic, class-differentiated zones of competitive survival." Jacob Blumenfeld, "Climate Barbarism: Adapting to a Wrong World," *Constellations* 30, no. 2 (2023): 162–178. I will make a similar argument in the second section of this chapter.

[6] Robin Celikates, *Critique as Social Practice: Critical Theory and Social Self-Understanding*, trans. Naomi van Steenbergen (New York: Rowman & Littlefield, 2018), 7.

[7] My conception of "horizons of normative expectations" bears some similarity to Kim Sterelny's analysis that a necessary element for the success of our cognitive processes is that we can intervene in and engineer our environments to support our projects. Kim Sterelny, "Minds: Extended or Scaffolded?," *Phenomenology and the Cognitive Science* 9, no. 4 (2010): 466. My focus, however, will consider that our environments are not solely up to us as individuals and thus constrain our activities and expectations. See Valerie Soon, "Implicit Bias and Social Schema: A Transactive Memory Approach," *Philosophical Studies* 177, no. 7 (2019): 1866: "Expectations shape our cognitive processes, which in turn lead us to respond in certain ways to the environment. Our responses subsequently shape the environment itself, influencing our own expectations as well as those of others."

form a practical relationship with the objective constraints in their life.[8] When we observe agents' behaviors within certain environments, we should be cautious about attributing specific ideologies or beliefs, explicit or implicit, as explanatory for why someone chooses one option rather than another. Instead we ought to examine the incentive structures of the environment in which they are embedded and how those enable or frustrate the attainment of specific needs and desires. My use of horizons of normative expectations will show that diverse agents may hold differing beliefs and yet still be induced to engage in similar behaviors due to a shared understanding of their constraints. In other words, horizons of normative expectations are not solely, or even primarily, reducible to the beliefs of individuals, but constitute a common ground for social practices between multiple agents.[9]

It is when these horizons can no longer anchor an agent's rational justifications for their social practices that we can expect the possibility of social transformation. Social environments that can no longer support agents with insight into how they can meaningfully arrange their lives, that can no longer provide grounds for coherent social practices, will produce turmoil. Thus, a more robust theory of social transformation should take consciousness as actively producing norms while never being completely ignorant of how those norms relate to the surrounding social environment. I will elaborate on this experience of social disequilibrium as a moment when past practices fail to have a coherent relationship to the future.

To better understand these agential capacities, I contend that we should have two typologies of consciousness that will be operative in conjunctures where an extant form of life appears to be on the brink of breakdown. Drawing from the work of Brian Milstein and Ernst Bloch, I will describe these two forms of consciousness as

---

[8] Soon encapsulates my claim here in relationship to Rational Choice Theory and ideology: "Even if individuals are aware that they are acting in response to perverse incentive structures and disagree with the ideology embodied by these structures, it is not instrumentally rational for them to act otherwise as long as sufficiently strong incentive structures remain. . . . Ideology should be understood non-ideationally in terms of conventions, or equilibrium solutions to social coordination problems." Valerie Soon, "Social Structural Explanation," *Philosophy Compass* 16, no. 10 (2021): 6.

[9] Olúfemi Táíwò, "The Empire Has No Clothes," *Disputio* 10, no. 51 (December 2018): 309–314.

"crisis consciousness" and "utopian consciousness," respectively.[10] Consciousness comes to play a critical role in social transformation in a two-stage sequence, I will argue. First, when available epistemic and normative resources are no longer able to solve problems or functionally predict how to accomplish projects within a form of life, a *crisis consciousness* will form. Second, in the context of a crisis, if it is possible to grasp the social causes of dysfunction and develop insight into the real possibilities in the situation that would allow for the development of an alternative form of life that would displace the causes of dysfunction, then a *utopian consciousness* can take shape. By understanding consciousness as the activity of justification rather than merely awareness we will be able to develop a more plausible account of social transformation that takes seriously the structural constraints of a form of life and the necessity for political capacities that can overcome those constraints.[11] How we justify the constraints a form of life places on our social practices is central to the "progressive" expectations we develop for social life and also what we take to be possible. My hypothesis is that these justifications exercise power over our conduct and thus when they are in crisis there is an opening for new modes of critique to emerge.

In what follows, I will outline what I take to be a central problematic concerning the relationship between consciousness and form of life: if a form of life places constraints on consciousness, how can the latter fundamentally reshape the former? By reference to some arguments from the conservative neoliberal philosopher F. A. Hayek, I will

---

[10] Brian Milstein, "Thinking Politically about Crisis: A Pragmatist Perspective," *European Journal of Political Theory* 14, no. 2 (2015): 141–160; Ernst Bloch, *The Principle of Hope*, vol. 1, trans. Neville Plaice, Stephen Plaice, and Paul Knight (Cambridge, MA: MIT Press, 1995).

[11] My argument here is informed by Rainer Forst's notion of "justifying reason" and his argument that "[e]very social order must be conceived as an *order of justification*. It consists of a complex web of different justifications, some of which have congealed into justification narratives, that exercise hegemonic power—and provoke counternarratives, such as those put forward by the Levellers or by Locke against Filmer's defense of absolute monarchy as the exercise of paternal power. However self-enclosed such an order of justification may be, it always presents points of attack for critique through its claim to legitimacy . . . namely, the claim not to be subjected to any form of rule that cannot be adequately legitimized toward those who are subjected to it." Rainer Forst, *Normativity and Power: Analyzing Social Orders of Justification* (Oxford: Oxford University Press, 2017), 34–35.

demonstrate that the awareness model of consciousness is ill-equipped to answer the preceding question. I will then argue that a phenomenology of crisis consciousness offers a more plausible account of how agents come to challenge the constraints of their form of life. However, I will conclude that crisis consciousness is not sufficient, and we require recourse to utopian consciousness if we are to adequately explain how a form of life can be structurally altered. I then conclude with an assessment of the current struggle for racial justice in the United States.

On the Limits of the Awareness Model of Consciousness

A "form of life" is here defined as the relatively stable configuration of economic structures, political institutions, and interpretive frameworks that allow agents to make predictions about what actions stand the best chance of satisfying their needs and desires.[12] If we start with this conception of form of life, then we can see that taking consciousness to be primarily an organ of awareness and cognition does not take us very far in explaining why agents do what they do and how they come to participate effectively in social transformation. Living within a form of life is not only a matter of recognizing its substantive reality. First and foremost, an agent must justify their actions to themselves in light of their prediction that given the current configuration of the form of life this action will meet with success.

Certain argumentative strategies and pedagogical approaches take the obstacle of agents' consciousnesses to social transformation to be premised on false beliefs they hold about the substantive reality of the form of life.[13] The idea is that the distorted beliefs agents hold can offer a causal explanation for the actions they take and the persistence of

---

[12] See Jon Elster, *The Cement of Society: A Study of Social Order* (Cambridge: Cambridge University Press, 1995), 97–152 for an elaboration of how social norms coordinate behavior through the distribution of shame and expectation.

[13] Mills, *Black Rights/White Wrongs*; Charles Mills, "Global White Ignorance," in *Routledge International Handbook of Ignorance Studies*, ed. Matthias Gross and Linsey McGoey (Abingdon: Routledge, 2015), 217–247; Linda Martín Alcoff, "Epistemologies of Ignorance: Three Types," in *Race and Epistemologies of Ignorance*, ed. Shannon Sullivan and Nancy Tuana (New York: State University of New York Press, 2007), 39–59.

forms of life. Charles Mills argues, "The political economy of racial domination *required* a corresponding cognitive economy that would systematically darken the light of factual and normative inquiry."[14] Mills is most definitely correct in his contention that racial domination often attended assumptions about the innate characteristics of dominated populations. However, taking cognitive distortions as a requirement would suggest that the rectification of our awareness would remove a necessary condition for the continuation of racial domination.

What I have been describing as the awareness model of consciousness pervades commonsense diagnoses of ongoing racial injustice. These diagnoses implicitly assume that "at the heart of these patterns of racial injustice is a structure of social relations that is *ideologically sustained* in spite of legislative, judicial and individual efforts to change it."[15] The idea that our "collective epistemic failings" are sufficiently explanatory for why an unjust form of life remains in place suggests that what inhibits our collectively transforming our arrangements is that "individuals in the grip of an ideology fail to appreciate what they are doing or what's wrong with it, and so are unmotivated, if not resistant, to change."[16] Without denying that this does in fact happen, we should still ask what we should expect from agents once they are no longer in the grip of ideology. Do they feel differently? Think differently? Speak to others differently? Or act differently? One can imagine an agent thinking differently and still engaging in similar behaviors as before. I may be aware that air travel contributes to climate change, but that does not mean that I will hop on a bus to visit my mother who lives two thousand miles away.

It is for the following reason that I find the awareness model of consciousness limiting: it fails to provide a consistent explanation

---

[14] Mills, "Global White Ignorance," 217, emphasis mine. Mills goes on to say later that "'whiteness' must be operative in the right way in producing, at least tendentially, a particular cognitive orientation to the world, an aprioristic inclination to get certain kinds of things wrong" (218). Interestingly, Mills is more circumspect here where he claims that there is a *tendency* to get salient normative and empirical facts about the world wrong in a world dominated by the practices of racial domination.

[15] Sally Haslanger, "Culture and Critique," *Proceedings of the Aristotelian Society Supplementary* 91 (2017): 152, emphasis mine.

[16] Haslanger, "Culture and Critique," 152.

for why it seems possible for a form of life to remain in place even as the doxastic beliefs of agents within said order have shifted markedly. One explanation that could be offered is that extracognitive interests in the maintenance of the status quo tend to overwhelm moral awareness, and thus we have a problem of *akrasia* or weakness of the will. Another explanation might suggest that the cognitive awareness was not thoroughgoing enough and so did not produce a "true" conversion of consciousness. Either explanation risks admitting that awareness is not a very effective lever for transforming a form of life and therefore raises the question of why make it central to a theory of social transformation.[17]

The deeper problem of the awareness model of consciousness in a form of life is that it does not sufficiently distinguish a quotidian lack of awareness concerning the complexity of a form of life from the lack of awareness that frustrates social transformation. When I go to the grocery store and see that the price of milk has gone up relative to last week, I most likely do not have an awareness of all the macro and micro interactions that went into presenting this number before me. Instead, I may be frustrated at how this upsets the budget I had planned for myself. But let's say an economist sits me down with an assortment of graphs and the capacity to translate their expertise to me so that I become aware of what economic mechanisms most likely led to the price increase. I may understand my social world better, but when I return to the grocery store, I still have hard and complex choices to make given the constraints of my form of life. In other words, given that I am aware, now what do I do?

In the foregoing example we can see that the awareness of social facts does not necessarily furnish consciousness with practical knowledge. It might not even be enough to unseat the justifications imposed by

---

[17] The preceding point is made in Joseph Heath, "Ideology, Irrationality and Collectively Self-Defeating Behavior," *Constellations* 7, no. 3 (2000): 363–371 and Kirun Sankaran, "What's New in the New Ideology Critique?," *Philosophical Studies* 177, no. 5 (2019): 1441–1462. They raise the concern that an overemphasis on ideology as sufficiently explanatory for the continuance of unjust social arrangements fails to explain "the causal connection between the critique of ideology and social change" given that "they systematically ignore the role strategic considerations play in driving and preventing social change" (Sankaran, "What's New," 1449).

economic power.[18] Instead, these social facts may appear to me as *only* external constraints on my social activity that, however regrettably, I must learn to navigate. The limitation of conceptualizing awareness as one of the central obstacles to racial justice or social transformation is that this theoretical focus does not generate a convincing account of how agents come to have knowledge of their freedom over and above knowledge of their constraints. In the best-case scenario, we are often left with a picture of consciousness alienated from an external form of life over which it cannot exert much agency, rather than grasping the form of life as immanent to one's life and practical activity. There is a real, substantive difference between acquiring knowledge of a moral or social wrong and developing the knowledge of how to address that wrong. Why wouldn't increasing awareness of the depth and complexity of systemic racism, economic exploitation, and rampant environmental degradation lead to the conclusion that one's ideological beliefs matter very little when compared to entrenched incentive structures and practical considerations? Indeed, we can imagine that upon realizing how dependent and intertwined our social practices are with the existing form of life I may come to conclude that there is very little *we* could do. Somewhat surprisingly, the awareness model of consciousness tends to coincide with conservative arguments against the role consciousness can play in social transformation when confronted with the reality that most people do not agitate for the radical transformation of social life.

For instance, F. A. Hayek provides a sharp rebuke to conceptions of consciousness that entail the possibility that agents can ever fully cognize the conditions of their form of life.[19] For Hayek, consciousness is always nested within a complex set of traditions, institutions, and biological processes that limit what an agent can make explicit about their social world. Nevertheless, Hayek does not think our form of life functions as only a limit to the activity of consciousness; a form of life provides the tacit and abstract rules that make it possible

[18] Søren Mau, *Mute Compulsion: A Marxist Theory of the Economic Power of Capital* (London: Verso, 2023).
[19] F. A. Hayek, *The Constitution of Liberty* (Chicago: University of Chicago Press, 2011) and *Studies on the Abuse and Decline of Reason* (Chicago: University of Chicago Press, 2018).

for consciousness to provide expectations for itself, make predictions about the actions of others, and critically analyze limited regions of one's social life. Hayek inveighs against the conception of reason that he calls Cartesian which assumes "an independently and antecedently existing human reason that invented these institutions" in favor of understanding a form of life as having "evolved by a process of cumulative growth and that it is only with and within this framework that human reason has grown and can successfully operate."[20] It is important for Hayek that consciousness be put in its proper place. Consciousness can never become fully aware of all the rich complexity of its form of life insofar as that might throw the form of life into doubt. Hayek presumes that our capacity for awareness and knowledge already presupposes the validity of the very form of life that is to be critiqued and thus cannot logically surpass it. Hayek finds such wholesale critique to be implausible because it would assume that consciousness can self-generate an order of complexity greater than the form of life that made consciousness possible.

Following the insights of Burkean conservatism and the Scottish Enlightenment, Hayek sees forms of life as the accretion of generations of spontaneous and experimental activities that for one reason or another survived their environments against other models of social cooperation.[21] He challenges what he takes to be the hubris of individuals who believe they can replace such a complex and unplanned historical process by conscious fiat.[22] Hayek defends this position by claiming,

---

[20] Hayek, *The Constitution of Liberty*, 112.

[21] Bruce Caldwell, *Hayek's Challenge: An Intellectual biography of F. A. Hayek* (Chicago: University of Chicago Press, 2005), 288–323 provides a comprehensive summary of this aspect of Hayek's thought wherein he came to believe that forms of life were the slow accumulation of generations-long experimentation by individuals and social groups who were simply seeking their own advantage. Hayekian social theory presumes that no amount of knowledge could replace the delicate and complex mechanisms of self-organizing spontaneity and experimentation.

[22] This claim of Hayek's has invited the critique that he has an undue reverence for tradition and ends up in a political quietism. I think there is something to this criticism, but we can understand Hayek to be making the weaker claim that elements of our form of life survived because *at one time* it was most advantageous. However, it does not follow that as our environments change this will remain the case. See Gerald Gaus, "Hayek on the Evolution of Society and Mind," in *The Cambridge Companion to Hayek*, ed. Edward Feser (Cambridge: Cambridge University Press, 2006), 232–259. We can always critique *elements* of our form of life, but not the form of life as a whole.

"Far from assuming that those who created the institutions were wiser than we are, the evolutionary view is based on the insight that the result of the experimentation of many generations may embody more experience than any one man possesses."[23] For Hayek, attempts to replace forms of life with conscious planning inevitably court disaster. He inveighs against Marxists and positivists for what he considers the utopianism of their "constructivist" rationality that supposes alternative forms of life can be imposed once we have become sufficiently aware.

Hayek's epistemological conservatism (to say nothing of his political conservatism) offers an important challenge to the awareness model of consciousness in theories of social transformation because if he is right then it is neither possible nor advisable for agents to become wholly aware of their form of life and thereby critique the foundations of their form of life *in toto*. From an allegedly less conservative direction, Alasdair MacIntyre chides Descartes's presumption of "radical doubt" because no one can doubt everything in their tradition at once.[24] Instead doubt works by presupposing that some crucial elements of the form of life must remain provisionally undoubtable.

Hayekian social theory sets before theories of social transformation a crucial test that we ought not assume we have passed. The test is whether we can plausibly explain how and why it is that agents come to demand a structural rearrangement of their social life. I do not think moral or empirical awareness sufficiently answers this question. We can make a number of people aware of injustices that occur within a form of life, and we can even make them aware of alternative visions of social life, but awareness is not sufficient to encourage people to disrupt their practices of justification as they lead their lives. By Hayek's lights, agents do not enter into crisis voluntarily, but instead seek equilibrium in their social life. Nor should we expect that putting agents into crisis reliably leads to progressive social transformation. More often than not, if the form of life can restore some semblance of equilibrium in an agent's social life, radical challenges will dissipate even if the awareness does not.

---

[23] Hayek, *The Constitution of Liberty*, 122.
[24] Alasdair MacIntyre, "Epistemological Crises, Dramatic Narrative and the Philosophy of Science," *The Monist* 60, no. 4 (October 1977): 458.

My aim in turning to Hayek in this section is not to claim that he is wholly correct in his social theory, but to point out how the awareness model of consciousness tends to agree with Hayek in practice. After all, Hayek does not deny that we can make local reforms to our form of life. He just insists that these reforms always remain limited in scope. The awareness model cannot explain why agents would dissolve their links to a form of life that allows them to make reliable, local predictions of how to successfully navigate their social life. Because it cannot do so, awareness, in practice, often culminates in acts of token recognition of racial injustice or piecemeal reforms that aim to preserve our existing form of life. Undoubtedly certain piecemeal reforms can make agents' lives better, but then we are explaining how a form of life conserves itself rather than how it might be transformed.

Hayek represents a constellation of ideas and assumptions that regard the possibility of radical, democratic transformation with suspicion. These ideas and assumptions have become the background common sense against which struggles for racial justice are framed. Given that a central principle of Hayek's social theory is our systemically necessary and inalterable ignorance, the idea of collective, self-conscious transformation represents a profanation of the "natural" time of progress.[25] Hayekian social theory justifies a world where legal and cultural mechanisms prevent any sudden transformations of the rhythm of economic practices. In other words, it is important to discipline social time according to the supposedly unquestionable ebb and flow of economic progress.[26] Nowhere is Hayek clearer on this than

---

[25] "It is misleading to think of those new possibilities as if they were, from the beginning, a common possession of society which its members could deliberately share; they become a common possession only through that slow process by which the achievements of the few are made available to the many. This is often obscured by the exaggerated attention usually given to a few conspicuous major steps in the development. But, more often than not, major discoveries merely open new vistas, and long further efforts are necessary before the new knowledge that has sprung up somewhere can be put to general use. It will have to pass through a long course of adaption, selection, combination, and improvement before full use can be made of it" (Hayek, *The Constitution of Liberty*, 96).

[26] "The changes to which such people must submit are part of the cost of progress, an illustration of the fact that not only the mass of men but, strictly speaking, every human being is led by the growth of civilization into a path that is not of his own choosing. If the majority were asked their opinion of the changes involved in progress, they would probably want to prevent many of its necessary conditions and consequences and thus ultimately stop progress itself. And I have yet to learn of an instance when the deliberate

when he considers the example of a conservative European peasant who may "cherish their way of life, though it has become a dead end," but has become "too dependent on urban civilization, which is continually changing, to preserve itself."[27] What I want to draw attention to is how Hayek naturalizes and endorses economic processes as the mechanism for disciplining our social practices such that we are "not only the creatures but the captives of progress."[28] It is the function and evaluation of the mechanisms for organizing and discipling social time that characterize a form of life and its appearance of stability for consciousness.

Without endorsing Hayek's specific politics, what I have called the awareness model of consciousness tends to reproduce the Hayekian foreclosure on utopia by leaving undertheorized how our form of life disciplines our social time and thus makes "progress" little more than what Kathi Weeks describes as "better versions of the present rather than visions of radically different worlds."[29] Weeks distinguishes utopia from pragmatic reform by focusing on the ways political change conceptualize progress and temporality. Pragmatic reform tends to reify the world as what Bloch calls "the mechanical Time and Time again."[30] Conversely, utopia takes aim at the mechanisms of time discipline and seeks to bring them under the control of reason so that agents can truly direct their progress. My hypothesis is that the prospect of social transformation emerges when these mechanisms of time discipline (for Hayek, these are explicitly market relations) become dysfunctional. When this happens new expectations for progress may become practical because time has become "free" for self-direction.[31]

---

vote of the majority (as distinguished from the decisions of some governing elite) has decided on such sacrifices in the interest of a better future as it made by free-market society" (Hayek, *The Constitution of Liberty*, 104).

[27] Hayek, *The Constitution of Liberty*, 103.
[28] Hayek, *The Constitution of Liberty*, 105.
[29] Kathi Weeks, *The Problem with Work: Feminism, Marxism, Antiwork Politics, and Postwork Imaginaries* (Durham, NC: Duke University Press, 2011), 196.
[30] Bloch, *The Principle of Hope*, 286.
[31] E. P. Thomson's work on the evolution of time discipline and industrial capitalism is instructive here when he muses over what the possible conditions for a new form of life would have to be: "But if the purposive notation of time-use becomes less compulsive, then men might have to re-learn some of the arts of living lost in the industrial revolution: how to fill the interstices of their days with enriched, more leisurely,

This would mean that an objective crisis in a form of life offers a more plausible account of why protests emerge than an account that begins from the awareness of moral injustice.[32] A critical mass find their interpretive frameworks can no longer succeed in justifying how they live their lives and thus an objective crisis transitions into a subjective crisis for consciousness. Here we find an important limit to Hayekian social theory insofar as it cannot explain what happens when the form of life itself produces the crisis. For this I now turn to my description of crisis consciousness.

The Phenomenology of Crisis Consciousness

When we speak of a social system being in "crisis" we are generally designating two phenomena. Seyla Benhabib separates these two phenomena out as "systemic crisis" and "lived crisis."[33] A systemic crisis is the observation of dysfunctionality or breakdown in how a form of life distributes wealth, justice, or power. Thus, we may call it "objective." Lived crisis, on the other hand, is the experience for agents of needs, demands, and dissatisfactions generated by the form of life in which they live. In this manner it is "subjective." A systemic crisis may be the daily fines, harassment, arrests, and evictions carried about by the

---

personal and social relations; how to break down once more the barrier of work and life," E. P. Thomson, "Time, Work-Discipline, and Industrial Capitalism" in *Class: The Anthology*, ed. Stanley Aronowitz and Michael J. Roberts (Hoboken, NJ: John Wiley & Sons, 2018), 37.

[32] Allen W. Wood makes this point clearly when he explains, "A historically potent demand, a genuine and effective *need* for emancipation arises in an oppressed class only under certain conditions. This need does not appear merely as a social ideal ... it arises, according to Marx's theory, only where there is a disharmony or antagonism between the productive forces and the existing production relations." Allen W. Wood, "The Marxian Critique of Justice," *Philosophy & Public Affairs* 1, no. 3 (Spring 1972), 279. In other words, when the pandemic and economic slowdown made apparent that social needs could no longer be satisfied under the existing arrangements, new and fervent political activity formed. Rather crudely, we can say that *need* rather than ideals of *justice* provide a more robust explanation for the change in behavior that was witnessed in 2020. Of course, this does not deny that many participants in the protests used the language of injustice to describe what was done to George Floyd.

[33] Seyla Benhabib, *Critique, Norm, and Utopia: A Study of the Foundations of Critical Theory* (New York: Columbia University Press, 1986), 12.

police in a poor neighborhood.[34] The lived crisis would be the experience of blocked projects, being unable to reliably predict whether one will have job or housing security, and the moral indignation that one's life ought not be subject to such conditions. Separating out the general notion of crisis into two distinct phenomena allows us to analytically specify the relational structure immanent to crises and ask questions I contend are foreclosed by the awareness model of consciousness.

Schematically, if we accept Benhabib's criteria, we can see the crisis of a form of life and crisis consciousness are in a relationship of dependence. For there to be crisis consciousness there must at least be the sense for the agent *of* a breakdown somewhere in their social world. It simply would be incoherent to contend that there is crisis consciousness, yet the agent experiences their world as essentially sound.[35] For this reason, and assuming that agents do not typically invent a sense of crisis, we should suppose that systemic crises or objective crises of a form of life have analytic primacy in any social theory of crisis consciousness. However, it is important not to make the mistake in assuming that crisis consciousness is inessential. What I designate

---

[34] I flesh out what I take to be the formal criteria necessary for designating a constellation of practices as a "crisis" in this section. But in selecting this example, I hope two ideas become immediately clear. First, "crisis" is already a normatively thick concept that presumes an "ethical-functional understanding of norms of ethical life" (Rahel Jaeggi, *Critique of Forms of Life*, trans. Ciaran Cronin [Cambridge, MA: Harvard University Press, 2018], 128). In other words, through *immanent critique* we should be able to assess whether a nexus of social practices contravenes a form of life's putative ethical norms *and* whether these practices produce systemic dysfunction or rather solve social problems. Second, a crisis is *always* a crisis for specific, context-bound agents. Fines and evictions may not appear as crises for police and landlords, but for citizens undergoing them they present real problems for actualizing their freedom according to the constraints of the extant form of life. I should stipulate that this form of critique assumes that "a historically sensitive formal anthropology" (Karen Ng, "Ideology Critique from Hegel and Marx to Critical Theory," *Constellations* 22, no. 3 [2015]: 401) is necessary for us to adjudicate how and when capacities for freedom are being systemically blocked by the practices of a form of life.

[35] I will not focus on this possibility, but I believe this formulation leaves open the conceptual possibility of *manufactured crises* wherein agents may assume a breakdown exists because of ideological conditioning even though in fact the crisis does not objectively obtain. Examples include moral panics over Critical Race Theory being taught in schools and the United States government justifying its war powers by appeal to ever imminent terrorist attacks. However, I think a complex theory of crisis consciousness would not stop at the conclusion that the agents involved are "dopes" (Celikates, *Critique as Social Practice*, 1–19), but would inquire into whether there are actual dysfunctions in the form of life that consciousness has miscast.

as a general crisis is necessarily the objective fact of some dysfunction in the social world *and* a normative demand to resolve the source of dysfunction. As Brian Milstein puts it, "Crisis belies the traditional distinctions between empirical science and normative philosophy: it is an objective event, but it is one whose urgency demands a normative commitment on the part of those involved in it. It is an inherently *reflexive* concept."[36] While an objective crisis does not depend, in the first instance, on the existence of crisis consciousness there can be no general crisis without the interiorization of it by agents.

A general crisis has both ethical and functional components. It is crucial that both are at play when understanding how crisis consciousness can form. A form of life that is afflicted with only an objective crisis may be one in which the existing norms and practices do not function very well, but it does not appear to those who participate in the form of life that the crisis is *because* of one's social practices. For example, a heatwave may cause a drought that disrupts the agricultural practices of a community. This is no doubt a crisis insofar as crops cannot be grown and sold, but agents may not see anything wrong with how they live their lives. It is just that misfortune happens. However, once droughts appear to be the result of social and economic practices that lead to a warming planet, then a form of life appears to not only be failing, but unjustifiable. The loss of justification, at the very least, leads to a crisis of confidence in one's form of life insofar as the bridge between one's past practices and one's presupposed future collapses.

The generation of crisis consciousness is crucial because it indicates that agents hold "normative presuppositions and expectations" that a form of life systematically violates or obstructs.[37] A form of life functions or retains some patina of legitimacy insofar as its violations of normative expectations are experienced as local and isolated rather than widespread and systemic. If a form of life is experienced as no longer capable of or justified in resolving normative problems of social life, then a decision will have to be made by agents as to why this form of life should be kept in place. I am not suggesting that this indicates that social transformation is imminent since there may be relevant

---

[36] Milstein, "Thinking Politically about Crisis," 143.
[37] Milstein, "Thinking Politically about Crisis," 146.

objective and subjective constraints to the development of an alternative form of life. I will cover these constraints in detail in the following section. My only point is that the form of life is put into question rather than being tacitly assumed as the background condition for normative expectations.

The central difference between the awareness model of consciousness and crisis consciousness is that the latter generates a degree of alienation from a form of life whose severity goes far beyond moral indignation. When agents are in crisis, they characterize their form of life not only as unjustifiable according to the ethical norms of the form of life, but *unlivable* in light of its functional norms.[38] This social arrangement of economic imperatives, political institutions, and moral categories systematically obstructs an agent's normative expectations of how to carry out their life projects. Contrariwise, if we imagine one of the goals of social justice is to make those with privilege aware of injustices then we must also admit the possibility that these agents may be persuaded that their form of life is unjust, but they can still find it quite livable in terms of planning their livelihood and security.[39] It is possible to argue that these agents have a moral duty to address injustices upon becoming aware of them, but that is not the focus of my argument. I am suggesting, more pragmatically, that awareness is not a sufficient causal explanation for social transformation. A higher-order condition must be met.

Assuming that horizons of normative expectations are essential for the activity of consciousnesses nested within a form of life, we should expect crises to incite agents involved in the situation to resolve the dysfunction. This is often felt as both a functional necessity *and* an ethical imperative. We need to solve this problem, but also social life

---

[38] "Indeed, one of the facts Hegel acknowledges is that however contradictory a form of life may be, and however much of an impact that way of being untrue may have on the lives of its participants, people live with those contradictions and whatever anguish they bring with them for centuries. If anything, that seems to be a fact about human psyches. However, for Hegel, the more interesting question has to do with when such contradictions become so compelling that we must acknowledge them and thus when the anguish in living within those contradictions becomes too much. At that point, the lives in a form of life become uninhabitable." Terry Pinkard, *Hegel's Naturalism: Mind, Nature, and the Ends of Life* (New York: Oxford University Press, 2012), 118.

[39] David Kinney and Liam Kofi Bright, "Risk Aversion and Elite-Group Ignorance," *Philosophy and Phenomenological Research* 106, no. 1 (2023): 35–57.

ought not be this way. Awareness or consciousness-raising does not necessarily meet these criteria. My awareness may lead me to conclude that the police ought not treat citizens in a certain manner or that banks should be fairer in how they distribute mortgages to black people. However, this type of consciousness can often take for granted that the institutions being critiqued are necessary for the functioning of our form of life and the problems occur at the point of distributing rights and goods.

Rahel Jaeggi's distinction between a moral critique and an ethical critique of capitalism is helpful here. A moral critique or "a *narrow* one of internal distributive justice" tends to assume that the configuration of social life functions well, but second-order distortions have accrued to its practices.[40] There is no necessary disruption of an agent's horizon of normative expectations. Indeed, an agent can coherently argue that what the form of life is for them it should be for everyone. In the aftermath of highly publicized police shootings of black citizens there are always white people who will write columns detailing how when they were in a similar situation the police let them off with a warning or a mere fine. The argument appears to be "the police should treat black people the way they treat white people." The fact that the police shoot white citizens as well leads one to suspect that there is either a fundamental misunderstanding of the functional role of policing in our current form of life or that justice demands having a statistically better chance of having a non-violent encounter with the police.

An ethical critique, according to Jaeggi, addresses "*the rationality and ethical standing of a form of life*" as such. It would not assume that problems of racial injustice, for instance, are second-order problems of distribution, but that the constitutive relations of social life are both ethically deficient *and* functionally deleterious to social life as a whole.[41] The experience of such a crisis whereby the very conditions of one's life are taken to be ethically deficient and functionally deleterious is different in kind from the distance of abstract awareness.

---

[40] Rahel Jaeggi, "What (If Anything) Is Wrong with Capitalism? Dysfunctionality, Exploitation and Alienation: Three Approaches to the Critique of Capitalism," *Southern Journal of Philosophy* 54 (Spindel Suppl. 2016): 58.
[41] Jaeggi, "What (If Anything) Is Wrong with Capitalism?," 58.

In crisis consciousness there is the necessity of either reintegrating one's horizon of normative expectations into an existing form of life or generating a new horizon of normative expectations. Now simply changing one horizon of normative expectations is not the same as creating a new form of life that would anchor those expectations. It may be the case (and often is) that one lacks the knowledge or power to create new social institutions out of the social inertia of the status quo. All of this is to say that a crisis experience is a historical moment when reform of an existing form of life or its transformation enter into open conflict. It is a moment when the tendencies toward inertia and the tendencies toward an open future reveal the heterogeneity of social time.[42]

Both tendencies could be apprehended during the George Floyd protests. The response of politicians, local governments, and corporations involved symbolic recognition, charitable giving, and, in some cases, attempts to pare back police budgets (many of which seem to have been quietly restored in the interim); these were efforts at reintegrating citizens' horizon of normative expectations with the form of life.[43] These reforms were counterposed to the demands found under the slogan "defund/abolish the police." The ubiquity of the phrase "systemic racism" should not persuade us that those in power experience the exigency to construct an alternative form of life. In fact, systemic racism has come to mean that there is a second-order pattern of unfair distribution internal to our form of life and that what black citizens need is a *fair shot*.

We should note that these attempts to integrate radical critiques of a form of life by naturalizing an already existing horizon of normative expectations (à la the "free market") are not further evidence of the cynicism of those in power. Cynical though they may be, I am not interested in relying on a psychological account. Rather, we

---

[42] Karl Marx and Frederick Engels offer a description of this heterogeneity when they claim "consciousness can sometimes appear further advanced than the contemporary empirical conditions, so that in the struggles of a later epoch one can refer to earlier theoreticians as authorities." Karl Marx and Frederick Engels, *Collected Works*, vol. 5 (New York: International Publishers, 1976), 83.

[43] Fola Akinnibi, "NYC's Violent Crime Is Up; So Is the City's Police Budget," *Bloomberg*, May 6, 2021, https://www.bloomberg.com/news/articles/2021-05-06/new-york-city-s-police-budget-is-increasing-again.

should interpret this as the rational actions of agents who are aware of injustices but see no other plausible way we might organize our social life. It is not plausible to claim that these agents did not have *true* moral awareness and conclude that if they did, they would voluntarily transform their horizons of normative expectations. I think this shows that the fundamental limitation of the awareness model is that it cannot explain what good reason agents would have to restructure their horizons given the fact that the form of life remains reliable for them.[44]

Having said all of that, I do not think it is reasonable to assume that even crisis consciousness is *sufficient* to explain the process of social transformation. I want to avoid the risk of romanticizing crisis and the experience of dysfunction or breakdown. Invariably, the experience of the breakdown of one's form of life is distressing and violent, irrespective of whether observers removed from the situation think a breakdown will be, in the long term, for the "greater good." We should be wary of taking crises or revolutions as quasi-messianic events that move the arc of history forward with no reasonable account of the fact that actual persons underwent these painful transitions. People, generally, do not want crisis and will do what they can to avoid it. But beyond this point, we should affirm that crisis consciousness *has no necessary moral or political content*. The breakdown of one's horizon of normative expectations may lead agents to take any number of actions, some of which we may find regressive, unhelpful, or even repugnant. Analytically, crisis consciousness should be understood as a "negative" moment whose positive resolution in a new horizon of normative expectations requires another element. This element I call "utopian consciousness."

---

[44] My argument allows for the possibility that coming to understand injustice would mean coming to desire to change it. But even still we would have to ask under what conditions such a desire would play out in social practices that would directly contravene the reliable reproduction of one's life as they have known it. What insulates this desire from "the famous Hegelian charge of the 'impotence of the moral ought'"? Nancy Fraser and Rahel Jaeggi, *Capitalism: A Conversation* (Cambridge, UK: Polity, 2018), 121. In other words, knowledge of injustice does not furnish the thick understanding that the injustice is *immanent* rather than external to a form of life. Faced with such knowledge an agent may just as likely aver that life ought to be different, but, alas, things are the way they are.

Utopian Consciousness and the "Not-Yet" Form of Life

Crisis consciousness is not sufficient to explain how agents come to constitute a new horizon of normative expectations. If a form of life can stabilize a crisis and meet some of the demands of the agents in crisis then we might expect their horizon of normative expectations to be reintegrated into the form of life. However, in the period when a gap opens up between agents' horizons and the extant form of life it is possible that an alternative set of possibilities for a form of life may be grasped alongside new normative criteria by which a form of life ought to be judged. In other words, *time opens up*. Utopian consciousness distinguishes itself from crisis consciousness in that it develops new norms of justification for social practices and experiences *insight* into the "structural possibility" of a form of life that is "not-yet."[45] Breakdown and dysfunction appear to be the structural conditions for utopian consciousness, yet they do not exhaust its content.

I emphasize *insight* in order to address an ambivalence that is at the heart of conceptualizations of utopian consciousness. Modern criticism of utopian consciousness and utopia, more generally, go as far back as conservative critiques of the French Revolution and its enthusiasm. The normative expectation that a form of life should produce happiness for all and the hubris of thinking the many could, by fiat, bend life away from hierarchy and tragedy struck many critics as dangerous and lacking any insight into the real strictures of life.[46] The

---

[45] Erik Olin Wright, *Envisioning Real Utopias* (New York: Verso, 2010), 107.

[46] Domenico Losurdo, *Nietzsche, the Aristocratic Rebel: Intellectual Biography and Critical Balance-Sheet*, trans. Gregor Benton, intro. Harrison Fluss (Chicago: Haymarket Books, 2021), 86–108. Edmund Burke, for instance, interpreted the French Revolution as a disaster because it overthrew the wisdom of tradition and the participants presumed that they could willfully construct a rational order of happiness. Burke criticizes the French Revolution by noting, "The levellers therefore only change and pervert the natural order of things; they load the edifice of society, by setting up in the air what the solidity of the structure requires to be on the ground. The association of tailors and carpenters, of which the republic (of Paris, for instance) is composed, cannot be equal to the situation, into which, by the worst usurpations, an usurpation on the prerogatives of nature, you attempt to force them. . . . The occupation of a hair-dresser, or of a working tallow-chandler, cannot be a matter of honour to any person—to say nothing of a number of other more servile employments. Such descriptions of men ought not to suffer oppression from the state; but the state suffers oppression, if such as they, either individually or collectively, are permitted to rule. In this you think you are combatting

concern has been that such desires sidestep the complexities of social life. These desires may even misunderstand the necessary role some forms of unhappiness play in securing stability. Hayek, for instance, inherits this tradition that makes the argument that a healthy dose of pessimism is necessary for a stable form of life. We should restrain our expectations of what reason and consciousness can deliver. But distrust of utopian enthusiasm is not confined to more conservative philosophical traditions. We can find Adorno in "Marginalia to Theory and Praxis" criticizing student activists in Germany for their voluntarist enthusiasm to transform society that lacks an adequate thematization of the objective blockages to freedom. In other words, they lacked insight into how the world really was.[47]

Much as I wanted to avoid romanticizing crisis consciousness, I think it is imperative that we also resist romanticizing utopian consciousness as if it immediately follows that all enthusiasm is normatively praiseworthy and functionally successful. However, I register this ambivalence not in order to disavow what I take to be the necessary role of utopian consciousness in social transformation, but to explicate how critics from both the right and the left have painted utopian consciousness with too broad a brush.[48] What both sets of critics presume is that utopian consciousness and utopias are primarily of the order of the *imagination* and thus provide either no knowledge at all or, at the very least, a degraded form of knowledge. In "Socialism: Utopian and Scientific," Friedrich Engels juxtaposes utopia that is made up of fantasies and ephemeral desires against science that grasps objective reality.[49] I think this manner of carving up the distinction between

---

prejudice, but you are at war with nature." Edmund Burke, *Reflections on the Revolution in France*, ed. Frank M. Turner (New Haven, CT: Yale University Press, 2003), 42.

[47] Theodor Adorno, "Marginalia to Theory and Praxis," in *Critical Models: Interventions and Catchwords*, trans. Henry W. Pickford, intro. Lydia Goehr (New York: Columbia University Press, 2005), 270–271.

[48] See Hannah Arendt, *The Human Condition*, 2nd ed., intro. Margaret Canovan (Chicago: University of Chicago Press, 1998), 227–230, and Karl Popper, *The Open Society and Its Enemies*, intro. Alan Ryan (Princeton, NJ: Princeton University Press, 2013), 343–403 for critiques of utopia as totalitarian.

[49] Friedrich Engels, "Socialism: Utopian and Scientific," in *The Marx-Engels Reader*, ed. Robert C. Tucker (New York: W. W. Norton, 1978), 693–694.

utopia and knowledge has held sway for far too long. We would do well to move beyond it.

One of the key insights the Marxist philosopher Ernst Bloch offers is that traces of utopian consciousness inflect our everyday social practices in the form of daydreams, wishes, and even the somatic experience of hunger.[50] Critics such as Jürgen Habermas have cited Bloch's reliance on naturalistic interpretations of utopia as evidence that he is a romantic who indulged the imaginary and irrational. Habermas worries that Bloch's invocations of utopia preclude any revision from the sciences and verges on the "totalitarian." Habermas claims that Bloch must be anticipating a static future where all potential problems and conflicts have been solved.[51] But this is not what he is saying at all. Bloch argues that the phenomenological evidence of daydreams, for example, indicates that an extant form of life is not satisfying some desire the agent has.[52] Or to use the language I have been deploying: our horizons of normative expectations are never completely isomorphic with our form of life. Bloch contends that these average and everyday yearnings contain implicit knowledge of dysfunctions in one's social experience.[53]

[50] Bloch, *The Principle of Hope*, 11.
[51] Jürgen Habermas, "Ernst Bloch—A Marxist Romantic," *Salmagundi*, nos. 10–11 (Fall 1969–Spring 1970): 322. See also Alfred Schmidt, *The Concept of Nature in Marx*, trans. Ben Fowkes (London: NLB, 1971), 156–163 for a related critique of Bloch's supposition that nature and subjectivity could merge together in absolute unity.
[52] "As long as man is in a bad way, both private and public existence are pervaded by daydreams; dreams of a better life than that which has so far been given him. . . . And even where the ground, as so often before, may deceive us, full of sandbanks one moment, full of chimeras the next, it can only be condemned and possibly cleared up through *combined research* into objective tendency and subjective intention" (Bloch, *The Principle of Hope*, 5). The important point to take here is that for Bloch daydreams may contain ideological or distorted elements, but they are not *reducible* to mere false consciousness. Research and social theory can distill utopian knowledge from daydreams since both emerge from the same objective social relations. See Vincent Goeghegan, "Ideology and Utopia," *Journal of Political Ideologies* 9, no. 2 (2004): 127–131 for explication and criticism of Bloch's complex usages of ideology.
[53] I compare what Bloch is doing with the work of Michael Polanyi in *The Tacit Dimension* (Chicago: University of Chicago Press, 2009), 4 where he makes the argument that "*we can know more than we can tell.*" In the series of lectures that make up this book Polanyi attempts to demonstrate that knowledge cannot be reduced to explicit propositions, but must be subtended by an agent's background familiarity with a form of life that often resists explication. For my purposes, Polanyi offers a generative account of how Bloch's examination of daydreams and wishes are "tacit foreknowledge" (23) of novel solutions to as yet to be solved problems. If knowledge were only explicit

Bloch insists that we are not confined to any single order of time. On the one hand, our habits and practices have no set future trajectory and can be put to other purposes in alternative forms of life. Bloch gives the example of medicine that gives us a glimpse of life lived in good health even as its practices are warped by the imperatives of profit. On the other hand, Bloch contends that even our practices that we inherit from tradition or the past are never given once and for all, but require our active appropriation, and thus even the past can be opened up to the future.[54]

Bloch's project, at varying levels of success, was to argue that philosophy should thematize this everyday, implicit knowledge and bring it into contact with social scientific analyses of objective conditions rather than allow it to languish ineffectually in the sphere of imagination. Bloch concludes, "*Philosophy will have conscience of tomorrow, commitment to the future, knowledge of hope, or it will have no more knowledge.*"[55] The tendency of forms of life and elites toward inertia and conserving the status quo will often systemically distort the "not-yet" as an essential category of social experience.[56] For Bloch, the "not-yet" was not an abstract future that has not arrived, but bundles of tendencies and capacities that exist within a form of life that in everyday situations are suppressed and disciplined. Nevertheless, consciousness grasps them in diffuse, inchoate patterns.

Unfortunately, Bloch's dense literary style obscures the rather mundane and practical point he wants to make: a form of life's norms of justification never entirely convince everyone. Consciousness is never fully satiated and strives to both understand why and thematize what state of affairs would bring satisfaction. What frustrates projects of social transformation are a form of life's systematic attempts to separate utopia from

---

formulations then we would have to explain how problems straddle the border between being identifiable even as we do not yet have the knowledge to solve them. This is why Polanyi insists that "to see a problem is to see something that is hidden. It is to have an intimation of the coherence of hitherto not comprehended particulars" (21).

[54] See chapter 4 for more detailed explication of this claim.
[55] Bloch, *The Principle of Hope*, 7.
[56] "[B]ourgeois interest would like to draw every other interest opposed to it into its own failure; so, in order to drain the new life, it makes its own agony apparently fundamental, apparently ontological" (Bloch, *The Principle of Hope*, 4).

social reality, to render the former imaginary and the latter static. For instance, calls for abolishing prisons or the police are systematically met with the dismissal that these do not deal with actual social problems and are the exercise of imaginary ideals that may *inspire* us, but cannot give us any relevant knowledge of what is really possible.[57] Polling data that suggest the relative unpopularity of the "slogans" is marshaled as evidence of an objective limit to social transformation. And so, we have the "dreamers" and the "realists." But Bloch insists that for those of us interested in social transformation it is "a question of *learning* hope" and this means that hope can be a mode of knowledge production.[58] Perhaps even the essential mode of knowledge production for grasping objective tendencies and latent possibilities permeating a form of life.

I want to question the criteria we, as theorists, use to decide the difference between real possibility and objective impossibility. Bloch insists that no matter how central and essential one takes the objective sciences to be (what he calls the "cold stream" of Marxism) you will never find the "not-yet" form of life in those data. The specificity of the "not-yet" will only be found in agents' utopian consciousness at their points of frustration and breakdown.

None of this is to suggest that utopian consciousness spontaneously and automatically brings about a better form of life. What I claimed for crisis consciousness follows for utopian consciousness as well: it has no necessary moral or political content. In fact, Bloch was aware of this as well in his analyses of fascism in Nazi Germany.[59] The danger was

[57] Cf. Tommie Shelby, *The Idea of Prison Abolition* (Princeton, NJ: Princeton University Press, 2022).
[58] Bloch, *The Principle of Hope*, 3.
[59] Ernst Bloch, "Nonsynchronism and the Obligation to Dialectics," trans. Mark Ritter, *New German Critique* 11 (1977): 22–38. Oskar Negt provides a summary interpretation of this aspect of Bloch's thinking concerning utopia. He describes Bloch's philosophy of utopia as navigating "the *tendency towards revolutionary emancipation* of society, borne primarily by the working class and *fascism*, which emerged and grew out of the material nonsynchronous contradictions." Oskar Negt, "The Non-Synchronous Heritage and the Problem of Propaganda," *New German Critique* 9 (Autumn 1976): 48. What Negt calls "nonsynchronous" (a translation of the German *Ungleichzeitig*) accords with the phenomenological description I gave in the previous section of horizons of normative expectation becoming unmoored from a form of life. These crises of temporal and existential experience do not have any automatic or necessary political direction and indeed "in intensified crisis situations, when the solution of the contradictions within the logic of capital is limited" regressive political formations may emerge (48).

that a form of life oriented utopian desires back to a nostalgia for a lost homeland that had been humiliated. A more robust account of utopian consciousness would take it to be crucial to the social learning process of what alternative forms of life would allow for the establishment of shared horizons of normative expectations and well-being. I follow Jaeggi here when she concludes, "A successful form-of-life would be one that has the *feature of not hindering, but facilitating successful collective learning processes*."[60] A form of life that systematically and actively suppresses utopian consciousness deprives itself of *practical knowledge* as well as desiccates the capacity for imagination.

I am insisting that theories of social transformation should take stock of the loss or distortion of knowledge as much as the potential harmful effects a dysfunctional form of life can have on agents' imaginative capacities. Bloch differentiates between knowledge that distills what has already occurred from prospective knowledge that examines "what is becoming [and] decisively contributes to this becoming."[61] Hegemonic forms of life often turn the "not-yet" into disciplinary injunctions to slow down and trust the process since a better order cannot yet emerge. However, for utopian consciousness the "not-yet" is not a limit, but an epistemic task to understand what tendencies and capacities could establish an alternative form of life. In this way, consciousness does not outstrip the present form of life by fleeing into the space of imagination, but instead delves deeper into it and inquires after real possibilities of social life.

These are two different dispositions toward social time. On the one hand, time can appear to be a barrier against which agents must acquiesce. The present is never ripe for radical transformations because everything we would need and all the knowledge we require does not yet exist. What-has-been becomes the primary source of justifications for our social practices, and thus a true leap from one form of life to another seems impossible. On the other hand, Bloch counsels us to understand the "not-yet" as both a promise and an imperative that exists in the present. For him, utopian consciousness is the disposition of social practices whose aim is to take control of our social time and direct

---

[60] Jaeggi, "What (If Anything) Is Wrong with Capitalism?," 65.
[61] Bloch, *The Principle of Hope*, 132.

it toward the goal of social freedom. He thinks this impulse already animates how we comport ourselves as reasoning agents, but our form of life blocks our apprehension of these latent forces.

I think this provides us with a plausible response to the Hayekian quandary of epistemic pessimism. Hayek takes our reliance on implicit or tacit knowledge of our form of life as a *limit* to what consciousness can grasp and effectuate. But if Bloch is right that this implicit knowledge also contains a not-yet explicated apprehension of the problems of a form of life *and* the immanent resolution to those problems, then we are not resigned to the conservative position as concerns tacit knowledge. For Hayek, we imperil the stability of our form of life when politics endeavors to self-consciously bring about new forms of social organization that have little correspondence to the tacit knowledge of our past experiences. Such a form of "utopian" politics risks engineering crises of knowledge that will make social systems dysfunctional and inefficient. I think there is more to Hayek's worry, however. If tacit knowledge is no longer an unsurpassable limit, then historical processes of hierarchy and inequality may increasingly seem unjustified or illegitimate.[62]

Bloch endorses the possibility that utopia can outstrip our present knowledge but thinks that by linking tacit knowledge with objective analyses of the social world we could, hypothetically, establish utopian learning processes from which new forms of problem-solving and social life could emerge. This would allow us to develop a more grounded critical theory that illuminates the complex relays between needs, social environments, and political practice. Indeed, it would require that we incorporate work from the social sciences on how actions become meaningful for us given the environments in which we are embedded.[63]

---

[62] "But if the material achievements of our civilization have created ambitions in others, they have also given them a new power to destroy it if what they believe is their due is not given them. With the knowledge of possibilities spreading faster than the material benefits, a great part of the people of the world are today dissatisfied as never before and are determined to take what they regard as their rights" (Hayek, *The Constitution of Liberty*, 105).

[63] I am here thinking of work on "affordances" as found in Bert H. Hodges and Reuben M. Baron, "Values as Constraints on Affordances: Perceiving and Acting Properly," *Journal for the Theory of Social Behavior* 22, no. 3 (1992): 263–294, as well as more recent work by Roy Dings, "Meaningful Affordances," *Synthese* 199 (2021): 1855–1875.

Crisis consciousness and utopian consciousness should be understood as mutually supportive of the learning process that can crystallize new horizons of normative expectations. Without utopia, crisis consciousness cannot grasp alternative possibilities of normative expectation. Without crisis, utopian consciousness will not understand the breakdowns and dysfunctions that shape social life. These two typologies of consciousness more adequately explain potential processes of social transformation than models that explicitly focus on moral awareness and ignorance.

The temporal rhythms of these two forms of consciousness differ, however. The emergence of crisis consciousness is necessarily anchored in the inadequacy of *past experience* for solving present problems. When I am in crisis the fund of accumulated habits and practices upon which I draw to make my way through social life are outstripped by the new problems I am tasked with solving. This can happen because of social, political, or economic changes in our form of life.[64] For instance, the historian Reinhart Koselleck analyzes the modern concept of "progress" where the development of new technologies, global exploration, and the dissolution of old forms of life by industry and capital severed past experiences from future expectations.[65] More contemporarily, we might think of how the COVID-19 pandemic introduced millions of people to expectations in social life concerning public health and work that had little correspondence to their past experience of the "normal" rhythms of social life. Crisis consciousness is more than being confronted with problems. After all, if a carpenter is called to fix a cabinet door, they most likely experience little to no crisis because this problem is well within their horizon of normative expectations. It is when I no longer know how to go on, but must go on, that crisis sets in.

---

[64] Jürgen Habermas offers an overview of different types of crises in his *Legitimation Crisis*, trans. Thomas McCarthy (Boston: Beacon Press, 1975), 45–92. For an analysis that critiques Ernst Bloch on the basis of the speed and scale of technological change, see Hans Jonas, *The Imperative of Responsibility: In Search of an Ethics for the Technological Age*, trans. Hans Jonas and David Herr (Chicago: University of Chicago Press, 1981), 1–25.

[65] Reinhart Koselleck, *Futures Past: On the Semantics of Historical Time*, trans. Keith Tribe (Cambridge, MA: MIT Press, 1985), 279.

Alternatively, utopian consciousness is anchored in the emergence of *future expectations* that do not "fit" within the settled horizons of experience. Utopian consciousness is not an already recognized experience, but the provocation to leave behind past experiences for the prospect of a better form of life. What is distinctive about utopian consciousness is that it tends to challenge the justifications that underwrite a form of life and proffer new justifications for how we may organize ourselves. For instance, societies were once organized around the justification of black people as non-citizens or second-class citizens The experience of treating black people in such a manner of course accumulated in personal habits and institutional practices. Struggles for racial justice that lay claim to the expectations of equal citizenship confront the wider polity with a new vision of social life where the background experience of racial subjugation will have been foreclosed.[66] Whatever the practical success of a given form of utopian consciousness it always draws a limit on a form of life by separating past experience and future expectations. It makes clear the organizing habits and justifications of a form of life by relativizing them through the juxtaposition of alternative normative expectations. Arguments for prison or police abolition make this point by critiquing whether society must be organized around carcerality.[67]

However, a word of caution is needed here. We should not understand crisis consciousness as inevitably leading to utopian consciousness, as if there were an automatic progressive teleology between the experience of crisis and the transformation of a form of life. Past experiences and future expectations may be out of sync for two possible reasons. First, crisis consciousness is *positional*. One is in crisis vis-à-vis one's social location, and thus not all members of a form of life will find that there is a gap between their past experiences and future expectations. This unevenness in social time will be the subject of the following chapter, where I examine the work of

---

[66] See chapter 3 for an analysis of black nationalism and the expansion of the concept of "citizen."
[67] See Angela Y. Davis, *Are Prisons Obsolete?* (New York: Seven Stories Press, 2003) and Derecka Purnell, *Becoming Abolitionists: Police, Protests, and the Pursuit of Freedom* (New York: Astra House, 2021).

W. E. B. Du Bois. But for now, it is enough to state that the emergence of crisis consciousness does not entail that everyone will agree that a form of life is in crisis. Second, utopian consciousness may transform horizons of normative expectations without provoking agents to organize new institutions because either the costs are too high or the utopian desire is relatively thin.[68] It is important not to confuse raising horizons of normative expectations with the creation of a new form of life. The hard question is how crisis consciousness and utopian consciousness may be synchronized to enable new social practices in the struggle for justice. This will be a recurring question of the book. For the moment, I turn to contemporary struggles for racial justice and how they can be informed by crisis and utopian consciousness.

Crises and Utopias of Racial Justice

In the United States, calls for racial justice and critiques of systemic racism as it concerns policing, prisons, and poverty have only become more urgent in the wake of the COVID-19 pandemic and the George Floyd protests of 2020. It is not uncommon to hear the language of crisis being used when describing the situation of impoverished black communities. In fact, it is hard to think of a time when talk of race, racism, and the United States' sordid history with non-white peoples was more ubiquitous. For better and for worse, few are unaware of discourses concerning racial justice. One might expect that after the severe challenges to its legitimacy brought on by a mishandled pandemic and nationwide protests, the form of life of the United States was on the cusp of transformation. However, the opposite has proven to be the case. The form of life of the United States has proven itself to be

---

[68] "In contexts of complex social interdependence, new institutions often entail high fixed or start-up costs, and involve considerable learning effects, coordination effects, and adaptive expectations. Established institutions generate powerful inducements that reinforce their own stability and development." Paul Pierson, "Not Just What, but *When*: Timing and Sequence in Political Processes," *Studies in American Development* 14 (Spring 2000): 78.

remarkably durable even as trust in the government reaches historic lows.[69]

Now this does not imply that the crises and dysfunctions were not real and that the social situation in the United States was in actuality going well. One can point to any number of data points such an increased debt held by the young, decreasing life expectancy among white people, and deteriorating democratic mechanisms to suggest that there are real crises within the United States form of life. Instead, what follows is that a form of life can persist even as there are widening rifts between it and agents' horizons of normative expectations.[70] My hypothesis is that the general crisis facing racial justice is not a crisis of moral ignorance or a lack of knowledge concerning the situation of black people, migrants, or other minorities, but to borrow a famous phrase from Antonio Gramsci, "The crisis consists precisely in the fact that the old is dying and new cannot be born; in this interregnum a great variety of morbid symptoms appear."[71] The increased reliance on what I have called the "awareness model on consciousness" in discourses of racial justice expresses the real lack of political and organizational capacity to resolve the systemic dysfunction of our form of life. If we cannot change the world we can at least change ourselves seems to be the idea. Our moment is a moment of breakdown and transition when new horizons are forming, yet old social relations persist. The aim of racial justice needs to be the establishment of a new common ground for meaningful action or else we will witness the diminishing returns of our struggles in the guise of increased bureaucracies, token representation, and the decay of knowledge of how to organize ourselves.

There is not enough space to give full and specific details of the social cause of our interregnum, so a broad outline will have to suffice.

---

[69] Pew Research Center, "Public Trust in Government: 1958–2024," June 24, 2024, https://www.pewresearch.org/politics/2024/06/24/public-trust-in-government-1958-2024/.

[70] I should be clear that I do not think a form of life can persist indefinitely in a legitimation crisis, but for some time relations of coercion, inertia, and disorganization on the part of agents in crisis will allow a form of life to remain in place. See Habermas, *Legitimation Crisis*.

[71] Antonio Gramsci, *Selections from the Prison Notebooks*, ed. and trans. Quintin Hoare and Geoffrey Nowell Smith (New York: International Publishers, 1971), 276.

In the form of life of the United States, norms of legitimation and allegiance no longer have a rational structure for many citizens, and yet nothing has come to replace those norms that would bind together some minimal life that we could call the common good.[72] The fragmentation of social life is not only due to market pressures that continue to destabilize increasing swaths of the general populace with insecurity, but that this form of life ideologically takes itself to be "postracial" despite much empirical evidence to the contrary. I would call this, following Terry Pinkard, a *systemic* form of alienation whereby a form of life "can no longer sustain allegiance because of the incompatible entitlements and commitments such a way of life puts on its members."[73] The increasing absorption of a black elite and political class that attempts to represent and legitimate this form of life while presiding over apparatuses of violence and humiliation that disproportionately targets black citizens and other minorities only heightens a sense of alienation.[74] And so, projects of racial justice find themselves struggling within a social form of life in which fewer people believe, but continue to lack the structural capacity to achieve a new form of life.

However, we do *not* lack vision or imagination in this moment. Activists, philosophers, and even some politicians have been writing and envisioning worlds without police or prisons, ecologically sustainable and just worlds, and worlds without borders and with the right to free movement.[75] It may be difficult to apprehend from within what

---

[72] Alasdair MacIntyre, "The Privatization of the Good: An Inaugural Lecture," *Review of Politics* 52, no. 3 (1990): 351.

[73] Pinkard, *Hegel's Naturalism*, 148.

[74] Cedric Johnson provides an exemplary history of this shift in the post–civil rights/Black Power era in *Race Revolutionaries to Race Leaders: Black Power and the Making of African American Politics* (Minneapolis: University of Minnesota Press, 2007). See also James Forman Jr., *Locking Up Our Own: Crime and Punishment in Black America* (New York: Farrar, Straus and Giroux, 2017).

[75] I take my project here to be different from those of Robin D. G. Kelley, *Freedom Dreams: The Black Radical Imagination* (Boston: Beacon Press, 2002) and Alex Zamalin, *Black Utopia: The History of an Idea from Black Nationalism to Afrofuturism* (New York: Columbia University Press, 2019), who in their work elucidate the relationship between political oppression and the aesthetic imagination of utopia found in black thinkers. I think this is important work, but I want to emphasize that utopia gives us not only visions and imagination but knowledge and insight into our social capacities and the objective possibility of a restructured form of life.

seems to be a dystopian interregnum, but we are also living through a *utopian renaissance*. Utopias, as I have argued, often attend moments of crisis. These visions are crucial especially since we can expect regressive visions of utopia to emerge that will demand a "return" to a purer nation-state and ought to be contested. Nevertheless, vision is not enough if we do not grasp the shape of crisis before us.

There is no telling how long interregna will persist. Given this, if I am right that we are in an interregnum, then racial justice requires both normative critiques *and* functional analyses of why it is so difficult in our present moment to establish an alternative form of life that accords with our new horizons of normative expectations. Without such analyses the project of racial justice risks becoming an ineffective slogan, vulnerable to capture by elites (black or otherwise) who will attempt to mold its horizons according to their interests in the extant form of life.[76] The utopian consciousness of racial justice should allow us to specify the difficult terrain and new problems we face in the interest of repairing and nurturing our social learning processes. No doubt this is an immensely complex endeavor, but if we are to identify real utopian possibilities in our current crisis, we need much more than the awareness of racial injustices. In what follows, I describe and analyze the contours of utopian consciousness in past struggles for racial justice. What I will show is that all of them, in diverse ways, contest or illuminate how time and progress are disciplined in racially unjust societies. I look at the past in the hopes that a critical theory of utopia will reconstruct the learning processes of utopian consciousness in future struggles for racial justice.

---

[76] Olúfẹ́mi O. Táíwò describes this phenomenon as "elite capture" where those who are in positions of power within a social structure are able to substitute their concerns and analyses as representative of the concerns of an oppressed group in a manner that reconsolidates the status quo. Olúfẹ́mi O. Táíwò, "Identity Politics and Elite Capture," *Boston Review*, 2020, https://bostonreview.net/race/olufemi-o-taiwo-identity-politics-and-elite-capture. See also A. Phillip Randolph, "The Negro in Politics," in *African American Political Thought, 1890–1930*, ed. Cary D. Wintz (New York: Routledge, 1996), 249–250 for a historical example of this phenomenon of capture where he critiques the contradictions of black "representation" in the Republican Party from the late 19th to early 20th century. Randolph specifies that representation can be authentic and resist capture if and only if the representative shares the interests of their constituents, belongs to an organization controlled by the constituents, and, finally, is knowledgeable enough to understand their interests. All three conditions rarely obtain in social life as it is arranged presently.

From Consciousness to Social life

None of this is to suggest that we can remain at the level of consciousness even with my modified account of crisis and utopian consciousness. We still have not seen what it would mean to grasp the logic of social action for a form of life. All the preceding has shown is how individuals engage and become disengaged from the norms that anchor their form of life, but I have not yet developed an account of what it would mean for agents to be in control of the mechanisms that discipline their time. Nevertheless, it was fruitful to begin with consciousness and how the world comes to appear to agents in order to offer a grounded account of the problems facing racial justice. In what follows, I will turn to the work of W. E. B. Du Bois and examine how he grapples with the tensions that emerge between social knowledge and forms of life. What the next chapter will show is that Du Bois argues that an investigation into the cultural dynamics of social groups and their conflicts with one another can bring to the consciousness of the critical theorist the underlying forms of life in a situation. Helpfully, these inevitable conflicts within the context of racial domination also present an outline of what racial justice will require.

2
Race and the Fragmentation of Time
Critical Theory and the Utopian Hermeneutics of *The Souls of Black Folk*

Introduction

The Souls of Black Folk, W. E. B. Du Bois's famous examination of racial oppression at the turn of the 20th century in America, presents the United States as a disharmonious republic. I would even venture that *Souls* operates as a reverse image of Plato's *Republic*. In one of the most important utopian texts of "Western" civilization, Plato's Socrates claims that there is a definitional analogy between the just harmony of the soul and the just harmony of the city.[1] Du Bois's America manifests disordered souls by virtue of being built upon the great lie of racial hierarchy or, as Du Bois called it, "the color line."[2] The affinity Du Bois had for the classics of Western culture is seeded throughout *Souls*.[3]

My claim will be that Du Bois's use of classics in *Souls* provides a crucial architecture for what I will describe as Du Bois's utopianism. Du Bois intends for *Souls* to be a bridge between a currently ill-formed black culture and a Western classical tradition that has lost its way. By bringing both together, a new harmony in the American republic can be established. For this reason, I will read *Souls* as following in a long political tradition of Western utopian texts. Both Plato's *Republic* and Du Bois's *Souls* emerge from a context of social crisis and breakdown.

---

[1] Plato, *The Republic*, ed. G. R. F. Ferrari, trans. Tom Griffith (Cambridge: Cambridge University Press, 2013), 368d, 369a.
[2] W. E. B. Du Bois, *The Souls of Black Folk* (Mineola, NY: Dover, 1994), 9.
[3] Mathias Hanses, "Cicero Crosses the Color Line: *Pro Archia Poeta* and W. E. B. Du Bois's *The Souls of Black Folk*," *International Journal of the Classical Tradition* 26, no. 1 (2019): 10–26; Carrie Cowherd, "The Wings of Atalanta: Classical Influences in *The Souls of Black Folk*," in *The Souls of Black Folk: One Hundred Years Later*, ed. Dolan Hubbard (Columbia: University of Missouri Press, 2003), 284–298.

Utopias, I will insist, are rarely blank slates, but attempts to repair real frustrations in social life. Accordingly, whatever utopianism Du Bois defends will not be a dream of starting over, but rather the careful insight into spaces of possibility that have been carried forward by the waves of history. These spaces of possibility are immanent to the disharmony of the American polis. In other words, if the *Republic* is, at least partially, a critical attempt to work out how one can know the ideals of good governance from the disarray of contemporary political life, *Souls* harbors a similar inclination with the added difference of historical racialization.[4]

My argument in this chapter will be that *Souls* contains a latent social ontology of time which posits the existence of a truer society from within the false society of racial domination. The truer society, what Du Bois calls "the kingdom of culture," is as yet unknown given the current conditions of racial hierarchy in the United States.[5] The upshot of my reconstruction will be that *Souls* provides a preliminary framework for understanding racially unjust societies as *temporally out of joint* or, borrowing a concept from the Marxist philosopher Ernst Bloch, as forms of life afflicted with "non-synchronicity [*Ungleichzeitigkeit*]."[6]

---

[4] On the relationship of Du Bois to Plato, see David Withun, *Co-workers in the Kingdom of Culture: Classics and Cosmopolitanism in the Thought of W. E. B. Du Bois* (New York: Oxford University Press, 2022), ch. 3; Stephanie J. Shaw, *W. E. B. Du Bois and The Souls of Black Folk* (Chapel Hill: University of North Carolina Press, 2013), 151–157, 173–175; Shamoon Zamir, *Dark Voices: W. E. B. Du Bois and American Thought, 1888–1903* (Chicago: University of Chicago Press, 1995), 172.

[5] Du Bois, *Souls*, 3.

[6] Ernst Bloch, *Heritage of Our Times* (Cambridge, UK: Polity Press, 1991), 97–117. The clearest formulation Bloch offers of this concept comes near the beginning of *Heritage of Our Times* when he writes, "The times are in decay and in labour at the same time. The situation is wretched or despicable, the way out of it is crooked" (1). See also Oscar Negt, "The Non-synchronous Heritage and the Problem of Propaganda," *New German Critique*, no. 9 (Autumn 1976): 46–70; Cat Moir, *Ernst Bloch's Speculative Materialism: Ontology, Epistemology, Politics* (Leiden: Brill, 2019), 21; Peter Thompson, "Ernst Bloch, *Ungleichzeitigkeit*, and the Philosophy of Being and Time," *New German Critique* 42, no. 2 (August 2015): 49–64; Peter Thompson, "Introduction: The Privatization of Hope and the Crisis of Negation," in *The Privatization of Hope: Ernst Bloch and the Future of Utopia*, eds. Peter Thompson and Slavoj Žižek (Durham, NC: Duke University Press, 2013), 15–17; Vittorio Morfino, "On Non-contemporaneity: Marx, Bloch, Althusser," in *The Government of Time: Theories of Plural Temporality in the Marxist Tradition*, ed. Vittorio Morfino and Peter D. Thomas (Chicago: Haymarket Books, 2017), 117–148; Wayne Hudson, *The Marxist Philosophy of Ernst Bloch* (New York: St. Martin's Press, 1982), 43–44; Jack Zipes, "Traces of Hope: The Non-synchronicity of Ernst Bloch," in *Not-Yet: Reconsidering Ernst Bloch*, ed. Jamie Owen Daniel and Tom Moylan (New York: Verso, 1997), 1–15.

Du Bois, I will argue, offers a dual methodology that both *diagnoses* the causes of racial injustice and *anticipates* their future resolution.

The concept of "non-synchronicity" will be key throughout the book so I will briefly spell out how I will be using it. Bloch uses the concept of "non-synchronicity" as an analytical tool for understanding how it was possible for fascism to take root in Germany. His thesis is that Germany was a temporally out of joint society with different classes such as peasants and the petit-bourgeoisie living in relationship to distinct histories, practices, and visions of the future that emerged from their position in the class structure of German society. The transformative dynamics of capitalism deepened the alienation of these classes by eviscerating or making obsolete their forms of life and bending them toward the ends of accumulation. Fascism, Bloch contends, was a regressive response to these temporal fractures that promised a "return" to stability and a nostalgia for the past where these classes could feel unified again—if on a racial basis. I will show that such a hypothesis is also at work in Du Bois's thinking and thus provides a useful framework for developing a critical theory of utopia that looks at the diverse temporal dynamics that shape and break forms of life. This problem of "non-synchronicity" exists not only within critical theory and within social life, but *between* critical theory and social life.[7]

Du Bois surveyed an American form of life that was growing in economic power, yet stubbornly held onto the racial hierarchies that were formed under slavery. American society was rife with racial domination and economic chaos. In *Souls*, we find Du Bois struggling with the temporal contradiction of a black proletariat that had neither the leadership nor the skills needed for the advancement of a modern economy.[8] Moreover, writing at the turn of the 20th century, Du Bois

---

[7] Adorno, though perhaps overly hyperbolic, touches on a real problematic when he notes, "If theory and praxis are neither immediately one nor absolutely different, then their relation is one of discontinuity. No continuous path leads from praxis to theory.... But theory is part of the nexus of society and at the same time is autonomous. Nevertheless praxis does not proceed independently of theory, nor theory independently of praxis.... The dogma of the unity of theory and praxis, contrary to the doctrine on which it is based, is undialectical: it underhandedly appropriates simple identity where contradiction alone has the chance of becoming productive." Theodor W. Adorno, "Marginalia to Theory and Praxis," in *Critical Models: Interventions and Catchwords*, trans. Henry W. Pickford (New York: Columbia University Press), 276–277.

[8] Du Bois, *Souls*, 64.

was well aware of the differing temporal dynamics between black people in rural areas and black people in urban areas and between formally educated black people such as himself and black people in the working class. Du Bois explicitly struggled against the racial perception of black people as becoming obsolete or condemned to the past. The systematic misalignment of "horizons of normative expectations"[9] fatally compromised social cooperation among black peoples and within society as a whole. Both Bloch and Du Bois understood these "non-synchronicities" as providing fertile ground for what I will call "racial fetishism" in chapter 4. The sense that one's form of life is no longer adequate to the historical movement of economic life while feeling that one does not have control over where that society is going creates the social conditions for rage, paranoia, and certainly violence.

Nevertheless, in Bloch and Du Bois I find the possibility of mobilizing these "non-synchronicities" in a socially progressive direction.[10] However, unlike Bloch, Du Bois at this time was no Marxist and thus could not rely on a social vision of Communism to reflect on the temporal pathologies of the American form of life.[11] Du Bois looks at culture as the vehicle for organizing social time and opening the way for a more just future. He analyzes black folks' cultural practices as "non-synchronous" by virtue of the fact that they have not been fully

---

[9] See chapter 1 of present volume.

[10] Bloch insists that Communists must learn to "master" the secondary non-synchronous contradictions of social life if they are to build a social movement that can resolve the primary contradiction of capitalist social relations (*Heritage*, 114). As I described in the introduction, we can make this distinction between primary and secondary contradictions if we assume that there are practices to which all forms of life must respond, even if differentially. The distinction of primary and secondary does not assume either moral priority or even strategic priority. Indeed, Bloch, a dyed-in-the-wool Marxist, did not think it was possible to avoid dealing with problems of culture, nationalism, and race if fascism and capitalism were to be overcome.

[11] David Withun argues that even when Du Bois turned toward Marxist thinking he retained his foundations in Platonic and classical thought: "Du Bois's praise for the income equality of these communist societies also has a basis in the thought of Plato. In *The Republic*, Plato bans the ownership of private property from his ideal state on the basis that it is the cause of conflict between nations and citizens.... For Du Bois, Marx's great insight was in pointing to the economic factors rather than solely the moral factors that were the causes behind the inability of the world to attain his Platonic vision of the future" (*Co-workers*, 124–125). See also Keith E. Byerman, *Seizing the Word: History, Art, and Self in the Work of W. E. B. Du Bois* (Athens: University of Georgia Press, 1994), 64.

integrated in the drive for wealth accumulation and thus offer a different set of social virtues from which black citizens can develop their social agency. The utopian element of Du Bois's critical theory emerges from his understanding of culture as offering a vision of harmonious temporality where all peoples can learn from and share in ennobling human achievements.

The question is why Du Bois would take himself to be justified in positing a future "kingdom of culture" or that "one far off Divine event" of historical reconciliation in the first place.[12] Du Bois does not take this new *topos* to only be subjectively desirable; it is also true in some objective manner. What Du Bois means by "true" is not limited to epistemic veracity concerning facts, but also includes the normative character of a justly governed form of life.[13] Du Bois, it seems to

---

[12] W. E. B. Du Bois, "The Conservation of Races," in *The Idea of Race*, ed. Robert Bernasconi and Tommy L. Lott (Indianapolis, IN: Hackett, 2000), 112. In the essay, Du Bois suggests not only that there is a culturally coherent concept of race, but that there is a conceivable teleology to history where each "race" offers a "gift" or distinct message to humanity that will inaugurate an era when all peoples can share in the knowledge of others. I think this essay already suggests the temporal focus of Du Bois and his yearning for a historical moment when all "races" will be able to live side by side in the present. For the cultural emphasis of "Conservation," see Chike Jeffers, "The Cultural Theory of Race: Yet Another Look at Du Bois's 'The Conservation of Races,'" *Ethics* 123, no. 3 (2013): 403–426. For alternative readings of this crucial essay, see Kwame Anthony Appiah, "The Uncompleted Argument: Du Bois and the Illusion of Race," *Critical Inquiry* 12, no. 1: 21–37; Lucius Outlaw, "'Conserve' Races?," in *W. E. B. Du Bois on Race and Culture*, ed. Bernard W. Bell, Emily R. Grosholz, and James B. Stewart (New York: Routledge, 1996), 15–37; Robert Gooding-Williams, "Outlaw, Appiah, and Du Bois's 'The Conservation of Races,'" in *W. E. B. Du Bois on Culture and Race*, ed. Bernard W. Bell, Emily R. Grosholz, and James B. Stewart (New York: Routledge, 1996), 39–56; Kimberly Ann Harris, "W. E. B. Du Bois's 'The Conservation of Races': A Metaphilosophical Text," *Metaphilosophy* 50, no. 5 (2019): 670–687; Nahum Dmitri Chandler, *X—The Problem of The Negro as a Problem of Thought* (New York: Fordham University Press, 2014), 32–40.

[13] Robert K. Williams argues that Du Bois develops a theory of good democratic governance which takes as foundational the "individual unknowability" of corporeal others given their social identities. I cannot know all the relevant experiences, beliefs, and knowledge of another person given I do not share their embodiment. This unknowability requires that we accept our epistemological limitations as it concerns speaking for others, and thus if democracy is to be guided by true knowledge then more citizens must be allowed to speak. But Williams, with his focus mostly on writings of Du Bois after *Souls*, does not address how Du Bois comes to believe that a better state of affairs is a *real* possibility. Robert W. Williams, "A Democracy of Differences: Knowledge and the Unknowable in Du Bois's Theory of Democratic Governance," in *A Political Companion to W. E. B. Du Bois*, ed. Nick Bromell (Lexington: University of Kentucky Press, 2018), 197.

me, understood a just society to be one in which the various historical habits and expectations that comprise the cultures of different groups are brought into harmony with one another *and* the economic capacities of a society. Truth, in this context, does not refer to this or that proposition as factually correct, but the moral vision of a just society which does not obtain at present.

The hermeneutical task of *Souls* takes the "non-synchronicity" of black people as a sign of what the truer society could be. Ernst Bloch in his 1972 book *Atheism in Christianity*, defines the hermeneutical task of Marxist utopian epistemology as the search for "the Tomorrow within the Today."[14] Du Bois extends the temporal coordinates of this principle from "Today" to "Yesterday" because the color line is not only a present problem, but a historical problem of memory and racial fetishism. I will have more to say about how I understand the concept of "racial fetishism" and how it works in chapter 4. At present, we can say that racial fetishism names the tendency for race to appear as a facet of social life that is outside the control of our social practices. In Du Bois's time, racial fetishism often took the form of the putatively "natural" division of humanity into higher and lower races. Du Bois is sensitive to how a racist society tends to make it seem as if something called "race" sorts different populations into hierarchical relationships rather than the practices and institutions of human beings. This has the effect of alienating the present from the past by obscuring the true origins of our social relations.

Writing in 1925, Du Bois says of the time during World War I that "to more human beings than ever before at one time in the world's history, there came ... a vision of the Glory of Sacrifice, a dream of a world greater, sweeter, more beautiful and more honest than ever before; a world without war, without poverty, and without hatred." One might think that this proclamation commits Du Bois to the idea that utopia can lead to moral catastrophe and thus we would be better avoiding it. I do not think this is convincing if we understand that the emergence of World War I was precisely due to our contradictory form of life rather than the attempt to transform it. Du Bois wants to insist that we find what can be rescued from historical tragedy so that the world

---

[14] Ernst Bloch, *Atheism in Christianity*, trans. J. T. Swann (New York: Verso, 2009), 54.

can be put right. Indeed, as I will argue, it is precisely because of his Platonism that Du Bois is able to insist on the eternal value of truth and justice. After his utopian reflection on World War I, Du Bois proclaims, "I am glad it came. Even though it was a mirage it was eternally true. To-day some faint shadow of it comes to me again."[15] *Souls* is most concerned with the need to find the true within the mirage, utopia within historical disaster. In other words, Du Bois hopes to mobilize the truth of the not-yet in service of cultural and political emancipation rather than destruction.[16]

My concern in this chapter is to explicate the form of critical inquiry that utopia requires by attending to Du Bois's recursive strategy of insight in *Souls*.[17] This form of critical inquiry, I argue, is nonsynchronous insofar as utopia prospectively searches for the true possibility of living otherwise from within the webs of racial mystification and ideology that ensnare our forms of life. This assumes that the structure of the world is not yet settled, but instead is composed of "non-synchronous" social strata moving along different political, cultural, and economic rhythms.[18] Du Bois, controversially, viewed

---

[15] W. E. B. Du Bois, "Worlds of Color: The Negro Mind Reaches Out," in *The New Negro: Voices of the Harlem Renaissance*, ed. Alain Locke (New York: Touchstone, 1997), 413.

[16] "Not yet" is not a simple phrase since its temporal meaning can range between the reference of something that is not actual at this moment to something that is partially existing, but has not fully developed to the designation of an event that was begun in the past that has still not ended. For my purposes in this chapter I am primarily focusing on "not yet" as the past events of freedom struggles that have still not been fully accomplished. I will expand the sense of the not-yet truth of utopia further on in this book. Wayne Hudson provides rich detail of the many senses of *noch nicht* (not yet) in *The Marxist Philosophy of Ernst Bloch* (London: Macmillan, 1982), 19–20. I will also return to this thematic in chapter 5.

[17] See Robert Gooding-Williams, "Philosophy of History and Social Critique in *The Souls of Black Folk*," *Sur les Sciences Sociales (Social Science Information)* 26 (March 1987): 99–114.

[18] Alfred Schmidt criticizes Bloch on this notion of the not-yet structure of the world insofar as he thinks Bloch believes that even the laws of nature are incomplete and can be modified by human agency. This position not only seems fantastical, but it would put Bloch at odds with the mature Marx's own views of nature as a realm of necessity that can never be eradicated Alfred Schmidt, *The Concept of Nature in Marx*, trans. Ben Fowkes (London: NLB, 1971), 156–163. Du Bois does not have this problem since for him the structure of the world is unsettled insofar as it has not achieved the temporal harmony that is adequate to truth and justice. For better or for worse, the eternal nature of truth both makes possible social transformation and limits the extent of human creativity.

the racialization of black people as making them non-synchronous with "Western" civilization. Their lack of both broad education and Victorian manners struck him as social pathologies that needed to be arrested if black people were to advance as a group.[19] But for all that he also thought their historical experience of enslavement and struggle disposed them toward a different vision of freedom than what was on offer from the broader society of the United States. This vision has been frustrated and distorted by the color line, so Du Bois sets himself the task of distilling it from the racial dross of historical mystification. I want to lay out the hermeneutical fundamentals of utopic inquiry and apply them to Du Bois's writings in order to show that there are strata to Du Bois's own thinking of which he may not have been aware that can illuminate the darkness of our own present.

In the section that follows, I defend the utility of utopia for social theory by showing how Du Bois incorporated utopia into his sociology of knowledge to allow for a rigorous thinking of how possibility permeates contemporary reality. In the next section, I detail Du Bois's phenomenology of how racialized consciousness can come to learn of its "non-synchronous" status through its education by Western civilization. I then move on to show that Du Bois, in fact, has been making an argument in favor of a black educated elite, the Talented Tenth, whose knowledge of harmony tasks them with bringing order to the rest of the uneducated black folk. In the last section, I argue that Du Bois's elitism is not without its own disharmony. By turning to his reflections on black spiritual music, Du Bois stages the tomorrow of utopia as arising from the social practices of black folk rather than the erudition of a select few.

---

[19] W. E. B. Du Bois, "The Talented Tenth," in *The Future of the Race*, ed. Henry Louis Gates and Cornel West (New York: Alfred A. Knopf, 1996). See also Saidiya Hartman, *Wayward Lives, Beautiful Experiments: Intimate Histories of Riotous Black Girls, Troublesome Women, and Queer Radicals* (New York: W. W. Norton, 2019). Du Bois's insistence on the language of "pathology" does risk placing socially conservative constraints on his thinking insofar as he seems to presume some unitary standard of health for the body politic of black people. For more on the potential risks and benefits of social pathology see Frederick Neuhouser, *Diagnosing Social Pathology: Rousseau, Hegel, Marx, and Durkheim* (Cambridge: Cambridge University Press, 2022).

Reading Du Bois, Reading Utopia

My argument has two sides. The first is my interpretation that utopia was a consistent element in Du Bois's social analyses in *Souls* and his other writings around the turn of the 20th century. His search for truth amid a sea of mirages was driven not only by the sensibility that our lives are incomplete, but that there could be a space of existence where we are reconciled with ourselves and each other. In *Souls*, Du Bois names this space as the time when black people will be allowed to be a "co-worker in the kingdom of culture" rather than being forced to be the racialized outcasts of the American polis.[20]

My second argument shows that to read utopia effectively we must analyze it as contiguous with real social problems *and* the promise of their resolution. I argue against the supposition that utopia is a dream set apart from actual social practices. More to the point, as it concerns Du Bois in particular, I aim to show that utopia is the insertion of unrealized possibility into our forms of life that does not die away with the passage of time. This attitudinal comportment of critical theory is the conceptual work of the non-synchronous which resonates with Marx's exhortation in a letter to Arnold Ruge that "it will transpire that the world has long been dreaming of something that it can acquire if only it becomes conscious of it. It will transpire that it is not a matter of drawing a great dividing line between past and future, but of carrying out the thoughts of the past."[21] I do not mean to suggest that critical theory must only awaken the thought of freedom and then material freedom will follow in due course. But I am proposing that the activity of discerning unrealized possibilities in history is a critical element in black struggles for freedom insofar as it elucidates the violence of our lived moment as contingent.

Taken together, my two arguments critically elaborate the limits of Du Bois's thought in order to overstep them. What is important is to be able to develop an account of how the possibility of freedom can

---

[20] Du Bois, *Souls*, 3.
[21] Karl Marx, "For a Ruthless Criticism of Everything Existing (Marx to Arnold Ruge)," in *The Marx-Engels Reader*, 2nd ed., ed. Robert C. Tucker. (New York: W. W. Norton, 1978), 15.

emerge from a web of necessity. In "Sociology Hesitant," an essay that developed his vision of social science, we find Du Bois observing, "Looking over the world, we see evidence of the reign of Law; as we rise, however, from the physical to the human there comes not simply complication and interaction of forces but traces of indeterminate force until in the higher realm of human action we have Chance—that is actions undetermined by and independent of actions gone before. The duty of science, then, is to measure carefully the limits of this Chance in human conduct."[22] Du Bois was at the cutting edge of social science and wished to push its limits of analysis beyond observation of what is actual toward an appreciation of real possibility.[23] Thus, his wager is that sociology can show that human behavior cannot be fully reduced to calculable laws. In this manner, I take Du Bois as intent on showing that what may seem to be unalterable in the immediate present cannot tell us what may come.[24]

Now this notion of "Chance" is relatively useless when it is not related to existing, observable social dynamics. We can always imagine that a state of affairs could have been otherwise. For instance, one may

[22] W. E. B. Du Bois, "Sociology Hesitant," *boundary 2* 27, no. 3 (Fall 2000): 44. For the German influence on Du Bois's sociological methods, see Barrington S. Edwards, "W. E. B. Du Bois between Worlds: Berlin, Empirical Social Research, and the Race Question," *Du Bois Review* 3, no. 2 (2006): 395–424.

[23] Aldon D. Morris, *The Scholar Denied: W. E. B. Du Bois and the Birth of Modern Sociology* (Oakland: University of California Press, 2015). One of the first American sociology courses was taught by W. I. Thomas in 1894 at the University of Chicago. Émile Durkheim give his first sociology course in 1887, and the Sociological Society in Britain was not founded until 1903. Ruth Levitas, *Utopia as Method: The Imaginary Reconstitution of Society* (New York: Palgrave Macmillan, 2013), 85.

[24] Du Bois insists on the metaphysical underpinnings even of his explicitly sociological work in a letter to Herbert Aptheker: "I gave up the search of 'Absolute' Truth; not from doubt of the existence of reality, but because I believed that gradually the human mind and absolute and provable truth would approach each other . . . nearer and nearer and yet never in all eternity meet. I therefore turned to Assumption—scientific Hypothesis. I assumed the existence of Truth, since to assume anything else or not assume was unthinkable. I assumed that Truth was only partially known but that it was ultimately largely knowable. . . . Also of necessity I assumed Cause and Change. With these admittedly unprovable assumptions, I proposed to make a scientific study of human action, based on the hypothesis of the reality of such actions, of their causal connections and of their continued occurrence and change because of Law and Chance. I call Sociology the measurement of the element of Chance in Human Action." See W. E. B. Du Bois, "W. E. B. Du Bois to Herbert Aptheker, January 10, 1956," in *The Correspondence of W. E. B. Du Bois*, vol. 3 ; *Selections 1944–1963*, ed. Herbert Aptheker (Amherst: University of Massachusetts Press, 1978), 395.

imagine a history where Europeans never descended upon Africa and helped create the transatlantic slave trade. But in his *Encyclopedia*, Hegel warns against being satisfied with the proof that something is logically possible because all that would be revealed is an empty truth.[25] I think Du Bois is more careful on this score. He does not claim that science should insist that it has knowledge of "Chance" in itself, but that the practice of social science should be aware of its own limits when confronted with the postulate of human freedom in social reality.[26] In other words, Du Bois asserts that there are critical limits on what reason may claim to know and that to venture beyond those limits is to engage in speculation. Du Bois's reference to Kant in this essay is key insofar as Du Bois seems to affirm that thought and being, knowledge and reality, are not necessarily synchronous.

For Du Bois, Kant provides a methodological example of how to combine systemic rigor and human freedom in social science. He decries as preposterous any sort of definitional analogy between "Heat as a mode of motion" and "Shakespeare as pure Energy."[27] "Heat" and "Shakespeare" exist at two distinct levels of action. Du Bois notes that the attempt to produce a science that would take humanity as its object led to a problem: "A Categorical Imperative pushed thought to a Paradox: 1. The evident rhythm of human action; 2. The evident incalculability in human action."[28] Du Bois concludes that any social science that is attempting to understand human beings as they actually are must negotiate this paradox and "determine as far as possible the limits of the Uncalculable—to measure, if you will, the Kantian Absolute or Undetermined Ego."[29] What Du Bois seems to have in mind here is

---

[25] "For this reason there is nothing emptier than the talk of possibilities and impossibilities of this kind. And in particular, there should be no talk in philosophy of proving *that something* is *possible*, or *that something else* is *possible*, too; and that something, as people say, is 'thinkable.' And the warning not to use this category which has already been shown up as untrue even on its own account applies just as immediately to the historian. But the subtlety of the empty understanding takes the greatest pleasure in this pointless invention of possibilities." G. W. F. Hegel, *The Encyclopedia Logic (with the Zusätze)*, trans. T. F. Geraets, W. A. Suchting, and H. S. Harris (Indianapolis, IN: Hackett, 1991), §143.
[26] Williams, "A Democracy of Differences," 195–196.
[27] Du Bois, "Sociology Hesitant," 41.
[28] Du Bois, "Sociology Hesitant," 41.
[29] Du Bois, "Sociology Hesitant," 42.

how to make space for human freedom when one is an embodied creature beholden to firm laws such as cause and effect, whether physical or historical.[30] "Chance" not only allows him to claim that the motive force of the human creature exceeds whatever empirical knowledge we may have of their body, but also objective human reality is non-synchronous.

The postulation of "Chance" demands of the investigator a sensitivity to the discordant rhythms of our lived moment, or what I have called above "non-synchronicity." These rhythms, to stay with Du Bois's metaphor, frustrate the idea that we have immediate knowledge of ourselves or all the forces that are at play in a given moment. I may look at an event like a revolution and see only the inexorable forces of history working themselves out. Or, conversely, I may see the triumph of incalculable human freedom bursting forth, free from the determination of historical laws. Choosing either interpretation, Du Bois suggests, releases one horn of the dilemma and will not give us adequate knowledge of human action. Neither seeing determinism everywhere nor leaping arbitrarily ahead as if anything were possible, Du Bois develops a form of investigation and idea of education that strives to go to the limits of necessity and chance to open a space for reason and free action.

Du Bois never mentions race in this essay, but given the historical context we can surmise why he would claim this should be the paradigm of social science. Given that black people were often cast to the side of predetermined nature, Du Bois argues that there can never

---

[30] Paul C. Taylor understand Du Bois's positivism thusly: "Du Bois was a positivist in an older and more Comtean sense than we are now accustomed to using. He believed that there are facts about the social world, and that there are humanly accessible truths about these facts. He believed also that empirical investigation was the key to uncovering these facts, and that once they were uncovered, some of the truths about them could be stated abstractly, in the more or less formal terms of law-like generalizations (as opposed, say, to requiring poetic or symbolic expression). And, finally, he believed that some of these facts have to do with patterns, or, as he put it, 'rhythms,' in human conduct." Paul C. Taylor, "William Edward Burghardt Du Bois," in *Wiley-Blackwell Companion to Major Social Theorists*, ed. George Ritzer and Jeffrey Stepinsky (Malden, MA: Wiley-Blackwell, 2011), 433. I depart from Taylor in my interpretation of Du Bois on two counts. First, I think the "rhythms" of which Du Bois speaks should be analyzed in relation to one another and not only in respect to themselves and thus we can have an apprehension of "non-synchronicity." Second, Du Bois's theory of truth remains anchored in his Platonic belief in the reality of eternal, harmonious truths.

only be nature when human creatures are concerned. The color line brackets out the postulation of "Chance" or the rhythm of incalculable action as it concerns the "Negro" and the racially dominated. Their destiny has been determined by the laws of nature. Du Bois saw social science failing not only because it was racist, but because it was insufficiently attentive to the diverse rhythms and temporalities of social life. Obscuring these shifting and often conflictual rhythms is a central mechanism of what I describe as "racial fetishism" in later chapters.

The "Negro problem" was increasingly an object of social scientific inquiry after the failure of Reconstruction. The 1890s, with the publication of Harvard scientist Nathan Shaler's "Science and the African Problem," was a watershed moment for social science and the collection of statistical information to determine the supposedly innate character of black people. In this article Shaler announces, "Statistics will lead the way to a new understanding of black people's 'true racial capacity.'"[31] Six years later, Frederick L. Hoffman would make good on this prophecy in his *Race Traits and the Tendencies of the American Negro* where he writes, "I have given the statistics of the general progress of the [black] race in religion and education for the country at large.... Whatever benefit the individual colored man may have gained from the extension of religious worship and educational processes, the race as a whole has gone backwards rather than forwards."[32]

Du Bois was well aware of this text and its attendant black inferiority thesis. He indicts Hoffman's abuse of statistics along with Hoffman's fallacious reasoning for not realizing that the facts did not "pertai[n] to 'the race' but its various classes, which development since emancipation has differentiated."[33] In other words, Hoffman did not take seriously the internal differentiation or non-synchronicity within black forms of life. Robert Bernasconi argues that Du Bois took very seriously the harm race science could do to black political efforts and so

---

[31] Quoted in Khalil Gibran Muhammed, *The Condemnation of Blackness: Race, Crime, and the Making of Modern Urban America* (Cambridge, MA: Harvard University Press, 2010), 33.

[32] Frederick L. Hoffman, *Race Traits and the Tendencies of the American Negro* (New York: American Economic Association, 1896), 236.

[33] W. E. B. Du Bois, review of "Race Traits and Tendencies of the American Negro, by Frederick Hoffman," *Annals of the American Academy of Political Science* 9, no. 1 (1897): 132.

set himself the task of "giv[ing] hope to blacks at a time when scientists were questioning their future [and] their capacity to survive their struggle for existence."[34] Now Bernasconi's focus here is on Du Bois's "The Conservation of Races" where Du Bois seems to offer a defense of the concept of race for black people which does not disavow the model of Darwinian biological science. But this defense is located in the primary rhythm of the empirical sciences. In other words, he claims that even calculable natural laws do not establish that black people are inherently inferior at any biological level.

In "Criteria for Negro Art" Du Bois specifies a different order of truth for the secondary rhythm of art which searches "not for the sake of truth, not as a scientist seeking truth, but as one upon whom truth eternally thrusts itself as the highest handmaid of imagination, as the one great vehicle of universal understanding."[35] The point is that Du Bois deployed epistemological strategies at the level of both science and art to encourage social acknowledgment that black people were not locked in the realm of natural necessity. He searched for cleavages within the accepted discourses of knowledge that would provide intimations of a superior and truer reality for black people.

Du Bois, as early as "Sociology Hesitant," attempted to bring the realm of empirical science and art into harmony because these two rhythms of truth most fully capture human reality and they push the investigator over seemingly settled limits on knowledge. What this means is that these limits are always questionable. The black inferiority thesis could not capture the whole social reality, and Du Bois wagers social science has not adequately captured the emancipatory

---

[34] Robert Bernasconi, "'Our Duty to Conserve': W. E. B. Du Bois's Philosophy of History in Context," *South Atlantic Quarterly* 108, no. 3 (Summer 2009): 536.

[35] W. E. B. Du Bois, "Criteria of Negro Art," *The Crisis* 32 (October 1926): 293. Paul C. Taylor insightfully reconstructs Du Bois's notion of "truth" here as "shared and evolving *domain of discourse*"; a "*commitment to 'getting things right'*"; and, finally, "*a particular body of truths.*" Paul C. Taylor, *Black Is Beautiful: A Philosophy of Black Aesthetics* (Malden, MA: Wiley Blackwell, 2016), 94. He takes this to mean addressing themselves to "reigning ethical standards" or shared normative commitments (96). The secondary rhythm of culture encourages higher-order reflection on the status of a community's normative commitments so that they may be refined and made to adjust more closely to a better world.

tendencies, however imperfectly actualized, that have shaped the social practices of black peoples. Whatever refutation Du Bois can offer to the black inferiority thesis would have to take the form of a hypothesis with a concomitant methodology that would be sensitive to the real possibility of progress in the black community and the American republic as a whole. To do this he will show that the rhythms of American society are disharmonious and unethical. Accordingly, they are neither conducive to justice nor freedom. In order to capture the rhythm of chance Du Bois would have to leave the settled paths of established race science that had been laid down as it concerned black people. For Du Bois utopia would light the way. But whether this light is a mirage or true will be the question that animates Du Bois's understanding of utopian education.

To Learn What Is Missing: Du Bois's Utopia of Education

In the preceding section, I was concerned with demonstrating that Du Bois, in the early years of his work, insisted on a form of critical investigation that juxtaposed empirical existence and real possibility. If Du Bois took seriously the Kantian form of critique which establishes the proper limits of thought and knowledge, he nevertheless insisted that there was an epistemological and political imperative to transgress those very limits.

How does one do this responsibly? How do we avoid, on the one hand, irresponsible flights of fancy and, on the other, the racist projection of knowledge that Du Bois had accused Frederick Hoffman of? Du Bois's answer is to cast the problems that limit our knowledge as already containing, *in potentia*, their own resolution. The shape of utopia is never abstracted from the concrete problems which impinge upon us and so the establishment of limits is the transgression of those limits. It is from problems that we learn what is missing from our social existence. I will now spell out the specific vision of education Du Bois develops from this notion of "problem."

In a conversation with Theodor Adorno, Ernst Bloch suggests that the core of utopian consciousness is the capacity to discern that "something's missing" from our form of life.[36] In the previous chapter, I described the development of this insight as the reconstruction of a social learning process. Problems are not only an impediment to social functioning; they are the spur for developing new forms of life.[37] Without problems social consciousness becomes fused to the world as it is and forecloses insight into the normative possibilities of new forms of life.[38] Bloch, rightly, insists that utopias are historically dependent on present social conditions.[39] I understand Du Bois as advancing such a conception of critical theory *avant la lettre* insofar as the task of *Souls* was to raise the problem of the color line as a problem that hinders the proper flourishing of social freedom.

For Du Bois, problems are more than contingent phenomena that tragically befall us. Problems make it possible for us to define our historical situation and strive to become clear on what is true or what ought to exist. The two most famous lines from *Souls* contain the word "problem." The first is when he opens *Souls* with "They approach me in a half-hesitant sort of way, eye me curiously or compassionately.... How does it feel to be a problem?"[40] And the second comes a little later as the announcement "The problem of the twentieth century is the

---

[36] Ernst Bloch, *The Utopian Function of Art and Literature: Selected Essays*, trans. Jack Zipes and Frank Mecklenburg (Cambridge, MA: MIT Press, 1988), 15.

[37] Drawing on the pragmatism of John Dewey, Rahel Jaeggi describes problems as both given (objective) and made (subjective) insofar as problems do arise out of reality, but for them to appear as a problem they must be interpreted as such for them to be an object of our actions. "If the 'indeterminate situation,' hence a situation marked by fragmentation, inconsistency, and obscurity, is the starting point for the process of inquiry, then here to begin with something still quite undifferentiated and indeterminate 'announces' itself as a crisis—indeed, it is precisely the indeterminateness of the situation that makes it crisis-prone. If identifying the problem is already the first step toward solving it, it is because this makes it possible to work one's way out of the indeterminates and to achieve the first intimations of orientation, identification, and hence determinacy." Rahel Jaeggi, *Critique of Forms of Life*, trans. Ciaran Cronin (Cambridge, MA: Harvard University Press, 2018), 142.

[38] Adorno, in his conversation with Ernst Bloch, puts it this way: "Whatever utopia is, whatever can be imagined as utopia, this is the transformation of totality.... It seems to me that what people have lost subjectively in regard to consciousness is very simply the capability to imagine the totality as something that could be completely different. That people are sworn to this world as it is and have this blocked consciousness vis-à-vis possibility" (*The Utopian Function of Art and Literature*, 3–4). I will argue below that Du Bois offers a very similar critique of the split consciousness of the Talented Tenth.

[39] Bloch, *The Utopian Function of Art and Literature*, 4.

[40] Du Bois, *Souls*, 1.

problem of the color line."[41] There is a subtle difference between the two uses of "problem" here. By formulating the same "Negro problem" in subjective and objective terms, Du Bois positions the subjective frustration of a black individual as correlated to an objective limit of the historical world. At least part of the project of *Souls* is to make this unanswered question of a black identity an eminently historical issue. The resolution of the subjective problem contains the promise of a reorganized social world. Du Bois elevates the "Negro" from the status of an unfortunate creature who is a problem as such to a historical subject from which a truer and more just society can emerge.

Du Bois comes to this insight from his travels and studies in Berlin in the 1890s. In one of his earliest essays, titled "The Afro-American," Du Bois describes the estranging experience of his black body in what he took to be the heart of civilization, when he encounters a German man on a railway who hears Du Bois's accent and attempts to figure out where he is from. In the course of the dialogue, Du Bois realizes the man never thinks he is an African-American because he assumes black people from the United States are uniformly ignorant and could not learn a language like German. Du Bois recounts that "it gradually dawns upon my inquisitive friend that he is face to face with a modern 'problem.'"[42] The homology between this scene and the opening pages of *Souls* indicates that Du Bois understood the problem-space of the color line was not only restricted to the borders of the United States.[43] More importantly, he learns that the objective conditions of the world are such that they limit him to being identified as a problem. Yet these encounters with relatively benign racism are taken by Du Bois as moments when he has the dim recognition of how deeply racial injustice has been woven into various forms of life as well as how they would have to be transformed. This is due to Du Bois's implicit philosophy of history wherein "[a]ll social growth means a succession of

---

[41] Du Bois, *Souls*, 9.
[42] W. E. B. Du Bois, "The Afro-American" (1894), in *The Problem of the Color Line at the Turn of the Twentieth Century: The Essential Early Essays*, ed. Nahum Dimitri Chandler (New York: Fordham University Press, 2015), 34.
[43] See Nahum Dmitri Chandler, "Introduction. Toward a New History of the Centuries: On the Early Writings of W. E. B. Du Bois," in *The Problem of the Color Line at The Turn of the Twentieth Century: The Essential Early Essays*, ed. Nahum Dimitri Chandler (New York: Fordham University Press, 2015), 8–9.

social problems ... they denote that laborious and often baffling adjustment of action and condition which is the essence of progress."[44]

Rahel Jaeggi argues that forms of life ought to be understood as "problem-solving entities."[45] Problems give forms of life their normative character insofar as a problem appears not only as a feature of the objective world, but as part of collective practices of interpretation. Something is never a problem *as such*, but a problem for some putative end or goal. Jaeggi rightly notes that problems not only disrupt a form of life, they can also *generate* forms of life as agents collectively work to find solutions to social crises. Jaeggi notes that "problems have ... histories. A problem that arises at a particular point in history and in a particular sociocultural environment is always marked by the attempts previously made to solve it. In this sense, history becomes sedimented in the problems themselves and the problems become enriched."[46] What this means is that grasping the historical genesis of forms of life *and* their supersession must inquire into the sedimented problems that have accumulated in social life.

Indeed, Du Bois consistently describes historical eras as finding their truth in the resolution of specific social problems they inherit. For instance, he claims that the problem of the 1700s was the problem of monarchy and the problem of the 1800s was the relationship of the state to the laboring classes.[47] The two rhythms of chance and imposed condition are entangled together, to be sure, but more to the point, problems are both a frustrating limit for, and enabling condition of, action.

For Du Bois, "action" must involve proper knowledge to guide one's practical conduct. Action without knowledge is liable to exacerbate problems by misrecognizing the actual character of the objective limitations of the world. This explains why so much of *Souls* is dedicated

---

[44] W. E. B. Du Bois, "The Study of Negro Problems" (1894), in *The Problem of the Color Line at the Turn of the Twentieth Century: The Essential Early Essays*, ed. Nahum Dimitri Chandler (New York: Fordham University Press, 2015), 81–82.
[45] Jaeggi, *Critique of Forms of Life*, 133.
[46] Jaeggi, *Critique of Forms of Life*, 145.
[47] W. E. B. Du Bois, "The Present Outlook for the Dark Races of Mankind" (1900), in *The Problem of the Color Line at the Turn of the Twentieth Century: The Essential Early Essays*, ed. Nahum Dimitri Chandler (New York: Fordham University Press, 2015), 120–121.

to defending the claim that black people ought to have access to institutions of education. To freely act is to know, and without insightful knowledge one's actions will most likely be reduced to reflexes or reactions against objective conditions.[48]

Utopia emerges early in *Souls* when Du Bois proclaims that black people are striving to become "co-worker[s] in the kingdom of culture, to escape both death and isolation, and to husband and use [their] best powers and [their] latent genius."[49] "Culture" is a difficult concept to precisely define in Du Bois's thinking in this period. This is mostly due to the fact that he uses it to cover a wide array of social phenomena such as historical practices, aesthetic ideals, social mores, and even political struggle. Nevertheless, we can isolate the most relevant feature of culture as its capacity to develop the faculty of *recognition*. Du Bois most likely adapts some aspects of Gottfried von Herder's understanding of culture as the process of expressing a social group's distinct historical character, their soul, in the context of a broader human family.[50] But the social/historical role of culture only obtains because of culture's epistemological function. Throughout his life, Du Bois insisted on the necessity of education to "address and resolve social, economic, and political problems."[51] Social recognition from others will only be possible once black people have the capacity to accurately recognize the social problems which beset them.

---

[48] The problem of reflex and reaction is core to the account of racial fetishism that I develop in chapter 4 in my interpretation of Frantz Fanon. Though Du Bois does not draw the same conclusions as Marx on what would make a rational society, he does agree with the epistemic argument that Marx makes whereby rational conduct will only become possible once "the practical relations of everyday life between man and man, and man and nature, generally present themselves to him in a transparent and rational form." Karl Marx, *Capital: A Critique of Political Economy*, vol. 1, trans. Ben Fowkes, intro. Ernest Mandel, (New York: Penguin Classics, 1990), 173. Problems, for Du Bois, initially present an obscurity in the social world, but they must be converted into the task of elucidating the Truth of the world.

[49] Du Bois, *Souls*, 3.

[50] Sieglinde Lemke, "Berlin and Boundaries: *Sollen* versus *Geschehen*," *boundary 2* 27, no. 3 (Fall 2000): 60–64; Kwame Anthony Appiah, *Lines of Descent: W. E. B. Du Bois and the Emergence of Identity* (Cambridge, MA: Harvard University Press, 2014), ch. 2; Mitchell Aboulafia, *Transcendence: On Self-Determination and Cosmopolitanism* (Stanford: Stanford University Press, 2010), ch. 5.

[51] Derrick P. Alridge, *The Educational Thought of W. E. B. Du Bois: An Intellectual History* (New York: Teachers College Press, 2008), 41.

To not be able to recognize the objective problems of one's situation is to lack "true self-consciousness."[52] Du Bois claims this lack prevents black people from discerning their historical self and their historical situation. Without a refined culture as opposed to what Du Bois understands to be the folk culture that black people already possess, black people will lack the capacity for *anagnorisis*. In Greek tragedy this denotes the moment where the hero attains insight into the true nature of how things are, the transition from ignorance to truth.[53] *Anagnorisis* reflects the creative capacity of thought to comprehend not only the world as such, but the part one plays in the world. The tragic knowledge of how one has been conditioned and limited actually makes way for truly acting rather than reacting. The two scenes where Du Bois claims to have learned that he was a problem for others are not passive moments of alienation, but Du Bois peering into his memory and gaining subjective insight into the objective problem of the global color line.[54]

As Nahum Chandler puts it, Du Bois constantly displays his "general theoretical disposition toward the inductive study of the example," and here Du Bois offers himself as an example.[55] Du Bois takes his own historical life as a premise from which to build his argument for the unjust racial constitution of the American republic. But beyond this, he offers his life, at least how he reconstructs it, as an example of what is presently possible for black people as a whole. In other words, he recognizes tomorrow in his own yesterday.

Du Bois assumes that the capacity for historical insight of oneself and one's world must be trained through classical liberal education of science *and* art.[56] But not just any art. The young Du Bois finds in the

---

[52] Du Bois, *Souls*, 2.
[53] The dramaturgical content of this concept in no way takes away from Du Bois's clear insistence on the role of scientific inquiry and the objectivity of the world. Indeed, as I have claimed earlier, Du Bois defends the possibility of a harmony between the arts and the sciences.
[54] Du Bois, *Souls*, 1; Du Bois, "The Afro-American," 34.
[55] Nahum Dimitri Chandler, *The Problem of the Negro as a Problem for Thought* (New York: Fordham University Press, 2014), 20.
[56] "The riddle of existence is the college curriculum that was laid before the Pharaohs, that was taught in the groves by Plato, that formed the *trivium* and *quadrivium*, and is today laid before the freedmen's sons by Atlanta University. And this course of study will not change; its methods will grow more deft and effectual, its content richer by toil of scholar and sight of seer; but the true college will ever have one goal,—not to earn

yesterday of Western civilization critical fragments of utopia that the color line has distorted and submerged. In one chapter of *Souls* Du Bois concludes, "I sit with Shakespeare and he winces not. Across the color-line I move arm in arm with Balzac and Dumas.... I summon Aristotle and Aurelius and what soul I will, and they come all graciously with no scorn nor condescension. So, wed with Truth, I dwell above the Veil. Is this the life you grudge us, O knightly America?"[57] Du Bois dramatizes a utopic space wherein he plumbs the Western archive for its latent, yet unrealized "Truth." In it he finds the truth of his capacity for recognizing how he could be woven into a society intent on limiting his black body and the true recognition of how to express the desire to go beyond these artificial limits.

This is crucial for understanding the epistemological function of Du Bois narrating scenes of benign racism: he has already acquired the refined sensibilities of culture that allow him to see what was happening. In other words, he is not recounting an *immediate* access to the phenomenological experience of everyday racism as if he were claiming that *every* black person immediately knows when they've encountered racism. Du Bois demonstrates his critical capacity to mediate his individual experience as a data point on a broader map of the color line.[58] Yet he is only able to engage this retrospective/prospective

---

meat, but to know the end and aim of that life which meat nourishes" (Du Bois, *Souls*, 51). The invariance of the university institution as fixed in time and through history demonstrates Du Bois's insistence on the eternal image of Truth.

[57] Du Bois, *Souls*, 67.
[58] I think Du Bois's project here has crucial similarities to Frederic Jameson's concept of "cognitive mapping." For Jameson, cognitive mapping was the aesthetic effort to deal with the growing spatial contradiction between "a phenomenological description of the life of an individual and a more properly structural model of the conditions of existence of that experience." Fredric Jameson, "Cognitive Mapping," in *Marxism and the Interpretation of Culture*, ed. Cary Nelson and Lawrence Grossberg (Urbana: University of Illinois Press, 1988), 349. The problem of the color line works both as an empirical description and as an aesthetic device that situates the lived experience of a racial problem with a global structure of life. Du Bois, in other words, opens lines of practical action and analysis by designating a social totality that must be understood and against which one must struggle. Du Bois needs to create a *topos* of study because it is neither self-evident that the "problem" black people feel has anything to do with a global color line nor that the assumed color line of the world is a problem that must be resolved. That being said, Du Bois does think we need to start from problems and work up toward an apprehension of the broader social totality.

activity of *anagnorisis* because he has already acquired the necessary type of education.

Culture, at least partly, is the institution of practices that would refine the capacity for *anagnorisis* of black people as a whole social group. It generates a *form of life*. The issue here is that Du Bois realizes culture is not an automatic process but can be waylaid. Those who know have a duty to act and encourage culture. If Du Bois saw Western civilization as temporally out of joint and in need of resynchronization, he perceived an analogous problem with what he derisively called the "Mass" of black people. Inheriting a model of education from Plato, Du Bois insists that a healthy culture must proceed from an enlightened leadership class.[59] Du Bois will ask "Was there ever a nation on God's fair earth civilized from the bottom upward?" and then answer, "Never; it is, ever was and ever will be from the top downward that culture filters."[60] Du Bois, at this stage of his thinking, turns utopia into a form of elitism that he will struggle to overcome throughout his life. In the following section I will analyze the fraught relationship of education between Du Bois's enlightened leadership class, called "the Talented Tenth," and the black masses. While I do not think Du Bois can be completely defended from the charge of elitism, I will show that there are "non-synchronous" elements to Du Bois's social theory that will allow us to better understand the untimely relationship between utopia and education.

The Role of the Talented Tenth and Black Salvation

In the same year Du Bois published *Souls*, he wrote an article called "The Talented Tenth" for a collection of essays entitled *The Negro Problem*. Here he proclaims, "The Negro race, like all races, is going to be saved by its exceptional men."[61] Perhaps Du Bois's most infamous concept, there have been no shortage of arguments against Du Bois's defense of a black intellectual aristocracy tasked with leading

---

[59] Withun describes this as Du Bois's "egalitarian elitism" in *Co-workers*, 79–91.
[60] Du Bois, "The Talented Tenth," 139.
[61] Du Bois, "The Talented Tenth," 133.

and molding the black masses.[62] For instance, Adolph Reed insists that we must understand Du Bois's advocacy for an enlightened black aristocracy from within the economic context that emerged after the Civil War where "the related dynamics of urbanization and industrialization increased the social need for scientific and technical knowledge."[63] Thus, the role of intellectuals in the social division of labor was transformed. Situating Du Bois in his historical context should limit the tendency to render Du Bois's thinking as an abstraction in order to make him more palatable for our present sensibilities. Or, worse, uncritically inheriting the Du Boisian model of leadership and politics. For one only needs to look at Du Bois's stated end of education to see that he conceived of the relationship between the Talented Tenth and the black masses in relatively paternalistic terms: "The problem of education, then, among Negroes must first of all deal with the Talented Tenth; it is the problem of developing the Best of this race that they may guide the Mass away from contamination and death of the Worst, in their own and other races."[64]

In *Souls*, Du Bois implies the mass of black people are akin to the prisoners in Plato's Allegory of the Cave.[65] He sees them as trapped in a world of appearances, cut off from one another, and ruled by those who do not have their best interests at heart. They are ruled by others because they have not mastered their own appetites. The black masses, according to Du Bois, mostly live in darkness without true *anagnorisis* and so they are trapped in such a way that their hopes are oriented toward immediate, carnal gratification. Their only hope for advancement "lies in the correction of [sexual] immorality, crime and laziness among the Negroes themselves, which still remains as a heritage from slavery."[66] Saidiya Hartman affirms that "Du Bois blamed lax morals,

---

[62] See Adolph L. Reed Jr., *W. E. B. Du Bois and American Political Thought: Fabianism and the Color Line* (Oxford: Oxford University Press, 1997); Robert Gooding-Williams, *In the Shadow of Du Bois: Afro-modern Political Thought in America* (Cambridge, MA: Harvard University Press, 2009); Joy James, *Transcending the Talented Tenth: Black Leaders and American Intellectuals* (New York: Routledge, 1997), 15–35; Cornel West, *The Cornel West Reader* (New York: Basic Civitas Books, 1999), 87–119.

[63] Reed, *W. E. B. Du Bois and American Political Thought*, 16.

[64] Du Bois, "The Talented Tenth," 133.

[65] Du Bois, *Souls*, 59. I am indebted to Shamoon Zamir's interpretation in *Dark Voices* here.

[66] Du Bois, "The Conservation of Races," 117.

promiscuity, children born out of wedlock, and the disregard of marriage for the social crisis of revolution of black intimate life that was taking place in the slum."[67]

Du Bois's Talented Tenth are black philosopher kings and queens who balance the group soul of black people and correct their problematic form of life. The Talented Tenth function as both the theoretical and the practical solution to the non-synchronicity of the past and future, of black forms of life and the wider society. This view is constitutive of his philosophy of progress as shown when he declares, "Progress in human affairs is more often a pull than a push, surging forward *of the exceptional man*, and the lifting of his duller brethren slowly and painfully to his vantage-ground."[68] He invokes a heroic mythology of a cultured elite dragging the black masses up to the light of culture. Joy James helpfully notes the persistent danger of this legacy of the Talented Tenth for "most contemporary black intellectuals [who] rarely ask to what extent they intentionally or unintentionally fulfill the nineteenth-century missionary mandate for race management."[69] Du Bois did not advocate for elitism arbitrarily. It was part and parcel of his understanding of social reform within the bounds of reason.[70] Du Bois inherits a tradition of Enlightenment philosophy that insists the autonomy of reason ought to be the guiding force behind social change. Society, having reached a level of knowledge that would allow social reformers to consciously guide civilization into the "kingdom of culture," must allow those with the skills and knowledge to rise to positions of leadership.[71]

If we strip away Du Bois's vanguard politics, we find Du Bois making a striking claim as concerns social ontology. Du Bois asserts the present moment is composed of differential rhythms. It would appear that slavery has shunted the black population off onto a different historical and cultural rhythm than the rest of society. Du Bois diagnoses the regressive temporality afflicting black people such that they are not

---

[67] Hartman, *Wayward Lives*, 90.
[68] Du Bois, *Souls*, 59, emphasis mine.
[69] James, *Transcending the Talented Tenth*, 17.
[70] See Peter Gay, *The Enlightenment: An Interpretation*, vol. 2: *The Science of Freedom* (New York: Alfred A. Knopf, 1969).
[71] Du Bois, *Souls*, 3.

modern, they are out of step with the rest of society. The color line does not structure social relationships synchronously, but rather maintains them in non-synchronous domination. In other words, forms of life become not only spatially differentiated through segregation, but temporally fractured insofar as the practices and habits of distinct social groups become oriented toward divergent horizons of expectation. Social groups closer to whiteness are pulled forward while social groups associated with the darker races are pushed into social conditions which vitiate their capacity for political organization and self-knowledge. The conflict-ridden temporality of race introduces systemic dysfunctions into the body politic.

Recall that Du Bois intends to account for problems as they are subjectively experienced and as they objectively exist.[72] If black people are forced to exist non-synchronously by being constrained by poverty, racial derision, and exploitative working conditions then this will affect how they see and understand themselves. The Talented Tenth, as an "advance guard of the renaissance of culture," must lead black people away from the sources of regression by furnishing the educational institutions that would clear away the false and give them insight into the true.[73] Put more strongly, it is up to the Talented Tenth to descend back down into this discordant rhythm armed with cultural insight so that they may lead black people toward true self-consciousness.

Now this conception of top-down social change has as much to do with Du Bois's "Greek" philosophical influences as well as the increasing reorganization of society around corporate industries. The economic form of industrial capitalism that was partially ushered in by the end of the Civil War and Northern industries expanding into Southern markets transformed social problems around labor. This shift required intellectuals who could view society holistically. Du Bois sees the challenges of nominally "free" black labor as two-sided.[74] First, the black "masses" do not have the requisite moral habits and knowledge to fully participate in this historical stage of civilization. And

---

[72] Seyla Benhabib describes this as the distinction between "lived crisis" and "system crisis" in *Critique, Norm, and Utopia: A Study of the Foundations of Critical Theory* (New York: Columbia University Press, 1986).

[73] Du Bois, "Outlook," 123.

[74] Du Bois, "Study," 82.

second, white prejudice and the violence of American society prevents the cultivation of black intellectuals who could solve the first problem by foreclosing the well-funded establishment of black universities. These dual regimes of ignorance and violence, respectively, disrupted not only the harmony of black people as a social group, but prevented them from developing culture in the richest sense. No doubt Du Bois saw black people as an ill-formed public and the Talented Tenth as the social class that would know how to encourage proper ideals in the black masses.

Du Bois's utopian longing to "sit with Shakespeare" expressed his search for an alternate rhythm of thought no longer compressed into the density of the racist contemporary moment. Moreover, it reflects his belief that all cultures have eternally useful ideals which can be reappropriated for the resolution of historically variant problems. In the realm of culture, therefore, we find "the ever necessary combination of the permanent and the contingent—of the ideal and the practical in workable equilibrium" which is "a matter of infinite experiment and frequent mistakes."[75] The Talented Tenth bring black people into an alternate historical space where they recognize themselves and experiment with their limits. In so doing, they will discover the cultural gift they will leave for the "kingdom of culture." But without culture black people will either sink into their own inequity or lack the critical capacities to refuse being led astray by opportunistic leaders. Either way society will founder because "no secure civilization can be built in the South with the Negro as an ignorant, turbulent proletariat."[76]

Permanent ideals are group imperatives toward justice and self-worth. They are guiding values for the constitution of forms of life and thus operate as a compass to navigate the contingent terrain of problems. These ideals and how to strive for them are generated through a healthy formation of culture that encourages critique and rethinking among the group. Du Bois analyzes black culture as presently incapable of putting forth worthy permanent ideals. Instead, black culture has been reduced to focusing on the ever-contingent goal of wealth accumulation that typified the broader form of life of

---

[75] Du Bois, *Souls*, 57.
[76] Du Bois, *Souls*, 64.

American society. Ironically, this meant that black people, in a crucial sense, were *synchronous* with the rest of society. They were synchronous with the general structure of values of their historical situation and they lacked the cultural power to resist the materialist ethos that surrounded them. Mere synchronicity or integration is not praiseworthy, according to Du Bois; black people must be integrating into a true and just form of life. Thus, Du Bois critiques not only the spiritual character of black people, but the spiritual character of his times. Once again, Du Bois's Platonism offers him the utopian vantage point whereby he can see that "temporal laws were subordinate to a transcendent moral law."[77]

Du Bois criticizes what he takes to be the ethos of the city of Atlanta as a den of corruption and materialism. He proclaims, "The need of the South is knowledge and culture,—not in dainty limited quantity, as before the war, but in broad busy abundance in the world of work; and until she has this, not all the Apples of Hesperides, be they golden and bejeweled, can save her from the curse of the Bœotian lovers."[78] The use of Classical Greek mythology identifies the ideology of materialism, the golden "Apples of Hesperides," as one of the threats to black culture and group coherence.[79] It is up to the Talented Tenth to teach the black masses ideals and moral character that will dissuade them from seeing money as the only reasonable end of life. Du Bois affirms a university whose curriculum is rooted in what was taught in "the groves by Plato."[80] In it students can "follow the love song of

---

[77] Manning Marable, *W. E. B. Du Bois: Black Radical Democrat* (London: Routledge, 2016), 66.

[78] Du Bois, *Souls*, 53. In Greek mythology, Atalanta was the daughter of Schoeneus of Bœotia and a huntress. Du Bois is clearly drawing on the part of her myth where she offered to marry any man who could beat her in a race and killed any who lost to her. She eventually lost to Hippomenes, who laid golden apples of Hesperides in her way to distract her. The fate of the two lovers concludes with them making love in the shrine of Zeus or Cybele and being turned into lions for the misdeed. For an insightful reading of this line, see Carrie Cowherd, "The Wings of Atalanta," 289–290.

[79] "Here stands this black young Atalanta, girding herself for the race that must be run; and if her eyes be still toward the hills and sky as in the days of old, then we may look for noble running; but what if some ruthless or wily or even thoughtless Hippomenes lay golden apples before her? What if the Negro people be wooed from a strife of righteousness, from a love of knowing, to regard dollars as the be-all and end-all of life?" (Du Bois, *Souls*, 50).

[80] Du Bois, *Souls*, 51.

Dido ... listen to the tale of Troy divine," and "wander among the stars ... wander among men and nations,—and elsewhere other well-worn ways of knowing this queer world." Crucially he goes on to extol that there is "[n]othing new, no time-saving devices,—simply old time-glorified methods of delving for Truth, and searching out the hidden beauties of life, and learning the good of living."[81]

But why should we assume the Talented Tenth have acquired the requisite knowledge and character to perform these roles as culture workers? Du Bois's mobilization of Plato's Allegory of the Cave runs into the same unasked question one can find in the *Republic*: who frees the first prisoner? Robert Gooding-Williams points out this paradox in *Souls* and asks, "On what grounds can he believe that he has overcome the false, estranging double consciousness"?[82] While Du Bois recognizes that "[t]he number of group leaders of ability and character is far behind the demand," the thought behind *Souls* founders, splits in two, as he is forced to resolve why the Talented Tenth are not, as a group, fulfilling their purpose.[83]

Much scholarship on Du Bois and the Talented Tenth assumes that in this early period he was completely consistent in his faith in this group of intellectuals and only explicitly rethought it in 1948 when he critiques his assumption that the Talented Tenth would naturally internalize the virtue of sacrifice.[84] In the following section, I argue that Du Bois was already coming to rethink the vanguard status he gave to the Talented Tenth because he realized their leadership could not perform the role of synchronizing black forms of life without the support of the so-called black masses. I will show that *Souls* is mostly concerned with saving the Talented Tenth from *their* vices and their non-synchronicity. Du Bois, without realizing it, reverses who is saving whom. In this reversal, he demonstrates that without the mass of black people supporting and guiding them, the Talented Tenth are nothing more than a small dinghy buffeted by the waves of the color line.

---

[81] Du Bois, *Souls*, 51.
[82] Gooding-Williams, *In the Shadow of Du Bois*, 130.
[83] W. E. B. Du Bois, "The Development of a People," *Ethics* 123, no. 3 (April 2013): 542.
[84] James, *Transcending the Talented Tenth*, 161–163. For an opposing view that argues that Du Bois never fully relinquished his belief in a Talented Tenth, see Gooding-Williams, *In the Shadow of Du Bois*, 167.

The Utopian Music of Black Folk: Du Bois's Phenomenology of the "Non-synchronous"

The effects of "non-synchronicity" as I have been describing them range from the political to the cultural to the phenomenological. Du Bois's holistic approach, as much a product of his interest in social science as his philosophical inclinations, examines the color line as an arrythmia beating within the heart of society. Where people live, what jobs they hold or are barred from holding, how they are educated, what history they learn, and the social practices they must develop in order to survive affect how a society articulates itself. *Souls* analyzes the diverse racial and social strata that have been shaped by history and economic transformations in the United States and searches for a path forward.

A well-functioning society, Du Bois insists, would have all of these strata working cooperatively toward greater civilizational harmony and peace. The color line prevents such striving epistemologically by making it exceedingly difficult to separate what is true from what is false concerning the nature of black people. In addition to the epistemological wrong of the color line there is the social wrong of producing an "ignorant and turbulent" black proletariat who cannot recognize their place in history.[85] Remnants of slavery remain lodged in the racial attitudes and institutional functioning of American society insofar as the social practices and technologies of that era persist in the very matter of life. At the heart of this maelstrom stands the Talented Tenth who must, heroically, extricate themselves from the false necessities of racial life and find the true of what ought to be.

I will elaborate on these two wrongs in later chapters, but it is worth specifying how they are distinct and how they relate to one another. The epistemological wrong of the color line is a *cognitive distortion* that not only shapes how the world appears to us, but also inhibits the development of social resources for distinguishing between well-founded and baseless *reasons*. Du Bois's critique of the social science and the use of statistics is emblematic of a broader problem of our practices as reason-giving creatures. The co-identification of Truth

---

[85] Du Bois, *Souls*, 64.

and harmony, for Du Bois, relates both to the veracity of the claims that we make to others and our collective processes of deliberation. Du Bois's concern that Truth is the most sorely needed remedy for the color line reflects his understanding of forms of life as primarily anchored in knowledge-producing practices.[86] Accordingly, the loss of Truth is both a functional and an ethical problem.

The second wrong of the color line is a *practical distortion* of the social practices that are available to black people. The arbitrary creation of an economic-social underclass prevents black people from having the necessary degree of autonomy that would allow them to transcend the weight of enslavement and become fully modern creatures. At the core of Du Bois's debate with Booker T. Washington concerning the emphasis of cultivating skills in manual labor over intellectual labor in the black community was the worry that racial domination would become entrenched rather than lessened via integration into labor markets.[87] In other words, developing skills that the "economy" needs is no guarantee for uplift. The phenomena of "split-markets" attests to this reality.[88] In other words, the sphere of equal exchange between labor and wages reproduced social inequality.

These two wrongs are clearly conjoined for Du Bois and reinforce ideologies of racial inferiority throughout the body politic. Taken

---

[86] For the centrality of truth and ignorance for Du Bois's thought, see Withun, Co-workers, 91–94; Arnold Rampersad, *The Art and Imagination of W. E. B. Du Bois* (New York: Schocken Books, 1990), 50; Marable, *W. E. B. Du Bois*, ix; José Medina, "Color-Blindness, Meta-ignorance, and the Racial Imagination," *Critical Philosophy of Race* 1, no. 1 (2013): 38–67; Brandon R. Davis, "The Politics of Racial Abjection," *Du Bois Review: Social Science Research on Race* 20, no. 1 (2023): 143–162; W. E. B. Du Bois, *Dusk of Dawn: An Essay toward an Autobiography of a Race Concept* (1940; Oxford: Oxford University Press, 2007), 2–3.

[87] Du Bois, *Souls*, 30–31.

[88] W. E. B. Du Bois, "W.E.B. Du Bois (1906), 'L'ouvrier Negre en Amérique [The Negro Worker in America],' *Revue Économique Internationale*, 3:298–348," trans. Aaron Major, *Critical Sociology* (2022): 1–25, https://doi-org.myaccess.library.utoronto.ca/10.1177/08969205221138011; Aaron Major, "Race, Labor, and Postbellum Capitalism in Du Bois's 'The Negro Worker in America,'" *Critical Sociology* 49, no. 3: 383–393; Cliff Brown, "Racial Conflict and Split Labor Markets: The AFL Campaign to Organize Steel Workers, 1918–1919," in "Migration and Labor Markets," special issue of *Social Science History* 22, no. 3 (Autumn 1998): 319–347; Salvatore J. Restifo, Vincent J. Rescigno, and Zhenchao Qian, "Segmented Assimilation, Split Labor Markets, and Racial/Ethnic Inequality: The Case of Early-Twentieth-Century New York," *American Sociological Review* 78, no. 5 (2013): 897–924.

together, these two distortions offer a preliminary account of what I call *racial fetishism*. Du Bois, on my view, sees resolving the cognitive distortion as the necessary mechanism for overcoming the practical distortion. We must first repair our social practices of reasoning in order to develop an economically just form of life. Put this way, we can see why the Talented Tenth as an engine for social transformation appeared so compelling to the young Du Bois.

However, the Talented Tenth are not immune to the effects of racial fetishism even if they have been fortunate enough to receive the liberal education Du Bois sees as necessary for *anagnorisis*. Du Bois describes these black intellectuals as "[t]he confused, half-conscious mutter of men who are black and whitened, crying 'Liberty, Freedom, Opportunity'" but "[b]ehind the thought lurks the afterthought—suppose, after all, the World is right and we are less than men? Suppose this mad impulse within is all wrong, some mock mirage from the untrue?"[89] The Talented Tenth are divided within themselves. They are black because of their race and whitened because of their education. Education elevates them; race debases them. The political nature of the color line shapes the epistemological problem of distinguishing between the true and the false. In fact, I take this this be the critical question of utopia: how do we discern if it is not "some mock mirage from the untrue"?[90]

---

[89] Du Bois, *Souls*, 56. The beginning of the chapter is telling for how Du Bois sees the immanent and dynamic contradiction of thought and material reality: "From the shimmering swirl of waters where many, many thoughts ago the slave-ship first saw the square tower of Jamestown, have flowed down to our day three streams of thinking: one swollen from the larger world here and overseas, saying, the multiplying of human wants in culture-lands calls for the world-wide cooperation of men in satisfying them [19th-century humanism]. Hence arises a new human unity, pulling the end of earth nearer, and all men, black, yellow, and white.... To be sure, behind this thought lurks the afterthought of force and dominion.... The second thought streaming from the death-ship and the curving river is the thought of the older South,—the sincere and passionate belief that somewhere between men and cattle, God created a *tertium quid*, and called it a Negro.... To be sure, behind the thought lurks the afterthought—some of them favoring chance might become men, but in sheer self-defence we dare not let them.... And last of all there trickles down that third and darker thought—the thought of the things themselves, the confused, half-conscious mutter of men who are black and whitened, crying 'Liberty, Freedom, Opportunity—vouchsafe to us, O boastful World, the chance of living men!' To be sure, behind the thought lurks the afterthought,—suppose, after all, the World is right and we are less than man? Suppose this mad impulse within is all wrong, some mock mirage from the untrue?" (55–56).

[90] Du Bois, *Souls*, 56.

Du Boisian phenomenology in *Souls* attempts to surmise under what conditions racialized consciousness can come to know what is true about itself and critique the social conditions which frustrate projects of freedom. The Talented Tenth are tasked with establishing the very educational conditions that would allow them to be educated in the first place. How does true historical consciousness get behind itself when it must emerge from the false? It seems that Du Bois's partial answer to this question is that cultural values of Western civilization are not, in principle, racialized, only contingently so. After all, the Truth they express, even partially, is invariant and eternal. Accordingly, the Talented Tenth can lift themselves out of the accumulated ignorance of their racially unjust society by reading the likes of Shakespeare and Dumas. The simplicity of this solution raises two deeper problems that Du Bois finds himself compelled to address.

First, if this cultural inheritance does have the salvific power Du Bois imputes to it then he has to explain why racism persists more generally. Second, he will have to answer why the Talented Tenth find themselves unable to mobilize the Truth they have glimpsed through their education. Du Bois intimates that the problem must go beyond the relation of self-consciousness that the Talented Tenth have within themselves. The root of the problem will be found in the non-synchronicity of social life that provides the foundation of consciousness. So long as the world is disordered, so too will be the souls of the Talented Tenth.

Another way to put the problem is to say that Du Bois sees the Talented Tenth as heteronymous because they live in a heteronymous form of life. They can hardly legislate for themselves, let alone for the black culture they are supposed to lead. In the one piece of fiction in *Souls*, the chapter titled "Of the Coming of John," Du Bois acknowledge the limits of the Talented Tenth. He provides us with the story of a black character named John who goes north to receive an education and returns to his home in the South in order to educate his people and save them. When he gives these rural black folks a speech about the importance of culture he realizes, "Little had they understood of what he said, for he spoke an unknown tongue."[91] The liberal education John received transformed him at the expense of having concrete

---

[91] Du Bois, *Souls*, 148.

insight into the black community he left behind. The rhythms between John and the black community are not synchronized, which leads to his alienation from them.

Moreover, he can no longer abide by the social norms of segregation and deference. Upon his return, a powerful white judge in the town asks, "Now, John, the question is, are you, with your education and Northern notions, going to accept the situation and teach the darkies to be faithful servants and laborers as your fathers were,—I knew your father, John, he belonged to my brother, and he was a good Nigger."[92] Now what Du Bois dramatizes is how self-consciousness cannot be obtained by only having a single individual attain education. John's own people do not understand him, and the social-historical distance between the present and enslavement is too narrow. The story ends with John's lynching when he kills another white character, also named John, who assaulted his sister. Black John stares out toward the ocean, humming "The Song of the Bride" from Richard Wagner's opera *Lohengrin*, while he awaits the white mob that will kill him.

The invocation of music from Western culture as violence descends on this member of the Talented Tenth crystallizes the tragic fate of those caught between the rhythms of society. Kevin Thomas Miles insists that we must understand this story and its music as a repetition of Greek tragedy.[93] John is undone by his own yearning for truth and the reader attains critical and affective insight into social reality. The failure of John has as much to do with education as the fact that he could not join himself with the black community that might have been able to protect him. The utopia John finds in the music of Wagner leaves him nowhere, with no concrete home. His consciousness may be free, but his body remains vulnerable to the violence of the color line. All of which is to say that "non-synchronicity" in itself is not progressive without attaining some sort of practical mastery over it. Du Bois provides the reader with *anagnorisis* in this moment. The

---

[92] Du Bois, *Souls*, 150.
[93] Kevin Thomas Miles, "Haunting Music in *The Souls of Black Folk*," *boundary 2* 27, no. 3 (Fall 2000): 211–212. See also R. A. Judy, "Lohengrin's Swan and the Style of Interiority in 'Of the Coming of John,'" *CR: The New Centennial Review* 15, no. 2 (Fall 2015): 211–258 and Russel A. Berman, "Du Bois and Wagner: Race, Nation, and Culture between the United States and Germany," *German Quarterly* 70, no. 2 (1997): 123–135.

secondary rhythm of truth presses against the fantasy that individual self-knowledge will be enough for progress and safety. Du Bois offers the insight that the Talented Tenth can confuse themselves about what it means to be free and what it means to serve the black community. Aesthetic uplift is nothing without a practical vision of tomorrow rooted in actually existing black life.

John, Du Bois's representative of the Talented Tenth, reveals how the color line frustrates the ability of black people to articulate their historical message. Moreover, I believe John somewhat recasts Du Bois's stance on the Talented Tenth. Even if he could support the Talented Tenth ideally, practically he found them wanting. The music of Wagner's *Lohengrin*, a synecdoche for "Western" culture, affords limited insight into one's unhappiness living as a problem along the color line. John's sister asks him, "'[D]oes it make every one—unhappy when they study and learn lots of things?'" and he answers in the affirmative while also expressing that he is glad that he did.[94] Unhappiness returns again when the white judge warns black John not to make the black people of the community "discontented and unhappy" by giving them ideas about freedom and equality.[95] Unhappiness or, more precisely, indignation is aroused by feeling the interdiction of society against the apprehension of Truth and harmony. The Talented Tenth have a false utopia in their hands. They know enough to know they live among falseness, but they do not know enough to get closer toward what is true: freedom. Du Bois appears to give a racial body to Hegel's "Unhappy Consciousness," which is "the consciousness of self as dual-natured, merely contradictory being."[96] The problem exists, first, between John and the world and then, subsequently, between John and himself. John recognizes his tragic circumstances, but he does not have the recognition of a community that would allow his idea of freedom to become objective.

---

[94] Du Bois, *Souls*, 149.
[95] Du Bois, *Souls*, 150.
[96] G. W. F. Hegel, *Hegel's Phenomenology of Spirit*, trans. A. V. Miller (New York: Oxford University Press, 1977), §206. See also Terry P. Pinkard, *Does History Make Sense? Hegel on the Historical Shapes of Justice* (Cambridge, MA: Harvard University Press, 2017), 36–38.

In the wake of historical tragedy, utopia surges forth from an altogether different music than that of Wagner. The "sorrow songs" or "Negro folk-song," with rhythms quite distinct from those found in Western culture, are the subject of the concluding chapter of *Souls*. The split consciousness of the Talented Tenth hears "a haunting echo ... in which the soul of the black slave spoke to men."[97] Du Bois takes these songs to be a historical record of the true sorrow and hope buried in the mists of slavery. These spirituals that were sung by slaves working in the fields have been imprinted by the affective longings of those black people and, as they are still sung by black people, those longings for a world beyond the color line still reproduce themselves. They carry within their melodies, as transmuted African music, the intimations of forms of life that preceded the modern color line and thus introduce a possibly productive form of non-synchronicity into the education of the Talented Tenth. Du Bois somewhat mitigates his harsh criticisms of black culture and admits that there is a *true* fragment of "non-synchronicity" immanent to the social practices of black people.

Whatever truth is buried within these songs sung in the fields of slavery and passed down from ancestors with more direct connections to the continent of Africa must be drawn out and clarified with patient elucidation. Du Bois declares that his consciousness can only sense this truth rather than render it propositionally. This is so because the lyrics, caught up in "conventional theology," block the full expression of the music and distort it. Du Bois, as a member of the Talented Tenth, lacks the attunement to discern this "message [that] is naturally veiled and half articulate."[98] Du Bois avers, "I know little of music and can say nothing in technical phrase, but I know something of men, and knowing them, I know that these songs are the articulate message of the slave to the world."[99] He cannot place the songs within the firm boundaries of knowledge and so he must speculate about the *potential* content of this forthcoming black identity.

Once again, Du Bois establishes limits so that they may be responsibly overstepped. Stephanie Shaw describes Du Bois as moving

---

[97] Du Bois, *Souls*, 155.
[98] Du Bois, *Souls* 159.
[99] Du Bois, *Souls*, 157.

"the discussion of the songs from one about 'the experience of consciousness' and *learning* to one about 'the philosophy of spirit' and *knowing*."[100] What she means is that Du Bois supposes that he has an *intuition* concerning the truth of the songs rather than knowledge that arises from training in the empirical sciences. And so, from within the problematic limits of expression imposed by the color line, an as yet amorphous historical truth exerts pressure on his consciousness.

Music allows for the apprehension of the truth which language and racist ideology hide from the Talented Tenth. But Du Bois's reasoning for this is still troubling. The problem of the color line is an unnatural distortion of just and harmonious relations between groups, yet it is part of civilization. The music of the black folk, on the other hand, escapes this distortion because it arises from "black folk of primitive type."[101] The primitivism in Du Bois's thought understands music of the black folk as expressing, in raw form, the potential shared identity of black people. It reflects the historical stages of black identity through slavery from African music to "Afro-American" to its most developed form, "a blending of Negro music with the music heard in the foster land."[102]

Now it appears that Du Bois takes "Negro music" to be a part of the Western cultural inheritance, but if it has been, then the musical form and its message have been disavowed. It has been disavowed insofar as civilization has drifted into an untrue organization of human relationships. Du Bois implies that what secures the Negro spiritual against the mirage of the untrue is that it arises from the harmony of nature. He claims, "Like all primitive folk, the slave stood near to Nature's heart."[103] If civilization and culture are the processes by which human groups cease to be natural creatures and become historical creatures, then the music of the black folk is non-synchronous. The black folk are a problem insofar as they have not joined civilization or "the kingdom of culture."[104] But they are a promise because they are elsewhere from the lie produced by the color line.

---

[100] Stephanie Shaw, *W. E. B. Du Bois and* The Souls of Black Folk (Chapel Hill: University of North Carolina Press, 2013), 130.
[101] Du Bois, *Souls*, 156.
[102] Du Bois, *Souls*, 159.
[103] Du Bois, *Souls*, 159.
[104] Du Bois, *Souls*, 3.

Du Bois's primitivism notwithstanding, I suspect that he has captured a true aspect of how we can understand utopia. What Du Bois apprehends in the music of the black folk is the experience of a determinate otherwise. *The normal flow of time for his double-consciousness, the time of the color line, is interrupted by music which expresses another history and another concrete possibility of future life.* This otherwise is not arbitrary or concocted by the flight of his imagination, indeed there is no image since the message remains veiled, but this otherwise is grounded upon the concrete, historical activity of the black folk. Thus, it is determinate.

Du Bois describes his work being interrupted by the singing of young black people outside his window as "welling up to me from the caverns of brick and mortar." They fill him with the hope that "somewhere in this whirl and chaos of things there dwells Eternal Good [and] in His good time America shall rend the Veil and the prisoned shall go free."[105] Du Bois appears to reverse Plato's Allegory of the Cave here, and now it is the intellectual who is lifted up and saved by the imprisoned down below. The ongoing failure of black people to attain complete freedom does not mean that fragments of true freedom do not survive into the present. Social movements often leave behind legacies and ideas that are discordant with the governing economy of ideas and structures. They presuppose another world from within the present world as they struggle to make their message heard. Eva von Redecker describes this as "interstitial change" where "two practices overlap . . . and form a new pattern."[106] In the interstices of social life practices can emerge that question the false truths we have absorbed.

The promise of history interrupts Du Bois's salvific project for the future.[107] He does not fully overturn his belief that an elite cadre of intellectuals must save black people. Instead it seems that the Talented Tenth are charged with refining and elucidating the message embedded in the music of the black folk. They are the ones to bring civilization and the "Negro folk-song" into alignment by solving

---

[105] Du Bois, *Souls*, 163.
[106] Eva von Redecker, *Praxis and Revolution: A Theory of Social Transformation*, trans. Lucy Duggan (New York: Columbia University Press, 2021), 127.
[107] Alex Callinicos, *Making History: Agency, Structure, and Change in Social Theory* (Ithaca, NY: Cornell University Press, 1988).

the problem of the color line. However, what I find more interesting is the surreptitious glance backward of Du Bois in *Souls*. Many of his efforts in this period are focused on looking forward. However, in this moment, there is a split in Du Bois's thought. But this split is of a distinctly different nature than the unhappy split experienced by John and his education via Western culture. The split Du Bois phenomenologically describes is not of despair or bourgeois melancholia, but the pre-appearance of a just future that separates the shadows of racism from the light of reason. Du Bois insists, "Through all the sorrow of the Sorrow Songs there breathes a hope—a faith in the ultimate justice of things."[108] What Du Bois intends to do at the end of *Souls* is emancipate reason from the accumulation of historical irrationality, the justice of tomorrow from the injustice of yesterday. In other words, a rhythm of chance continues to persist in the realm of necessity. Utopia beckons to the consciousness of the Talented Tenth, hinting that the way back may also be the way forward. And so, Du Bois concludes, listening to the singing of black folk, that he "girds himself, and set his face toward the Morning."[109]

How would this work exactly? Du Bois, on this score, remains vague. I think we can reconstruct a hypothesis, however, from what he has said. Insofar as the music and the communal practices oriented around creating and preserving the music are still extant, then the member of the Talented Tenth will have to embed themselves in this social organization if they are to gain further clarity on the musical form and its submerged history. Listening to the music from afar will not be enough. Rather the Talented Tenth will have to learn how this community of black people have organized themselves and what harmonies they have engendered.[110] In doing so, one can attain a glimpse of a different public that will be guided by the best epistemic practices of both sides of the color line. Perhaps Du Bois did not fully

[108] Du Bois, *Souls*, 162.
[109] Du Bois, *Souls*, 164.
[110] Robert Gooding-Williams describes this aspect of Du Bois's political thinking as "political expressionism." It is the thesis that "the efficacy and authority of African American leaders requires that they, in directing the black masses, avow and embody (and so reflect) the collective, spiritual (folk) identity that antecedently unites black Americans" (*In the Shadow of Du Bois*, 14).

pursue this line of inquiry at this stage in his life because what would follow is the idea the black philosopher kings and queens no longer rule from their own wisdom, but will have to be swayed and formed by the very people they are meant to guide. Nevertheless, this "non-synchronous" truth makes its way into Du Bois's republic of thought even as he, for the most part, refuses it.

Emancipation and Insight: Limits of the Du Boisian Utopia

Utopia hovers at the borders of the mirage and the real. The utopianism which thrums through Du Bois's *Souls* and his other writings in this period is far from a fantasy of escape, but instead it has the epistemological function of beckoning for insight. Utopia and *anagnorisis* cannot be decoupled or else the investigator will lose the rhythm of "Chance" at play in human affairs. Du Bois fixates on the problem of the false and the true because black people have been approached as more myth than reality. They have been seen more as imaginary constructs than as fallible, yet human creatures. Having been obstructed in their drive for historical self-realization, Du Bois responds with a social ontology of "non-synchronicity" and a political program of uplift that will bring black people into harmony with the various social forces of American society and thereby reorganize social life in the vision of Truth and justice.

The utopianism of the Talented Tenth reflects Du Bois's classicism and his affinity for a harmonious polis which drew from figures ranging from Plato to Herder. The *prima facie* problem with Du Bois's elitism might appear to be the ungrounded supposition that this social class has any legitimate right to be the leaders of black people. As I have shown, Du Bois was not confident in the legitimacy of the Talented Tenth either practically or theoretically, but he made a wager that they were the primary lever for social reformation.

Still, I think we can find the problem elsewhere. The Talented Tenth expresses Du Bois's, at best, ambivalence toward chance or, at worst, outright distrust of chance left to its own devices. Du Bois is not keen to leave to chance its autonomy from reason and action, but rather he wants to bring it within the limits of thought. Du Bois's concern over the criminality, laziness, and sexual mores of black people had as much to do with his protests against an unfair American society that trapped many black people with few resources as it did with his sensibility that too much chance was being allowed to metastasize among these wayward folk.[111] The Talented Tenth had an epistemological and political function as well as a hygienic role for the black race. The tendency toward a vision of absolute social hygiene remains one of the most relevant risks of utopia.

None of this is to suggest that one should choose non-synchronicity over synchronicity. These are abstract oppositions without the aid of insight. Synchronicity with a social system is not in itself an admirable achievement if that social system strips groups of their autonomy. The Du Bois of *Souls* does not have as much to say about how the social system of industrial capitalism gradually winnows away the potential for group self-determination. Du Bois seems to have been limited in his recognition of the form of life that the utopia of the "kingdom of culture" presupposed. But for all that, we should not romanticize "non-synchronicity" as if it is *actually* good to be impoverished or locked out of governing social institutions. Such an idea risks falling into an abstract utopianism that imagines the possibility of living in a pure state that is untouched by the social forces of one time.

Souls and Du Bois's other writings in this period, even with their limitations, model a disposition toward social reality that takes seriously the role of social theory in attesting to the possibility of a more just society. The task of the rest of this book is to defend an account of critical theory which emphasizes this practical role of utopia in the constitution of social reality. Du Bois misconstrues how the process of emancipation should be brought about and upon what terms it must be premised, but his error should not distract us from his very real insight: we already hunger for a reconstructed world. The articulations of the "Negro folk songs" carry this historical hunger into the present. Du Bois did not fully capture the truth of this message because he

---

[111] Hartman, *Wayward Lives*, 102–114. See also Keith Byerman's conclusion that "Du Bois's radicalism ... is founded on traditional, conservative moral grounds" (*Seizing the Word*, 148).

did not adequately theorize how a racially just society ought to be anchored, what can give it permanency in our social life. However, Du Bois does demonstrate how a critical theory of utopia must elaborate on the latent tendencies toward emancipation already woven into our present form of life. Every emancipatory process necessarily contains this moment of *insight* that Du Bois so meticulously unpacks in his sociology and in *Souls*. In the next chapter I examine how black nationalism attempts to answer Du Bois's unanswered anchoring question.

3
Contesting the Polity
Black Nationalism, Utopia, and the Reconstruction of Racial Life

Introduction

In the previous chapter, I interpreted the work of the early Du Bois as providing the elements of a critical theory for understanding how racially unjust societies are *temporally out of joint*. This is what informs the problematic, and even *unreasonable*, character of their form of life that, in turn, shapes the forms of life internal to racially unjust societies. Progression and regression, integration and disintegration, live side by side. Racial injustice, I argued, not only fragments the historical patterns or "rhythms" of a given society, but subjects one group's rhythms to another's. The subjugation of a social group entails primarily one group having a dominating power over how life goes for another social group.[1] Exercising a dominating power does not mean that a social group intervenes at every moment in the individual lives of those they dominate, but that they have the ability, whether exercised or not, to arbitrarily shape the broad contours of the dominated group's life trajectory. Ruth Wilson Gilmore's famous definition of racism as "the state-sanctioned and/or extralegal production

---

[1] For republican accounts of freedom, see Philip Pettit, *Republicanism: A Theory of Freedom and Government* (Oxford: Oxford University Press, 1997), Quentin Skinner, "Freedom as the Absence of Arbitrary Power," in *Republicanism and Political Theory*, ed. Cécile Laborde and John W. Maynor (Oxford: Blackwell, 2008), 83–102.; Victoria M. Costa, "Neo-republicanism, Freedom as Non-domination, and Citizen Virtue," *Politics, Philosophy & Economics* 8, no. 4 (2009): 401–419; Alex Gourevitch, *From Slavery to the Cooperative Commonwealth: Labor and Republican Liberty in the Nineteenth Century* (New York: Cambridge University Press, 2015); William Clare Roberts, *Marx's Inferno: The Political Theory of Capital* (Princeton, NJ: Princeton University Press, 2018). I offer an extensive account of what I mean by power in chapter 5.

and exploitation of group differentiated vulnerabilities to *premature* death, in distinct yet densely interconnected political geographies" captures a central component of this dominating power.[2] Death, of course, is an inevitable occurrence for all living creatures. But Gilmore's contention that groups can be exposed to *premature* death tells us that we have expectations of what constitutes the "normal" course of a life or, at least, we can observe that some social groups tend to have more time than others. Phenomenologically, we might ask how divergent rhythms of life and death shape and sediment individual as well as group experiences given that death renders life intelligible.[3]

When analyzing the relationship between a more general form of life and specific forms of life in a racially unjust society, attention to differential patterns of mortality illuminates the reality of "nonsynchronicity." The social pattern of *premature* death may offer insight into whose lives are valued by society and according to what norms. Death becomes a *political* injustice when the state enforces policies that arbitrarily imposes it on others. We can understand this injustice as the infringement of a *right* to liberty, a right to be able to determine how one will spend the finite time one has. However, I think death can also be defined as a *social* injustice when the structure of a society arbitrarily generates conditions that devalue and constrain the lives of a social group absent direct state interference. To say that death is an injustice is not the same as saying a just society is one where no death occurs.

Instead, it is to interrogate conditions through which the finite time of our lives is formed. Adorno once insisted that a permanent

---

[2] Ruth Wilson Gilmore, "Race and Globalization," in *Abolition Geography: Essays toward Liberation*, ed. Brenna Bhandar and Alberto Toscano (New York: Verso, 2022), 107, emphasis added. See also Falguni Sheth, *Toward a Political Philosophy of Race* (New York: SUNY Press, 2009), 29–41.

[3] "My death is the horizon that renders intelligible all temporal relations of my life. If I actually believed that my life would last forever, I could not make any sense of the distinction between sooner and later in my life.... The horizon of my death is not a psychological projection, since it is not something I can 'choose' to project. Rather, the horizon of my death is a condition of intelligibility for my life.... The horizon of my death opens the question of what I should do with my finite time and thus makes it possible to lead my life in the first place." Martin Hägglund, *This Life: Secular Faith and Spiritual Freedom* (New York: Anchor Books, 2020), 200–201. See also Du Bois's reflection on death and life in a racially unjust society through the experience of the death of his firstborn child in *The Souls of Black Folk* (Mineola, NY: Dover, 1994), ch. 11.

feature of utopia was the abolition of death.[4] I think this is right, but in conjunction with Gilmore's definition, we can put this more specifically: utopia is the emancipatory struggle from socially imposed, arbitrary, and premature death. However, "death" need not be confined to biological death. The dominating practices of enslavement, for example, deprive the enslaved of rights and respect that are due to the free citizenry. Accordingly, the enslaved are denied any *generally* validated standing in social and political life even as they are forced to live under its norms and practices. This mode of internal exclusion that characterizes slavery has been described by Orlando Patterson as "social death."[5] The struggle against this condition of alienation and dishonor is *also* a struggle against a seemingly natural limit of life, broadly construed. This, I argue, is the value of utopia for critical theory.

The emancipation from socially imposed, arbitrary, and premature death brings into view the question of how a society values social life, what anchors these norms of value, and how civic identity mediates questions of social value and the practices that underwrite norms of social regard. Melvin L. Rogers, in his critique of neo-republicanism, argues, "There is little hope in changing individual minds if the broader cultural context continuously educates people to hold some in lower regard than others. Moreover, responses to these forms of domination, if confined to the domain of illegality, will obscure the deeper problems for standing that are anchored by the cultural context."[6] Black nationalism, I will show, is also animated by this problem of addressing how racial domination is "anchored" by a wider social context that goes beyond the state.

---

[4] "Indeed, death depicts the hardest counter-utopia. Nailing the coffin puts an end to all of our individual series of actions at the very least. In other words, it depreciates the before." Ernst Bloch, "Something's Missing: A Discussion between Ernst Bloch and Theodor W. Adorno on the Contradictions of Utopian Longing," in *The Utopian Function of Art and Literature: Selected Essays*, trans. Jack Zipes and Frank Mecklenburg (Cambridge, MA: MIT Press, 1988), 9.

[5] Orlando Patterson, *Slavery and Social Death: A Comparative Study* (Cambridge, MA: Harvard University Press, 2018); On the concept of "internal exclusion," see Sina Kramer, *Excluded Within: The (Un)Intelligibility of Radical Political Actors* (New York: Oxford University Press, 2019).

[6] Melvin L. Rogers, "Race, Domination, and Republicanism," in *Difference without Domination: Pursuing Justice in Diverse Democracies*, eds. Danielle S. Allen and Rohini Somanathan (Chicago: University of Chicago Press, 2020), 81.

Racially unjust societies block access to the social practices of rights that set the terms for what counts as civic life. Civic life is where human beings are acknowledged as capable of being more than mere natural creatures. They have *historical* standing. It is no wonder that justifications for racial domination often take the form of a temporal argument. Claims that the dominated are "backward" or "behind the times" may be wrongheaded, but they do get at the centrality of time for any form of life.[7] Cohering social practices cannot happen only for a single moment. They must be accomplished recursively. There is no other way to understand the sense of "this is what one does as a citizen" as it concerns the execution of rights and duties such as voting, protesting, and even paying one's taxes. Conditions of racial injustice take place against a backdrop of political progress that has been deemed appropriate for only one part of the wider public while the racially dominated must exist "out of joint" with these practices.

Black nationalism, I will show, emerges out of this "nonsynchronicity." Proponents of black nationalism, in one way or another, contest the capacity of the state to produce any lasting harmony between the forms of life of the dominant and the dominated. Sometimes these arguments insist upon some essential racial difference between, say, black people and white people as the necessary justification for a black nation, and at other times the black nation is a pragmatic tool for engendering solidarity.[8] However, I think focusing either on racial essentialism or pragmatism risks missing the utopian insight of black nationalism: the transformation of racially unjust societies can only occur through contesting the socially imposed and arbitrary death the dominant society asserts as a form of control over the social life of black peoples. This idea of control requires explanation and, as this chapter will show, it is controversial. Nevertheless, understanding control over the terms and boundaries of social life is essential for comprehending the utopian critique of black nationalism.

---

[7] See Justin E. H. Smith, *Nature, Human Nature, and Human Difference: Race in Early Modern Philosophy* (Princeton, NJ: Princeton University Press, 2015), ch. 9.

[8] Tommie Shelby, *We Who Are Dark: The Philosophical Foundations of Black Solidarity* (Cambridge, MA: Harvard University Press, 2005), 27–33.

Whatever the limitations of black nationalism (and there are many), it contributes the valuable insight that death and dishonor are not a *fait accompli*. Here, the thematic of black peoples having a national "destiny" acquires its ideological value. The utopian wager of black nationalism is that creating the conditions for self-determination beyond the existing state will allow the project of racial emancipation to attain some form of irreversibility. If one is dominated by not being accorded standing in civic life, then whatever political progress a social group may achieve is constitutively reversible by those with power in civic life. It is the problem of the reversibility of our social practices to which I turn in this chapter by examining the thought of Martin Delany and Marcus Garvey. Their arguments for black nationalism support the critical insight that racial emancipation is more than the *political* struggle for rights, but the *social* struggle over time.

Born in 1812, Martin Delany is widely seen as the progenitor of black nationalism. A proponent of black emigration from the United States before the Civil War, Delany expounds upon the problem of anchoring black political life in the American state. Delany was a journalist, military officer, and physician. In what follows, I will show why the latter matters for his account of black nationalism. There is a rich thematic link between Delany's black nationalism and Marcus Garvey's over half a century later.

The arrival of Marcus Garvey in the United States in 1916 coincides with a broader disillusionment with the promise of black liberation via liberal integration into the American state. Garvey, a Jamaican activist, publisher, and leader of the United Negro Improvement Association (UNIA), crystallizes this shift of utopia back into the problem-space of geo-political questions with his organized defense of black nationalism and the return to Africa. I in no way suggest that Garvey the individual should be seen as solely responsible for this shift. My purpose is to elucidate and emphasize the new constellation of questions and answers that we find with the rise of Garveyism and the UNIA.

In this chapter, I attend to the writings of Martin Delany and Marcus Garvey to examine the progressive and regressive features of black nationalism. I will argue that nationalism was taken by both figures to be the structuring principle of any polity. If the character of the nation is racialized then it will exclude those who are not a member of the dominant population. Delany's and Garvey's desire for an independent nation, I will argue, is premised on seeing the nation as a space of reasons that allows agents to both bind others to norms of civic regard *and* be the source of said norms. The utopianism of black nationalism is not the imagination of a perfect black polity somewhere else, but the work of opening an alternative space of reasons where black citizens can determine themselves.

Narrating Time: Race, Dishonor, and the Project of Justifying the Nation

Benedict Anderson, in his study of the rise of nationalism, notes that there is a paradox of temporality that often constitutes practices of nationalism. Nations tend to *feel* very old and deeply rooted when in fact they are relatively modern creations.[9] Whoever speaks of their nation often evokes themes of cultural distinction, historical honor, and a sense of destiny. The nation is a mode of address that both constitutes its audience and presumes that the audience was *already* a national people. By interpellating a population as a national unity, nationalism, retroactively, transforms their shared sense of time.[10] Where there was once an aggregate of individuals who may or may not have lived in close proximity to one another there is now the image of an "us" that not only can act collectively, but has been acting collectively for some time.[11] Where there was once the indistinction of my natural, mortal existence there is now my integration into a corporate, national body.

[9] Benedict Anderson, *Imagined Communities: Reflections on the Origin and Spread of Nationalism* (New York: Verso, 2003), 5.
[10] On interpellation, see Louis Althusser, "Ideology and Ideological State Apparatuses (Notes towards an Investigation)," in *Lenin and Philosophy and Other Essays*, trans. Ben Brewster (New York: Monthly Review Press, 2001), 85–127.
[11] Robert-Gooding Williams in *In the Shadow of Du Bois: Afro-modern Political Thought in America* (Cambridge, MA: Harvard University Press, 2009), 20–21 remarks on the young Du Bois's ambivalent admiration of Otto von Bismarck's unification of the German nation. He admired the leadership of Bismarck that brought together an inchoate mass of people as a nation, but criticized Bismarck's despotism that abjured any notion of popular right. In his autobiography Du Bois says of his own admiration of Bismarck that "[he] had made a nation out of a mass of bickering peoples. He had dominated the whole development with his strength until he was crowned emperor at Versailles. This foreshadowed in my mind the kind of thing that American Negroes must

Moreover, when I must inevitably die, I no longer perish as an anonymous organic being; I die *as* an American, a German, a South African. Indeed, even when I die the national body politic carries on and thus "I" or, more precisely, "we" attain some form of immortality. Anderson suggests that the monumentalization of the "Unknown Soldiers" is a specifically nationalist phenomenon. Those who die for the nation may not be remembered as individuals, but their deaths are recognized as *German* or *American* and thus attain a type of immortality. Indeed, their deaths are transformed from being ignoble and wretched into being dignified.[12]

That all of this is imaginary, that this "we" does not truly know one another, does not mean that the nation is not "real."[13] If by "real" we mean practices that have discernible effects on our lives, then the nation is very real. In fact, the riddle of the nation is that even as it is imaginary it can catalyze such intense affective bonds and motivational structures. Anderson suggests that we should find it puzzling "why people are ready to die for these inventions."[14] The nation can even appear to be truer or more real than any existing state and its laws. This is why Melvin Rogers insists that a fundamental tenet of African-American republicanism in the 19th century emphasized

---

do, marching forth with strength and determination under trained leadership." W. E. B. Du Bois, *The Autobiography: A Soliloquy on Viewing My Life from the Last Decade of Its First Century* (New York: International Publishing, 1968), 126. We will see that this thematic of forging a new people through leadership recurs in Martin Delany and Marcus Garvey.

[12] "The cultural significance of such monuments becomes even clearer if one tries to imagine, say, a Tomb of the Unknown Marxist or a cenotaph for fallen Liberals. Is a sense of absurdity avoidable? The reason is neither Marxism nor Liberalism are much concerned with death and immortality. If the nationalist imaging is so concerned, this suggests a strong affinity with religious imaginings" (Anderson, *Imagined Communities*, 10).

[13] Anderson isolates four necessary components of modern nations: (1) they are *imaginary* insofar as no member will actually know every single other member; (2) they are *limited* because no nation ever sees itself as encompassing all of humanity; (3) they take themselves to express the principle of *sovereignty* and therefore inherit the concept of autonomy that emerged from the Enlightenment and Age of Revolution; (4) they understand themselves as *communities* such that regardless of the inequality that may obtain within the nation there exists a deep, horizontal comradeship among the members (*Imagined Communities*, 6–7).

[14] Anderson, *Imagined Communities*, 141.

the "characterological propensities of the nation" since without the transformation of the national character, laws that aim to bring about justice will founder on the temperament and informal habits of the citizenry.[15]

I begin with this description of nations as imaginary because "nations" and "utopias" share many affinities.[16] Both are "unreal" descriptions of social space and time, yet they can have effects. They explicitly and implicitly recontextualize our relationship to death in its variety of forms. Finally, nations and utopias make fundamental claims about what counts as a dignified life. None of this is to say, as I will discuss in the following sections, that nationalism or utopianism are free from potentially regressive tendencies. What matters is analyzing if and how they anchor and motivate social practices. My point here is that the accusation of utopias as imaginary should not be conflated with the criticism that they are ineffective. It does not follow that something being imaginary must mean that it does not have real effects on our conduct.

Thus, I think investigating the similarity between nations and utopias will afford us a richer understanding of black nationalist critiques of racial domination. To begin, we should look at what makes the emergence of a nation possible and then move on to defining what a nation is. According to Anderson, the genesis of modern nationalism can be explained by the emergence of a new mode of apprehending social time.[17] The rise of the novel and the newspaper generated "wholly new ideas of simultaneity."[18] Reading a novel or a newspaper allows me to represent to myself the actions of others whom I will never meet as occurring alongside my everyday activities. For instance, while in State College, Pennsylvania, I may read about how the state government of Michigan has poisoned the water of Flint and feel indignanation at the injustice done to my fellow citizens. These people, who are strangers to me, appear to exist in the same "now" as I do and thus are not beyond

---

[15] Rogers, "Race, Domination, and Republicanism," 60.
[16] See Phillip E. Wegner, *Imaginary Communities: Utopia, the Nation, and the Spatial Histories of Modernity* (Berkeley: University of California Press, 2002) and Anderson, *Imagined Communities*, 69.
[17] Anderson, *Imagined Communities*, 24–26.
[18] Anderson, *Imagined Communities*, 37.

my horizon of concern. I imagine that what we have in common is the affordance of dignity or, more simply, *standing* due to us as members of the nation.

The conjunction of media such as newspapers and the distributional capacities of markets articulated the conditions for imagining that those anonymous individuals are not mere strangers, but members of a *shared public*. Anderson insists that the revolutionary thrust of capitalism alongside the expansion of print media created seemingly unified fields of communication through which people could imagine themselves as part of a public.[19] The language of the newspaper, the radio, or news anchors on television create the sense that *this* is the language of the nation. Whatever differences we may have we, at least, have this language and the concerns articulated through it in common.[20] We can assume that other members of the nation are legitimate participants in the concerns of the nation because they not only speak its language, but can see, debate, and critique its common concerns.

One of the critical possibilities opened up by the nation is the assumption of some concerns as common. These concerns open onto the possibility of public deliberation. The character of the nation becomes important because the citizenry must feel an appropriate sense of responsibility and trust if they are to resolve problems collectively. More to the point, the nation provides the conditions of possibility for agents to consider themselves as the type of people who can engage in public reason. Against the backdrop of the nation, certain speech acts and social practices are taken to be legitimate political actions. Speeches from politicians, voting, and *some* forms of protest are viewed as synchronous with the life of the nation. In other words, the nation is a *space of reasons*.[21]

---

[19] Anderson, *Imagined Communities*, 39–45.
[20] See chapter 4 for an analysis of the relationship between language and sociality in colonial societies.
[21] "[I]n characterizing an episode or a state as that of *knowing*, we are not giving an empirical description of that episode or state; we are placing it in the logical space of reasons, of justifying and being able to justify what one says." Wilfrid Sellars, *Empiricism and the Philosophy of Mind* (Cambridge, MA: Harvard University Press, 1997), §36.

The concept of "the space of reasons," as developed in the work of Wilfrid Sellars, captures the fact that when we judge an individual as knowing some fact, we are also claiming that they are *justified* in claiming that they do in fact have said knowledge. Chauncey Maher insists that for Sellars the practice of attributing knowledge to one another has inescapably normative dimensions.[22] For example, when the citizens in Flint raise the complaint that the poisoning of their water by the government was an *injustice*, we (in principle) respond to their claims with indignation because we take them to be justified in their demand for justice. Due to their *standing* in the life of the nation, they are right to expect appropriate treatment by their fellow citizens and, most importantly, they are the sort of persons that we acknowledge as being in the position to know when these expectations are betrayed. Du Bois makes a similar argument in *Darkwater* to justify the expansion of voting rights to women and black citizens.[23] No individual has direct access to another's self-understanding of their hurts and needs. If the nation is to remain healthy and responsive to the lives of its citizens, then these citizens must be acknowledged as both capable and justified in making their concerns known to the public. Without this knowledge the nation becomes poor and decays.[24]

I have offered a patently idealistic reconstruction of the nation as a space of reasons, premised on the production of simultaneity. The

---

[22] "To know that S knows that P is (roughly) to say that others (including oneself) are or would be right to rely on S in vindicating their own beliefs or claims that P. Thus, epistemic attributions have a crucial *normative* dimension; attribution of epistemic states or episodes are attributions of normative statuses.... The base idea is that knowing something or being justified in believing something is like having the *standing*, the *permission* or *authority*, to do something. ... Baseball umpires are authorized to call a pitch a strike; police officers of a jurisdiction are permitted to issue citations in that jurisdiction; legislators are allowed to propose and enact legislation.... When one says that knowledge is a normative status, one is saying that it concerns the permission or authority to judge how things are." Chauncey Maher, *The Pittsburgh School of Philosophy: Sellars, McDowell, Brandom* (New York: Routledge, 2012), 18.
[23] W. E. B. Du Bois, *Darkwater: Voices from within the Veil*, intro. Manning Marable (1920; New York: Verso, 2016), ch. 6.
[24] "In fact no one knows himself but that self's own soul. The vast and wonderful knowledge of this marvelous universe is locked in the bosoms of its individual souls. To tap this mighty reservoir of experience, knowledge, beauty, love, and deed we must appeal not to the few, not to some souls, but to all. The narrower the appeal, the poorer the culture; the wider the appeal the more magnificent are the possibilities" (Du Bois, *Darkwater*, 81).

course of justice rarely runs this smoothly. Furthermore, the norms of justified speech can be onerous and restrictive even for those who are ostensible members of a nation. However, even this idealistic reconstruction of the nation does clarify some immanent resources for the critique of racial injustice. Analyzing the nation as a space of reasons also means that we can recontextualize the inherently limited nature of any nation. A nation not only has geographical or cultural borders that set it off against other nations, but it also has borders that include and exclude who has the standing to express knowledge about the nation. It articulates *and* disarticulates who is taken to be a legitimate source of justification and who is not.

Taking this to be an accurate portrayal of the implicit workings of the nation, we can see that the nation is not necessarily coextensive with the occupants of a geographical territory. Black people lived in the same country as white people, but for much of the life of the nation they were not ascribed the normative status of citizens who could speak to or contest the common concerns of national life.[25] More importantly, not only were black people excluded from the space of reasons, they were bound to honor and obey the decisions of the nation as it concerned their lives. They were acknowledged as agents who could understand legal and informal prohibitions on their conduct but were not regarded as subjects who could bind white people to legal and informal prohibitions. To put the point more plainly, black people were treated as creatures who could receive reasons, but could not give them.[26] The nation does not disavow the truth of black people being

---

[25] Needless to say that it was not *only* black people who were excluded from the nation's space of reasons nor that the exclusions of women, immigrants, and Indigenous peoples have the same historical trajectories. I am merely taking the case of black people as an *example* that illustrates the non-universal character of the nation.

[26] Frederick Douglass captures this painful hypocrisy when he notes, "Must I undertake to prove that the slave is a man? That point is conceded already. Nobody doubts it. The slaveholders themselves acknowledge it in the enactment of laws for their government. They acknowledge it when they punish disobedience on the part of the slave. There are seventy-two crimes in the state of Virginia, which, if committed by a black man, (no matter how ignorant he be,) subject him to the punishment of death; while only two of these crimes will subject a white man to the like punishment. What is this but the acknowledgement that the slave is a moral, intellectual, and responsible being.... When the dogs in your streets, when the fowls of the air, when the cattle on your hills, when the fish of the sea, and the reptiles that crawl, shall be unable to distinguish the slave from a brute, then I will argue with you that the slave is a man!" Frederick Douglass, "What to the Slave Is the Fourth of July?," in *My Bondage and My Freedom*, intro. David

sensitive to reasons. Indeed, it presupposes that they have some rational character in order to exert power over them. To be addressed as a creature of reason yet prevented from making public use of it by the nation that has power over you is to be *dishonored*.

To be dishonored is to be marked as a subject deserving of lower esteem or social value. Importantly, the successful act of dishonoring requires three components: the *power* to enforce the act; a set of *values* that distinguish between the honorable and the dishonorable; and a coherent *justificatory narrative* for why the subject is deserving of dishonor. The racial domination that typified chattel slavery was comprised of the power of white people to determine black people as being of lesser social value. However, the *justificatory narrative* for why black people ought to be dishonored in this way has been historically variable and, more importantly, internally contradictory.[27] Reasons for racial dishonor have ranged from *theological* stories of black people as being marked by the curse of Ham to *biological* stories of black people descending from alternative origins of human evolution to *cultural* stories concerning the failure of black people to attain the value of modern civilization. The justificatory narratives for dishonor and domination have always been attacked in struggles for emancipation. By denaturalizing or revealing the arbitrary exercise of power, general values such as citizenship can be re-narrated to include black people as sources of power and equal social value.

One way to understand the recurrence of black nationalism is as a narrative response to a form of life that justifies black dishonor.[28]

W. Blight (1852; New Haven, CT: Yale University Press, 2014), 370–371. Douglass's explicit distinction between animals and humanity is meant to demonstrate what type of creatures a political community appeals to for justification. But it does something more here: it allows us to see that the space of reasons that is the nation makes "life" a *social* category rather than only a biological one.

[27] See Thomas McCarthy, *Race, Empire, and the Idea of Human Development* (Cambridge: Cambridge University Press, 2009).

[28] See Sylvia Wynter, "Unsettling the Coloniality of Being/Power/Truth/Freedom: Towards the Human, after Man, Its Overrepresentation—An Argument" *CR* 3, no. 3 (2003): 257–337 and "'No Humans Involved': An Open Letter to My Colleagues," *Forum N.H.I. Knowledge for the 21st Century* 1, no. 1 (Fall 1994): 42–71; William Michael Paris, "'One Does Not Write for Slaves': Wynter, Sartre, and the Poetic Phenomenology of Invention," *Journal of Speculative Philosophy* 33, no. 3 (2019): 407–421.

Justification narratives are not mere stories that we tell about ourselves: they are the historical narration of *how* such and such a form of life came to be and *why* it is indeed well-founded.[29] In other words, the general or abstract value of citizenship and the socially validated power to limit who counts as a citizen is mediated by historically developed reasons. These reasons are always, in principle, open to contestation and critique even if those in positions of dominance attempt to make it otherwise by, say, limiting the literacy and formal education of the dominated.[30] Power, in practice, is rarely exercised outside a given space of reasons where justification and historical narratives intermingle. Subjects must be habituated to the "appropriate" practices that cohere forms of life stratified by hierarchy and domination. Douglass's narration of being sent to the "negro-breaker" Covey is but one extreme example of this.[31]

Covey's power over Douglass was not primarily physical.[32] Douglass describes his degrading experience with Covey as both

[29] Rainer Forst describes the relationship between justification narratives and reasons thusly: "justifying reasons for normative orders are not simply connected with stories, but cannot even be fully understood without them. Reasons and justifications spring from historical constellations and experiences. When asked why a particular political institution exists, one will usually respond with a story that led to certain conclusions.... Stories provide the supporting basis for reasons, but the reasons also tower above any given story and raise it from the idiosyncratic into a universal space of justifications." Rainer Forst, *Normativity and Power: Analyzing Social Orders of Justification* (Oxford: Oxford University Press, 2017), 56.

[30] Frederick Douglass offers the clearest depiction of the necessity of social cultivation in any dominating order when he describes one of his owners, "Master Hugh," chiding his wife, "Mrs. Auld," for teaching Douglass to read. Douglass observes that Master Hugh was training Mrs. Auld in "the peculiar rules necessary to be observed by masters and mistresses, in the management of their human chattel" because education would "'[w]ould forever unfit him for the duties of a slave'" (*My Bondage*, 117, 118). A central theme of republicanism is an analysis of how domination instills habits of servility and compliance in the dominated. What Douglass aptly captures is how servility is reproduced through not only the threat of force, but the foreclosure of the space of reasons to the dominated.

[31] Douglass notes that Covey would often hide and spy on the enslaved in order to create an atmosphere of paranoia because "[m]ean and contemptible as is all this [spying on the enslaved], it is in keeping with the character which the life of a slaveholder is calculated to produce. There is no earthly inducement, in the slave's condition, to incite him to labor faithfully. The fear of punishment is the sole motive for any sort of industry with him. Knowing this fact, as the slaveholder does, and judging the slave by himself, he naturally concludes that the slave will be idle whenever the cause for this fear is absent. Hence, all sorts of petty deceptions are practiced, to inspire this fear" (*My Bondage*, 173).

[32] Douglass describes Covey as "not a large man; he was only about five feet ten inches in height, I should think" (*My Bondage*, 169).

physical and mental. The social practices of enslavement *and* its seeming permanence stole from Douglass any "*rational ground to hope for freedom.*"[33] The loss of this rational ground for expecting freedom alongside his previous memories for hope and happiness temporarily broke Douglass's sense of agency and autonomy. Douglass, here, vividly depicts the relationship between power and reasons. Even brutal regimes of domination such as slavery cannot deploy force at all times. Domination over a large group of people requires that the dominated lose the sense that there is a mediating link of reasons between principles such as freedom and power. They must become habituated to this narrative and thus bind themselves to reasons of the dominant.

I will have much more to say about the relationship between power and the space of reasons in chapter 5. For now, I want to suggest that black nationalism offers a more precise way of characterizing how utopia can be effective when contesting racial domination. The utopianism of black nationalism is the work of re-narrating the historical reasons that mediate abstract principles such as justice or citizenship and social power. Classical utopias often took a narrative form, but their purpose was to critique the naturalized justifications for a particular historical order. *When black people took themselves to be a nation, they attempted to develop an alternative space of reasons where they would no longer be bound by norms of dishonor.* Re-narrating themselves, their origins, their rights, and their social capacities had the effect of "transform[ing] narratively representable reality" such that a different world of just social relations could appear.[34] It is important to keep in mind that the catalyst for this utopianism does not occur outside history or even outside a space of reasons; it emerges from the conflictual temporality of being subjected *to* reasons, but not taken up as a subject *of* reasons.

Accordingly, we can add to Benedict Anderson's analyses of the rise of nationalism that at the same moment that the nation generated new modes of synchronicity it also promulgated new modes of *non-synchronicity* within these nations. The non-synchronicity of national dignity and social dishonor shaped what David Scott calls the

---

[33] Douglass, *My Bondage*, 178.
[34] Forst, *Normativity and Power*, 58.

"problem-space" of politics for the racially dominated. A problem-space is "an ensemble of questions and answers around which a horizon of identifiable stakes (conceptual as well as ideological-political stakes) hangs."[35] Black nationalism was the historical reaction against the problem of dishonor and social death (as well as literal death) that attended the rise of nations. Rather than reject the framework of the "nation" many black people attempted to found their own forms of national consciousness that would give them a sense of honor and unbind them from norms that imposed social death.

Adapting the terms of the "nation" to the struggle for social freedom does bring into relief the peculiar temporal dynamics of black nationalism. It is at once an attempt at exercising creativity and novelty and an expression of the settled terms for political life. Dean E. Robinson, in his study of black nationalism in the United States, claims that "the most politically consequential feature of black nationalism is its apparent inability to diverge from what could be considered the 'normal' politics of its day."[36] On the one hand, there is nothing more ordinary than noting how one cannot leapfrog one's own historical context. On the other hand, we should take seriously how the concepts and practices deployed to secure racial domination tend to frame the terms upon which freedom is understood. Racial domination is effective not only because of the physical force of the dominant (though this should not be underestimated), but because of the ability of the dominant to bind the dominated to the reasons of domination. The framework of the nation acquires the *appearance* of a natural and reasonable mode of organizing social practices such that to refuse recourse to the figure of the nation seems to commit oneself to social death.

The modern "nation" was an undeniable transformation of how time would come to be narrated not only for those who mobilized it for domination, but for the dominated as well. Nevertheless, we should not understate how this transformation also generated non-synchronous

---

[35] David Scott, *Conscripts of Modernity: The Tragedy of Colonial Enlightenment* (Durham, NC: Duke University Press, 2004), 4.
[36] Dean E. Robinson, *Black Nationalism in American Politics and Thought* (Cambridge: Cambridge University Press, 2001), 1. See also Michael C. Dawson, *Black Visions: The Roots of Contemporary African-American Political Ideologies* (Chicago: University of Chicago Press, 2001), 101.

experiences for the racially dominated. To do so would be to accept the racist ideology that sees the racially dominated as "backward" or "primitive." Instead, black nationalism was the attempt to appropriate that which had been refused: the life and dignity of citizenship. In this way, black people are as much "modern" creatures as everyone else. The painfulness—and possibility—of non-synchronicity is not that there is an absolute separation between the dominated and dominant, but precisely because there *is* a relationship. Non-synchronicity between forms of life could not appear if they were not anchored in a shared time that allowed for comparison and contrast.

My point is not to condemn black nationalism as derivative, but to suggest that its *revolutionary* aim of social freedom for black people also *conserves* the dominant terms of the polity. It is important to analyze the progressive and regressive rhythms of black nationalism in tandem. The effort to create a utopian space of reasons where black people could acknowledge each other's dignity and political life also reestablished the nation as commensurate with the space of reasons. In other words, black nationalism remains anchored in a particular form of political, economic, and social life. Nevertheless, black nationalism does contest how narrowly the borders of social life have been drawn and thus evinces an important type of creativity: the capacity to reappropriate the reasons that have bound them. The dilemma, as I will discuss in what follows, is whether the task of racial emancipation can be accomplished through reforming the nation or overcoming it.

Anchoring Emancipation: Martin Delany and the Problem of Reversibility

I propose that we begin analyzing black nationalism as a form of problem-solving. Following Rahel Jaeggi's suggestion that forms of life are problem-solving entities, we should ask: what is the problem for which the black nation is meant to be a solution?[37] The specific details of this answer will vary historically of course, but it is hardly deniable

---

[37] Rahel Jaeggi, *Critique of Forms of Life* (Cambridge, MA: Harvard University Press, 2013), 134–153.

that black nationalism is a persistent undercurrent of the background political discourses of black peoples in the United States.[38] Dismissals of black nationalisms as either politically ineffectual or utopian (in the pejorative sense) risk glossing over why the creation of a "nation" would even *appear* to be an effective solution to the problem of racial domination. My intention in this section is not to offer a defense of black nationalism, but to develop a theoretical analysis of black nationalism as an *anchoring practice*.[39] My hypothesis is that black nationalism is a response to the constitutive reversibility of freedom in a racial polity.[40] The idea is that in a racially unjust society political progress will always be contingent and precarious for the dominated because their advancement will proceed only insofar as it converges with the interests of the dominant.[41]

The writings of Martin Delany are fundamental for this insight. In an 1854 keynote address titled "Political Destiny of the Colored Race on the American Continent," Delany insists that black people can never have *rights*, but only *privileges* in white-dominated societies.[42] Whatever freedoms black people may have at the moment are not due to any inalienable claims they may make, but the permission of what he calls the "ruling element."[43] This distinction between rights and

---

[38] Shelby, *We Who Are Dark*, 24–25; Dawson, *Black Visions*; Robinson, *Black Nationalism*; Robert A. Brown and Todd C. Shaw, "Separate Nations: Two Attitudinal Dimensions of Black Nationalism," *Journal of Politics* 64, no. 1 (2002): 22–44; Angela Y. Davis, "Black Nationalism: The Sixties and the Nineties," in *The Angela Y. Davis Reader*, ed. Joy James (Cambridge, MA: Blackwell, 1998), 289–293; Harold Cruse, *The Crisis of the Negro Intellectual* (New York: Quill, 1984), 4–6;; Alphonso Pinkney, *Red, Black, and Green: Black Nationalism in the United States* (Cambridge, UK: Cambridge University Press, 1976); Theodore Draper, *The Rediscovery of Black Nationalism* (New York: Viking Press, 1970); Robin D. G. Kelley, *Freedom Dreams: The Black Radical Imagination* (Boston: Beacon Press, 2022), 13–36.

[39] Ann Swidler, "What Anchors Cultural Practices," in *The Practice Turn in Contemporary Theory*, eds. Theodore R. Schatzki, Karin Knorr Cetina, and Eike von Savigny (New York: Routledge, 2000), 83–101.

[40] Charles W. Mills, *Blackness Visible: Essays on Philosophy and Race* (Ithaca, NY: Cornell University Press, 1998), 119–139.

[41] See Derrick A. Bell Jr., "*Brown v. Board of Education* and the Interest Convergence Dilemma," in *Critical Race Theory: The Key Writings That Formed the Movement*, eds. Kimberlé Crenshaw, Neil Gotanda, Gary Peller, and Kendall Thomas (New York: New Press, 1995), 20–29.

[42] Martin R. Delany, *A Documentary Reader*, ed. Robert S. Levine (Chapel Hill: University of North Carolina Press, 2003), 245–247.

[43] Delany, *Documentary Reader*, 247.

privileges, I argue, can be characterized as a dispute over the anchoring practices that define a political form of life.

What is an anchoring practice? Think of the act of voting. What makes it possible for this act of slipping a piece of marked paper into a box count as the act of voting rather than, say, mailing a letter? Voting is intelligible as a political act because of a background structure that establishes schemata and resources that define the action of submitting a ballot at the appropriate time as a valid instance of voting.[44] There is not only the physical act of marking a piece of paper in a particular building or location; there are also accepted rules and norms that designate these locations as voting precincts that authorize them to participate legitimately in the political process. These schemata and resources are not brought together arbitrarily, but by the power and authority of *the state*. We may designate the state as an anchoring practice for the act of voting insofar as it is the background structure of the state that legitimizes voting as a political act rather than the mere action of slipping a piece of paper into a box.

However, there is more to voting than participation in a political process. There is also the understanding of *who* participates in this process and the reasons why it is legitimate for them to do so. The practice of voting is seen as a *right* that citizens have by virtue of belonging to *the nation*. As I will show, black nationalism does not understand this right as a metaphysical attribute, but a social practice that is underwritten by a space of reasons. What it means to be a citizen is anchored in norms and practices that have accumulated over history. An individual cannot simply decide for themselves what it means to be a citizen or who counts as a citizen. For instance, an individual cannot declare that they are a citizen of the United States, but refuse

---

[44] My use of "structure" as a combination of schemata and resources is drawn from William H. Sewell (*Logics of History: Social Theory and Social Transformation* [Chicago: University of Chicago Press, 2005], 133–137). He argues that structures are not inert states of affairs, but recursive processes where "material" resources are understood and organized toward definite ends by various "schemata" or, put differently, basic rules and norms. He offers the example of a factory and states, "A factory is not an inert pile of bricks, wood, and metal. It incorporates or actualizes schemas, and this means that the schemas can be inferred from the material form of the factory. The factory gate, the punching-in station, the design of the assembly line: all of these features of the factory teach and validate the rules of the capitalist contract" (136).

to pay taxes. Nor can an individual simply decide that people born in Ghana are also citizens of the United States. To be more precise, any individual *can* do these things, but they lack the requisite resources or legitimating schemata to enact these declarations. What matters is ascertaining who has the power to decide how far the boundaries of citizenship extend.

Delany takes up this question and explicitly highlights the tension between the state as anchoring practice and the nation as anchoring practice when it comes to the act of voting for black people. He begins by addressing his audience as "Fellow countrymen" but then continues, "We have not addressed you as *citizens*,—a term desired and ever cherished by us—because such you have never been."[45] What is the difference between "countrymen" and "citizen"? It is the distinction between those who are governed by a state and those who belong to a nation. Delany is, in effect, saying that black political life is anchored in a set of laws while not being fully incorporated into the norms and practices of citizenship. This ambivalence leads to the "false premises" that the "privilege of *voting* constitutes, or necessarily embodies, the *rights of citizenship*."[46] Some free black people in some states were allowed to participate in elections. However, Delany insists that his audience ought not confuse the meaning of voting for black people with the meaning of voting for white people. Some white people, unlike black people in general, could theoretically hold positions of power because they were deemed citizens of the nation.[47] In other words, black people (and nowhere near a majority of course since many were enslaved) "have the *privilege*—there is no *right* about it—of giving our *approbation* to that which our *rulers may do*, without the privilege on our part, of doing the same thing."[48]

The nation, Delany suggests, has a thicker duration than the state. From the anchoring practice of the nation it is decided who may

---

[45] Delany, *Documentary Reader*, 245–246.
[46] Delany, *Documentary Reader*, 246.
[47] Delany argues that the United States inherits its national form from ancient Rome where there were distinctions between the *cives ingenui*, who were unrestricted in their privileges, and the *jus suffragii*, who could only vote, but hold no office (*Documentary Reader*, 246). Delany compares free black people to the *jus suffragii*.
[48] Delany, *Documentary Reader*, 247.

occupy the role of ruling in the state and not vice versa. The state may execute laws, but it is the nation that decides who can and will develop these laws. What Delany calls the "ruling element" emerges from the historical nation and thus even though some black people may vote in the same way as white people may vote, black participation is akin to an indentured servant who may be "summoned to give his approbation to an act which would be fully binding without his concurrence."[49] The problem that Delany diagnoses is that black people do not control their political destinies. They are not acknowledged as co-members of the nation that may rule and thus whatever advances or regressions that are made as it concerns justice are ultimately anchored in the whims of white people who may rule. Here we can see why republican theories of domination are illuminating for understanding Delany's black nationalism. He is describing a form of life where the *potential* for arbitrary interference in black forms of life typify social relations.

Delany offers emigration and black nationalism as a solution to the problem of reversibility. The black nation would constitute an anchoring practice that would no longer define the act of voting coming from black people as a mere privilege, but as an objective right that follows from the subjective right of every individual to be their own sovereign.[50] What Delany helps us see is that black nationalism emerges from the tension between being governed by laws and belonging to a nation. The utopian critique that follows from black nationalism is underwritten by the pessimism about whether state governance and national belonging can be brought into sync with one another. Delany does not think that there is much black people can do to alter the historical weight of the nation even as they may give their assent to the policies executed by the state. He thinks it would take some "irresistible internal political pressure" to uproot the anchoring practices of white nationalism.[51]

[49] Delany, *Documentary Reader*, 247.
[50] On the distinction between objective right and subjective right see Derrick Darby, "XI—Rights Externalism and Racial Injustice," *Proceedings of the Aristotelian Society* 120, no. 3 (2020): 255–258.
[51] Delany, *Documentary Reader*, 269. Indeed this "irresistible internal political pressure" would arrive in the form of the American Civil War, which convinced Delany that emigration was no longer necessary and black people could participate in the nation as full citizens. I think it is important to see that it took an extraordinary amount of

Christopher J. Lebron in *The Color of Our Shame* helpfully articulates what I am describing as the anchoring practices of white nationalism as the problem of social value.[52] He argues that the national character of the United States is woven with historical patterns of narratives, power, and values that serve to reduce the normative standing of black people in the "scheme of normative attention and concern upon which our society depends in the first place to justify the distribution of benefits and burdens."[53] Lebron contends that the path-dependent evolution of institutions from contexts of racial oppression has distorted the character of the nation.[54] Lebron insists that character is the seat of practical judgment that allows us to decide what we will do when presented with moral or political choices. Given the corruption of the national character, the United States is afflicted with the condition of knowing what would be just (ideal judgment) but being unwilling to choose justice (practical judgment).[55] Much like Delany, Lebron characterizes the shape of abstract values such as citizenship as structured by the pattern of reasoning that is immanent to the national character.

Lebron carries on the tradition of critical theory's aim of isolating the first-order causes of domination and oppression. The answer Lebron offers is that our social practices are anchored in a normative framework that accords diminished *social value* to black people *qua* citizens. For him the reasons that guide our conduct are always articulated through a schema of values. If the character of our values has been distorted by legacies of racism, then our reasoning will become distorted as well. "Institutional processes and individual actions and

---

violence and devastation for Delany to become convinced that the structure of the nation had been sufficiently altered.

[52] Christopher J. Lebron, *The Color of Our Shame: Race and Justice in Our Time* (New York: Oxford University Press, 2013), 44.
[53] Lebron, *Shame*, 46.
[54] Lebron relies on the work of political scientist Paul Pierson to support his claim that institutions tend to retain the inertia of the values and practices that determined their historical emergence. See Paul Pierson, "Not Just What but *When*: Timing and Sequence in Political Processes," *Studies in American Political Development* 14 (Spring 2000): 72–92 and "Increasing Returns, Path Dependence, and the Study of Politics," *American Political Science Review* 94, no. 2 (June 2000): 251–267; Lebron, *Shame*, 58–60.
[55] Lebron, *Shame*, 45, 51.

attitudes are driven by reasons, and reasons are normative in nature—they direct actions in ways that we affirm being appropriate according to some aim or plan. So, what is the normative framework that serves to justify and motivate the actions and dispositions that result in systemic inequality?"[56] Lebron's answer bears a striking similarity to Delany's: the normative framework is one that does not take black people as having equal standing in the identity of the nation. Absent this standing, institutions and individual conduct will only contingently favor ensuring justice for black people. If national character anchors justice, then we can see why Delany would think it was imperative that black people form their own nation rather than rely on the privileges of a racist nation.

We need not accept that Delany was right on this score. But it is important to see how thinkers such as Delany and Lebron take themselves to be responding to the first-order cause or what I have been calling the anchoring practices of racial domination. My aim is not to show that black nationalism offers the right answer. Delany, as I understand him, insists that political freedom must be anchored in the capacity to rule. In order to rule, black people must live in a nation that has the type of character that acknowledges their equal social value as citizens. In other words, they must be fully included in the space of reasons. He understands this capacity to follow from the historical dimension of the nation. Fundamentally, Delany thinks the nation enshrines the irreversible status of sovereignty on citizens that binds what others may do to you. The utopia of black nationalism may be represented as distinct areas of land in Africa or South America, but its *reason* for being is the re-narration and acknowledgment of sovereignty for the racially dominated.

Unacknowledged Sovereignty: Black Nationalism as Rights Externalism

The question of rule, for Delany, amounts to a critical examination of what it means to have rights. The dominant tradition in

[56] Lebron, *Shame*, 46.

African-American political philosophy often makes recourse to some version of a natural law argument.[57] Slavery was wrong because it violated the human dignity of black people, whose moral worth was anchored in the law of God rather than the laws of humanity. Without a doubt Delany also believes black people have inherent rights due to them being children of God.[58] But the theological *source* of rights cannot sufficiently answer why Delany insists that for their rights to be secure black people must share in the "original identity" of the nation. After all, if all human beings *qua* children of God have rights, then it would seem that all people do in fact share in an original identity and thus all have the capacity to rule.

Delany would insist that this use of "original identity" is too abstract and ahistorical to anchor emancipation. What Delany refers to as the anchor of "original identity" is not the fact of mere resemblance or social descent, but historically shared practices of recognition. Rights are not free-floating claims, according to Delany. They acquire their effectivity from inherited forms of acknowledgment. It is not only that white people vote, but they vote with the acknowledgment that they do so as rightful citizens; they have the acknowledged capacity to delegate their sovereignty to another.[59] When black people vote, they do so without these background conditions of acknowledgment and thus they participate in a practice whose social conditions for success do not obtain. Delany proclaims that without the *"acknowledged right to govern* . . . [n]o one . . . can delegate to another a power he never possessed; that is, he cannot *give an agency* in that which he never had a right. Consequently, the colored man in the United States, being deprived of the right of inherent sovereignty, cannot *confer* a suffrage, because he possesses none to confer."[60]

But why is acknowledgment so important to Delany? There is a delicate knot that he presents in the above formulation. On the one hand, he affirms that there are *inherent* rights to sovereignty. This would mean that the right exists irrespective of historical contingencies and

---

[57] Vincent W. Lloyd, *Black Natural Law* (New York: Oxford University Press, 2016).
[58] Delany, *Documentary Reader*, 254.
[59] Delany, *Documentary Reader*, 247–248.
[60] Delany, *Documentary Reader*, 247–248.

developments. It is by virtue of being the type of creature one is, i.e., a child of God, that one has a right to sovereignty. On the other hand, this right is only *actual* once it has been historically acknowledged and validated through existing social practices. One must be seen as participating in the ruling element of the nation, and this ruling element only persists because it is anchored in the historical sedimentation of an original identity. Put another way, one must be taken as someone who has standing in the space of reasons of the nation.

This historically acknowledged right to sovereignty takes on an altogether different temporality than the supposedly inherent right to sovereignty whose source can be found in God. What Delany illustrates for his audience is that rights being God-given is not sufficient for the right being real or actual. I would go further and suggest that Delany's argument is that the historical acknowledgment of rights *precedes* rights being taken as natural and inherent.

Note that for Delany rights are a historically acquired power rather than an inherent attribute of the individual. A right to sovereignty is the power to bind others to appropriate norms of regard. On my understanding of Delany, he would think that to describe a right without a corresponding capacity for action would be a contradiction in terms. If I have a right to sovereignty this does not mean that I am stronger than others and thus have *power over* them, but that others recognize my *power to* determine myself or delegate my authority to another.[61] This means that individual rights have a social basis in a historical form of life. The right may be *mine*, but I can only claim it because I am part of a *we* that acknowledges this right. From this we can see why the discourse of the nation becomes so important for many oppressed groups.

Absent this historical form of life, I may make a claim for self-determination but it will not be acknowledged or taken up as my *right*, but as a potential privilege that is being conferred on me. Delany concludes, "Where there is no *acknowledged sovereignty*, there can be no binding power; hence, the suffrage of the black man, independently of the white, would be in this country unavailable."[62] The right

---

[61] In chapter 4, I will have more to say about this distinction between *power over* and *power to*.
[62] Delany, *Documentary Reader*, 247.

to sovereignty is a historical relationship that precedes a citizenry and anchors their actions as a *binding power* rather than mere supplication. Delany's address shares many features with the theory of *rights externalism* as defended by Derrick Darby.[63] According to Darby, the externalist position argues that "facts about how a subject is treated in a social milieu partly determine whether it possesses moral rights" rather than any rights-endowing properties (such as being a child of God or rationality) that a subject is presumed to have.[64] He contends that "recognition [that] is provided by social practices that proscribe, promulgate, and enforce ways of acting and being treated" are a necessary condition for having rights.[65] For Delany, black nationalism is an answer to the lack of social practices of regard that have historically developed in the United States. More than that, it is an attempt to see the world as it is and not how one wishes it would be. This might seem surprising given that we are trying to understand the *utopian critique* of black nationalism, but the concept of utopia that I have been defending emerges from within the breakdowns and conflicts between forms of life. And so Delany notes that even though *some* state governments may allow *some* free black people to vote, the fact of the matter is that for the majority of black people at the time neither the formal act of voting nor the substantive reality of freedom was a part of their lived experience.[66] The social significance of black peoples' skin color, especially after the

---

[63] See Derrick Darby, "Two Conceptions of Rights Possessions," *Social Theory and Practice* 27, no. 3 (2001): 387–417; Darby, "Unnatural Rights" *Canadian Journal of Philosophy* 33, no. 1 (2003): 49–82; Darby, *Rights, Race, and Recognition* (Cambridge, UK: Cambridge University Press, 2009); and Darby, "Rights Externalism." For criticisms, see Charles W. Mills, "Racial Rights and Wrongs: A Critique of Derrick Darby," *Radical Philosophy Review* 18, no. 1 (2015): 11–30 and David Lyons, "The Social Dimension of Rights" *Journal of Social Philosophy* 44, no. 1 (2013): 43–50.

[64] Darby, "Two Concepts of Rights Possession," 387.

[65] Darby, "Rights Externalism," 253.

[66] Darby emphasizes the important role of "lived experience" for the rights externalist position when he defends his account as more adequate for understanding the historical situation of chattel slavery than the "ontological conception" ("Rights Externalism," 253) of rights that presumes subjects have rights by virtue of their nature: "Whatever possessing a moral right to freedom amounts to, if it is a 'right' that one truly possesses then freedom must be a part of one's lived experience. In other words, possessing a right to freedom must make a concrete difference in the social world in terms of how one can act and be treated" (261). Darby's argument closely resembles Delany's supposition that rights are capacities for binding powers whose realization must be found in the historical practices of a given form of life rather than outside of history.

passage of the Fugitive Slave Act, prevents any widespread acknowledgment of sovereignty insofar as even a nominally free black person may be taken as a slave.[67]

Delany's utopian call for emigration proceeds from his realist analysis of the social practices that constituted the nation. "In the United States, among the whites, their color is made, by law and custom, the mark of distinction and superiority; while the color of black people is a badge of degradation, acknowledged by statute, organic law, and the common consent of the people."[68] This state of affairs could not be expected to change when a majority of the black population continued to live under enslavement. Even if particular state governments deigned to recognize a small minority of black people as free this could do nothing to undo the threat of broader *social unfreedom* that pervaded the nation. Until the state and its laws could cut loose from the anchor of the nation and its customary degradation of black people as a social class there could be no secure rights for black people at an individual level.

For Delany, the black nation is less than a real place, but more than a purely imaginary idea. It is a *prophetic* call for politically "free" black people to "act and judge appropriately" given that their social unfreedom is tied to the condition of the enslaved.[69] Melvin Rogers, in reference to David Walker's 1829 *Appeal to the Colored Citizens of the World*, describes prophetic practice as a rhetorical appeal to the audience that "honors the judgment of the recipients [and] exemplifies the logic of self-governance."[70] Delany follows in this tradition and uses the nation as a construction of call and response to incite black people to take up social practices of regard toward one another that would make rights real. These rights of which Delany speaks are *not*

---

[67] Delany, *Documentary Reader*, 272. Delany calls this a state of "relative *slavery*" because "save those who carry free papers of emancipation, or bills of sale from former claimants or owners" the Fugitive Slave Bill places "each and every one of us at the *disposal of any and every white* who might choose to *claim* is" (272). Delany effectively makes a republican critique of the U.S. polity insofar as black people are unfree because white people as a social class have the ever-present capacity to *arbitrarily* interfere with the freedom of black people even when they may not exercise this power.

[68] Delany, *Documentary Reader*, 248.

[69] Melvin Rogers, "David Walker and the Political Power of the Appeal," *Political Theory* 43, no. 2 (2015): 226.

[70] Rogers, "David Walker," 227.

yet established, but through the rhetorical figure of the nation they appear to be the necessary *destiny* for black people. What is peculiar for the black nation is that it appears as if it both precedes black people and must constantly be achieved or fulfilled. The nation is already here, but also yet to be discovered. Developing solidarity, under such extreme conditions of racial domination, seems to necessitate the rhetorical fusing of the past and the future to catalyze truly transformative social practices. Rights, for Delany, operate as a prophetic call for black people to become what they have always been in order to free themselves from the ossifying present of a racial polity.

We can gloss Delany's black nationalism as the attempt to create a form of life that emerges from the gap between the state and the nation. Delany highlights the potential limits of political freedom that is not anchored in a broader reconstruction of social emancipation. Confronted with a racial polity that is still shaped by slavery and racism, Delany endeavored to transform the anchoring practices of black people by constituting a new nation where they would have the power to acknowledge each other's sovereignty. He wanted to initiate a paradigm shift whereby the conduct of black people could no longer be taken up as the exercise of privilege rather than right.[71] Such a transformation would necessitate novel historical practices that would anchor the inherent rights black people were due. Delany well understood that states, much like rights, were not free-floating and for them to be effective they had to be anchored in ongoing social practices. Black nationalism attempts to interrupt this temporal flow of dominant social practices and create the space for a new foundation of rights to take root.

Notably, Delany did change his mind on the necessity of black emigration after the end of the Civil War. Rather than a change in principle I think we can see why this would follow from his understanding of the nation as the anchoring practice for the state. The Civil War, Delany presumed, shattered the "original identity" of the American nation

---

[71] Eva von Redecker offers a praxis-theoretical account of revolution that I attempt to build on here, where social transformation is obtained only once a new praxis has "become an anchor praxis" (*Praxis and Revolution: A Theory of Social Transformation*, trans. Lucy Duggan [New York: Columbia University Press, 2021], 192) that is repeated and continued.

once white citizen had turned against white citizen. With slavery abolished and the absence of an assumed unity of white national identity, history had been interrupted and, in that vacuum, a new form of life could emerge where sovereignty could be broadly acknowledged. There would still need to be some cohesive element that would ensure the stability of the state, but now that cohesion need not be *racial*, but truly *civic*. The point being that Delany changed his mind on black nationalism because of a radical disruption in the social practices of the nation.

We can imagine that Delany saw the founding narratives of the nation as in crisis. The war had unburdened the public from the inertia of slavery, and they could re-narrate the borders of the nation by acknowledging that black people could also call the nation to account for itself. Delany believed he had good reason to hope that black people would have standing in the space of reasons that now organized the nation and thus they would be able to begin the hard work of restructuring the character of the nation.

However, there are few, if any, "radical" breaks in history. Institutions and social practices are rarely able to strip themselves clean of the historical contexts in which they found their genesis. The nation, *if* it is the anchoring practice of the polity, presents a challenge for Delany's search for irreversible justice. The nation is comprised of dual temporalities insofar as it is often imagined as preceding the present and awaiting fulfillment in the future. This means that the rights that the nation grants are always historically mediated: inherited from the past and open to the future. There is no promise that the future will be more just than the present as our social practices may regress. Rights for racial minorities, as Delany understands them, are beholden to the vacillations of the nation's identity. They stand always on the horizon awaiting their fulfillment in a time that may never come.

What we can take from Delany is not the plan for emigration and colonization in other parts of the world, but the utopian creation of forms of life where sovereignty is acknowledged. By shifting our focus on rights away from their supposed inherence in our human nature, black nationalism highlights the social conditions necessary for the capacity to bear rights. Utopia is precisely the effort to break with the domination of historical practices and begin a new time. This is its prophetic element, as I discussed above. Delany makes this point when describing why his generation differs from the prior generation: "We are their sons, but not the same individuals; neither do we live in the same period with them. That which suited them, does not suit us; and that with which they may have been contented, will not satisfy us."[72] Delany overstates the supposed meekness of his black ancestors, but his central point still stands: once people take themselves to be sovereign they will no longer be satisfied with mere privileges. It is in this moment that rights have a chance to become actual.

However, we should not be too hasty to endorse the thesis that the state is primarily anchored in the temporal dynamics of the nation. Perhaps such an argument made more sense while chattel slavery still existed, but what does black nationalism have to offer once slavery is no more? I think the answer is that black nationalism still brings into view what I take to be a necessary condition for racial justice: institutions and social practices that anchor justificatory power against the arbitrary foreclosure of the space of reasons. Moreover, I think Delany's vision of black nationalism is correct that achieving this state of affairs requires a wholly new form of life over which there can be popular control. This was the utopian insight, but the social practices that are commensurate with nationalism cannot deliver on this promise.

From Body Politic to Body Politics

Black nationalism is a symptom of a racially unjust society. To be more precise, black nationalism is a response to crises of dysfunction and stagnation in social life.[73] Racial injustice is not only the experience of disrespect and unfreedom, but a broader sense that social life has ossified. The discourse of the "nation" as the necessary anchoring practice for social freedom aims at reinvigorating the social life of the dominated by constituting a new and autonomous "we" that need not remain encased in the decaying social body of the racist nation.

---

[72] Delany, *Documentary Reader*, 266.
[73] Robert L. Allen, *Black Awakening in Capitalist America: An Analytic History* (Trenton, NJ: Africa World Press, 1992), 89.

Throughout his address, Delany uses medical metaphors to justify his solution of emigration from the United States as the only avenue for social freedom. He tells his audience, "[W]e have discovered and comprehended the great political disease with which we are affected, the cause of its origin and continuance; and what is now left for us to do is discover and apply a sovereign remedy—a healing balm to a diseased body—a wrecked but not entirely shattered system."[74] Black nationalism attends to the problem not only of *political wrong*, but of *social disease*.

It is important not to collapse the concern for political wrongs with the concern for social disease because they point to two different facets of racial domination. *Political wrongs* refer to unfair legal policies that are enforced by the state, and the remedy here would be distinctly legislative. For black nationalism this does not go far enough and indeed misses the root of the problem. It is the stagnating *social disease* of non-legal norms or a lack of civic virtue that produces political dysfunction. Delany argues that the civic norms of the United States have been corrupted by racial identification such that the public good effectively excludes the well-being of black people. As discussed above, this is what Christopher J. Lebron and Melvin L. Rogers characterize as the problem of social value.[75] This would mean that the advancement of white peoples' interests is not taken to be partial or sectional, but common. Accordingly, Delany implies legal policy that would enshrine black peoples' freedom is unlikely or will be ineffective insofar as the broader social body will interpret the policies as unfair or contrary to the common good.

The utopian dream of emigration and separation fundamentally concerns the reconstruction of the civic norms that constitute the body politic. Black people have been deformed by adhering to civic norms that are only appropriate for a narrowly construed body politic. Delany worries that generations of slavery and racial domination have sapped the "vigor" of black collective practices.[76] They lack creativity, self-confidence, and ambition as civic norms of self-abnegation

---

[74] Delany, *Documentary Reader*, 249.
[75] Lebron, *Shame* and Rogers, "Race, Domination, and Republicanism."
[76] Shelby, *We Who Are Dark*, 34–38.

and servility have sunk into the habitus of the black social body. The very effort of dreaming, discussing, and planning the founding of a new black nation (irrespective of the actual act of claiming a piece of land) requires virtues that are antithetical to servility, thereby creating the conditions for new subjectivities to emerge. The utopian kernel of black nationalism that critical theory should rescue is not only the spirit of solidarity, but the impulse toward the emancipation of social life beyond the rectification of political wrongs.

Rescuing this kernel requires that we analyze how black nationalism reinscribes race into the life of the social body. The relationship of embodiment and nation is not particular to Delany.[77] As we will see in the work of Marcus Garvey and Garveyism in the 1920s practices of racial embodiment are what anchor the black nation. Black nationalism revalorizes race as a source of creativity and futurity rather than as an anti-modern weight that prevents social progress. Reacting against the racial domination of the white body politic, black nationalism endeavors to create a novel body politics that contests racist civic norms. Transforming how black people display themselves, comport themselves, and dispose themselves to each other is central to the supposed vitality of black nationalism. In its essence black nationalism is an *aesthetic* confrontation with the norms of the white body politic.[78] If race is going to be "seen" as a sign of *biological* backwardness, then black nationalism strives to reinscribe race as a sign of *aesthetic* creativity. For instance, one of the most distinct features of the Garveyite movement was the exuberance for public marches in military uniforms.[79]

---

[77] See Frantz Fanon, *The Wretched of the Earth*, trans. Richard Philcox (New York: Grove Press, 2004); Frantz Fanon, "Algeria Unveiled," in *A Dying Colonialism*, trans. Haakon Chevalier (New York: Grove Press, 1967), 69–99; Aimé Césaire, *Discourse on Colonialism*, trans. Joan Pinkham (New York: Monthly Review Press, 2000); William Michael Paris, "Gender and Technology in Fanon: Confrontations of the Clinical and the Political," *Philosophy Compass* 14, no. 9: 1–10.

[78] Mark Christian Thompson, *Black Fascisms: African American Literature and Culture between the Wars* (Charlottesville: University of Virginia Press, 2007), 41–44.

[79] Paul Gilroy interprets this aspect of Garveyism as fundamental because Garvey understood that "racial purity is a project, not a condition. Neither biology nor racial oppression is sufficient to generate purity of race: martial technologies of racial becoming—drills, uniforms, medals, titles, rallies—are necessary to standardize a racial outlook that cannot arise spontaneously." Paul Gilroy, "Black Fascism," *Transition* 9, no. 1 (2000): 70–91).

For black nationalism race is not a hidden historical essence that can only be discovered through the techniques of science. Race must show itself, and by showing itself in shared social practices it at least interrupts the dominant social practices that represent black people as backward or servile.[80] In other words, it is an effort to generate new justification narratives for black empowerment. The importance of the rights externalism position that I argued was crucial for Delany's black nationalism follows from the aestheticization of race. Race can anchor rights because race is primarily the fund of social practices that compose the nation. Insofar as these social practices do not appear or even decay then the actuality of one's inherent rights will also wax and wane.

The upshot of the aesthetic activities of black nationalism is that it reconfigures utopia as an already existing capacity in the practical efforts of one's body. The black nation does not have to wait for the implausible realization of full emigration and colonization of foreign lands. In a sense, black nationalism insists that the black nation already lives in the black body. Utopia is a *real* possibility because it is already embedded in the creative life process of race. If only black people could heal their bodies, they could collectively externalize this creative drive. The black nation gives form to the utopian possibility of transformation by reinvigorating the body politics of black subjects. No doubt Delany was sincere in his proposal for emigration, but this was because he thought the only chance for black people to develop enduring practices of dignity and respect was in the absence of the racial politics of the white nation. The calamity of the war, Delany wagered, had thrown these practices into disarray and exploded the machinery of the state upon which they were founded, thus paving the way for a healthy union between nation and state.[81]

---

[80] See Jacques Rancière, *Disagreement: Politics and Philosophy*, trans. Julie Rose (Minneapolis: University of Minnesota Press, 1999) for the close connection between aesthetics and politics.

[81] Delany associates the state with "machinery" in contradistinction with the organicism of the black nation (*Documentary Reader*, 253). Delany's realism views the state as an obstinate mechanism that follows law-like regularities and thus cannot be a source of vital creativity. Delany's ideas bear a striking resemblance to Friedrich Schiller's criticism of the state as a cold and mutilating machine in "Letters upon the Aesthetic Education of Man," in *Essays*, eds. Walter Hinderer and Daniel O. Dahlstrom, trans. Elizabeth M. Wilkinson and L. A. Willoughby (New York: Continuum, 1993), 90–95.

However, confounding the black body and the black nation is not without risks.[82] By burdening the black body with the task of carrying the nation, black nationalism necessitates the surveilling and disciplining of bodily expression. After all, if the aesthetic practices of the black body relate directly to the identity of the black nation, then individual deviations may imperil the health of the nation. Furthermore, the discourse of pathology and health tends to presume some "normal" mode of black body politics.[83] It is no wonder that black nationalisms have often been associated with rigid and conservative gender and sexual politics.[84] There seems to be an antinomy between the putative creativity of black body politics and the seemingly necessary conservatism of the body politic. I would suggest that this antinomy is not particular to *black* nationalism, but nationalism in whatever form it happens to take.

Given this tension between creativity and conservatism we might think that black nationalism makes sense in a historical moment when so many are formally enslaved, but once our form of life changes and new forms of racial domination appear it is conceivable that black nationalism should be relegated to the past. The fact that forms of black nationalism continued to persist suggests that the end of slavery did not fully resolve the problem of domination. By turning to the ideas of Marcus Garvey in the 1920s I will show that black nationalism, however limited, continues to offer potent resources for social critique under conditions of racial domination.

The Ideological Space of Garveyism

Without a doubt, Garveyism is most immediately known through the slogan "Africa for Africans." Before Garveyism currents of black

---

[82] Paul Gilroy, *Against Race: Imagining Political Culture beyond the Color Line* (Cambridge, MA: Harvard University Press, 2000), 137–177 and Gilroy, "Black Fascism."
[83] See Frederick Neuhouser, *Diagnosing Social Pathology: Rousseau, Hegel, Marx, and Durkheim* (Cambridge: Cambridge University Press, 2022), 7–10.
[84] E. Frances White, "Africa on My Mind: Gender, Counter Discourse, and African American Nationalism," in *Is It Nation Time? Contemporary Essays on Black Power and Black Nationalism*, ed. Eddie S. Glaude Jr. (Chicago: University of Chicago Press, 2002), 130–156.

nationalism had emerged in black politics and culture in the works of David Walker, Edward Blyden, and, as discussed, Martin Delany, but never had it crystallized into a mass movement that stretched from the U.S. and Canada through the Caribbean, Latin America, Europe, and Africa.[85] Garveyism and the Universal Negro Improvement Association (UNIA) carved out a new ideological space for black politics.

The success of Garveyism might be chalked up to the idiosyncratic charisma and personality of Marcus Garvey the man. No doubt Garvey believes this myth of himself when he recounts after reading Booker T. Washington's *Up from Slavery*, "[M]y doom—if I may so call it—of being a race leader dawned upon me in London after I had traveled almost half of Europe."[86] I think we have good reason to reject Garvey's self-professed messianism for two reasons. First, it reduces every discussion of Garveyism to the character of Marcus Garvey and tends to forestall philosophical analysis. If one does not like Garvey, then one can reject the movement of Garveyism as fruit of the poisonous tree.[87] Second, an overemphasis on individual personalities as the motive force in black politics deprives us of the insight that black politics emerges in a constellation of trans-individual historical forces and social processes.

In other words, black politics is a contest over the borders of a historical space of reasons. In this respect, Garveyism returns us to the immanent space of utopia and politics. The utopianism of "Africa for Africans" does not reside in the transcendent space of a future African state. Instead, we should understand its utopian success in its ability to

---

[85] See Steven Hahn, *The Political Worlds of Slavery and Freedom* (Cambridge, MA: Harvard University Press, 2009), 116–118.

[86] Marcus Garvey, *Philosophy and Opinions of Marcus Garvey*, vol. 2, ed. Amy Jacques-Garvey (Mansfield Centre, CT: Martino, 2014), 126.

[87] Hahn notes that the figure of Garvey has been "vilified, disparaged, scorned, and lampooned ... as a foreigner out of touch with American life; as a political dreamer who misled his followers; as a scam artist looking to fleece the masses and line his pockets; as something of a religious revivalist who traded on the traditions of faith and fraternalism; as a racial purist whose dangerous sensibilities led him to political associations with white supremacists; and as a self-absorbed and self-referential buffoon, outfitting himself and his African Legion with silly, resplendent military attire in a pathetic mimicry of the colonial powers that were. That he attracted so much attention makes Garvey all the more problematic and his movement something of an embarrassment" (*Political Worlds*, 120).

establish *communicative* spaces for black working-class people to understand themselves anew.

Garvey's black nationalism took inspiration from the contemporary movements of Irish nationalism and Jewish political Zionism.[88] These ideas were available to him and others, but more was needed. For Garveyite black nationalism to become an imagined community these ideas needed to be given institutional form through his newspaper the *Negro World*. The importance of this newspaper for the UNIA underscores Benedict Anderson's observation that oppressed groups within nations often worked to break into print and radio media in order to generate new national imaginaries.[89] Garveyism's energy for self-determination was not a historical anomaly, but the crystallization of disparate national struggles that were being transmitted across the globe with unprecedented speed.

Garvey's political awakening came from his interaction with print media and the dawning "information age" as well as his "travels in the West Indies and in South and Central America, where he discovered that conditions were no different than in Jamaica . . . white people ruled and black people were subordinate."[90] The rapid growth of international newspapers, radio, and other media transformed the

---

[88] Desmond Jagmohan, "Between Race and Nation: Marcus Garvey and the Politics of Self-Determination," *Political Theory* 48, no. 3 (2020): 275–276.

[89] Anderson, *Imagined Communities*, 45. Frantz Fanon, in "This Is the Voice of Algeria," describes a similar process as occurring during the anti-colonial war between Algeria and France where the radio, originally operating as a tool for transmitting French nationalism throughout Algeria, suddenly becomes a tool for anticolonial struggle by allowing Algerians to imagine that they were a part of a collective movement for freedom with Algerians they did not know and had never met. Frantz Fanon, *A Dying Colonialism*, trans. Haakon Chevalier (New York: Grove Press, 1965), 72–78; also in Frantz Fanon, *Œuvres* (Paris: Éditions La Découverte, 2011), 308–313. Fanon goes on to associate the dissemination of news, good or bad, over the radio concerning the war effort with the initiation of cycles of *will formation* and *enthusiasm*: "These manifestations, these attitudes of total belief, this collective conviction, express the determination of the group [*la volonté du groupe*] to get as close as possible to the Revolution, to get ahead of the Revolution if possible, in short *to be in on it* [*d'être dans le coup*]" (*Dying Colonialism*, 80/*Œuvre*, 315). The technology of the radio transforms the rhythms and sense of time of those who imagine themselves as part of the revolutionary nation. An alternative space of reasons emerges that contests the domination of French hegemony.

[90] Wilson Jeremiah Moses, *Creative Conflict in African American Thought* (Cambridge: Cambridge University Press, 2004), 235–236.

capacity for ideas to travel. Garveyism emerges not only as a distinct set of ideas concerning black nationalism, but within a distinctive set of conditions.

Garveyism reveals black politics to be essentially transversal and iterative. Richard Iton reminds us that "there is an autodiasporic quality to black life . . . that results from the impossibility of aligning culture and the borders of nation-states."[91] The transversality of Garveyism raises practical questions of how black people in different spaces can communicate with one another. How is it possible for them to interface when they are separated by borders, oceans, idioms, and languages? *Where* is this public to be found that will be the foundation of mass politics? Amy Jacques Garvey, Marcus Garvey's second wife, observed of Garvey's initial attempts to crystallize a political movement in his native Jamaica in 1914 that he was "'unable to get the masses to unite and cooperate for their own good.'"[92]

We should resist overlooking this initial failure of Garveyism as having only historical rather than philosophical value. Firstly, it disabuses us of the idea that black nationalism is an idea that is organic to black people, that it generates automatic lines of affinity between black subjects. Secondly, this failure suggest why Garveyism (and Garvey) had to find a different space for his political ideas. Movements for political transformation rarely catch fire on the first go. They are the culmination of prior efforts that may have appeared to have missed their opportunity or been out of joint with their contemporary moment. Part of the reason I have paired Marcus Garvey and Martin Delany together is to give a sense of the long historical trajectory of the search for the black nation. The disjointed temporality of the racial polity is an injustice, but it also testifies to the fact that ideological domination is never absolute. Learning processes that enable emancipation may be resumed in different historical contexts as the resources for utopian consciousness accumulate.[93] Thus far, I have suggested

---

[91] Richard Iton, *In Search of the Black Fantastic: Politics and Popular Culture in the Post–Civil Rights Era* (New York: Oxford University Press, 2008), 202. See also Paul Gilroy, *The Black Atlantic: Modernity and Double Consciousness* (Cambridge, MA: Harvard University Press, 1993).
[92] Quoted in Moses, *Creative Conflict*, 240.
[93] See chapter 1 of the present volume for an exploration of the argument.

that utopia is not a literal place, but a discordant rhythm or submerged temporality that animates struggles for racial justice. It is the idea that even failures may have their time.

Indeed, failure seems to be endemic to any politics that attempts to establish new frontiers of ideological space. The iterations of failure in black politics are lost when popular memory only recovers MLK's most popular sermons or a single moment when Rosa Parks refused to move. What we lose are the sermons that failed to instigate popular action, or the many times national media failed to report when Parks (and other black women) refused to be moved. There is the risk of mystifying black politics with the myth of organic success and spontaneity. The black nation never fully appears in history, never absolutely transcends its historical context, but, for all that, diverse justifications for freedom and self-determination course through the history of the body politic.

To return to the topic of Garveyism, we can see that its reiteration came in New York in 1916 where he found black people beginning their mass migration from the terror and lack of opportunity in the South, West Indian immigrants such as himself, a network of women's clubs, a newspaper industry, and an assortment of fraternal institutions.[94] Furthermore, Garvey found himself face-to-face with black people who were angry and cynical after the dismantling of Reconstruction, ongoing economic domination, persistent racial terrorism, and the erosion of civil rights. On top of all of this they would be asked in the years to come to "close ranks" and sacrifice themselves in the First World War by prominent black figures such as Du Bois.[95] The promise of the end of slavery and the emancipatory re-anchoring of the polity had been frustrated and felled by white supremacy and entrenched interests which led to the question "Where is hope to be found if not here?"

---

[94] Moses, *Creative Conflict*, 242–243.
[95] W. E. B. Du Bois, "Close Ranks," *Crisis* 16, no. 3 (July 1918): 111. For a historical reconstruction of Du Bois's complex motives for calling on black citizens to fight on behalf of the United States, see Mark Ellis, "'Closing Ranks' and 'Seeking Honors': W. E. B. Du Bois in World War I," *Journal of American History* 79, no. 1 (June 1992): 96–124.

Enter Garvey and his invocations of "a new Ethiopia."[96] We should remember that this call for a new space of black politics reiterates the nationalist movements for independence that could be found globally in Ireland and India at this moment. Nevertheless, Michael Dawson insists that Garvey's "mass movement . . . was based on a metaphysical view of a future utopia. . . . Garvey's movement was not a political one."[97] I agree that Garvey, the philosopher, was thoroughgoingly metaphysical, but I do not think this explains the success of *Garveyism* in this time period. Garveyism's good fortune was to find an ideological space among a mass of black working-class men and women who were hungry for alternative ideas precisely because of the repeated failures of the American government and extant organizations to speak to and address their material concerns.

Garveyism provided informational and communicative institutions like the newspaper *Negro World* that gave coherence to the broad dissatisfaction and fear that coursed through the black population of the United States. My point is that what was "new" about the space of Garveyism was not necessarily its ideas, but that it arrived at a conjunction of accumulating failures within the United States. The utopianism of Garveyism reached out and resonated with real hungers and needs that had gone unmet while moving them into a nationalist ideological space.

What was crucial for the "free-standing institutional life" that Garveyism would acquire was that its newspaper *Negro World* even spoke to those who were illiterate in the black population by being read aloud in "workplaces, beauty salons, barber shops, and Sunday schools."[98] The effectiveness of the space of Garveyism consists in the fact that it went to the spaces of black life where the vast majority of black people spoke, laughed, and deliberated. This diffusion of Garveyism into disaggregated spaces of black life cannot be adequately

---

[96] Marcus Garvey, *Selected Writings and Speeches of Marcus Garvey*, ed. Bob Blaisdell (Mineola, NY: Dover, 2004), 125.
[97] Michael Dawson, "Marcus Garvey: The Black Prince?," in *African American Political Thought: A Collected History*, ed. Melvin L. Rogers and Jack Turner (Chicago: University of Chicago Press, 2021), 268.
[98] Moses, *Creative Conflict*, 246, 253.

expressed with an exclusive focus on Garvey the man. I understand as utopic the construction of an alternative space of reasons with new theoretical terms, new imaginary borders of political life, and new institutions to keep these terms and borders in circulation.

Garvey's words would resonate differently in the United States than they did in Jamaica. His response to programs of adjustment as represented by Du Bois was to proclaim, "The white man of America will not, to any organized extent, assimilate the Negro, because in so doing, he feels that he will be committing racial suicide . . . to the white man the question of racial difference is eternal."[99] But it was not Garvey's racial pessimism nor the promise of repatriating to Africa that was the primary motive for black peoples' investment in Garveyism. There is little evidence that these ideas animated the mass movement that would go under the name of Garveyism.[100] In the following section, I will argue that it was his calls for self-mastery over, and self-knowledge of, one's black body that spurred black political imaginations throughout the globe. Garvey, in a short piece titled "Dissertation on Man," concludes, "I desire to impress upon 400,000,000 members of my race that our failings in the past, present and of the future will be through our failures to know ourselves and to realize the true functions of man on this mundane sphere."[101] Having established the political space of Garveyism we can now reevaluate his "metaphysical view of a future utopia," but contrary to most interpretations, I will argue that utopia for Garvey begins with the black body and not the geographical space of Africa.[102]

Producing the New Black Body: Marcus Garvey's Utopian Idealism

In what follows, I examine Garvey's personal metaphysical philosophy and its relationship to the "black body." I will focus on a set of lectures

---

[99] Marcus Garvey, *Philosophy and Opinions of Marcus Garvey*, vol. 1, ed. Amy Jacques-Garvey (Mansfield Centre, CT: Martino, 2014), 26.
[100] Moses, *Creative Conflict*, 248.
[101] Garvey, *Philosophy and Opinions*, vol. 1, 25.
[102] Dawson, "Marcus Garvey," 268.

he gave in 1937 entitled *Message to the People: The Course of African Philosophy*. In these lectures Garvey offers a philosophy that is thoroughly idealist and metaphysical. The central object of concern for liberation is not securing land or territory; Garvey focuses on the activity of the mind and intelligence to reform material life. Scant attention has been given to Garvey's metaphysical system in these lectures. I think this is unfortunate because what one finds in these lectures is that Garvey was not simply an opportunist but had deeply considered views and principles. More importantly, these lectures allow us to appreciate the internal philosophical contradiction within Garvey's black nationalism.

The rift between Garvey's metaphysics and his politics can be summed up in the fact that the black nation was never really "out there," it was never actually existing Africa. Utopia was always the interior self-mastery and emancipation of one's mind as well as the unleashing of the black body's endogenous capacities. The nation becomes coextensive with the physical body. If this is so, then the utopian kernel of black nationalism is a disciplined form of mindedness that takes oneself to be the legitimating source of self-activity. In reference to Malcolm X, who was raised as a Garveyite, Michael E. Sawyer describes this intellectual autonomy as "Black Mindedness." It is "a way of knowing about the self and in so doing, understanding the self to be a necessarily radical political subject."[103] For Garvey, emancipation begins not from claiming some territory and building a state, but from knowing oneself as a subject that has the capacity to rule. This principle of self-rule begins with the mind's regulation of the body against forces of heteronomy such as excessive love, anger, hunger, and uncleanliness.[104] From the individual's mind the character of self-rule radiates outward through the group until a collective nation is formed.

Garvey obsesses over the hygiene of the mind and body in ways that appear hyperbolic at first. He claims, "When a man is clean in body, appearance and mind, he feels like a giant and a master. He is afraid of nothing. If he lacks these qualities, he cringes, bows, and hides. He is

---

[103] Michael E. Sawyer, *Black Minded: The Political Philosophy of Malcolm X* (London: Pluto Press, 2020), 10.

[104] Marcus Garvey, *Message to the People: The Course of African Philosophy* (Mineola, NY: Dover, 2020), 46–47.

never himself."[105] However, Garvey's point here is that mind and body have an expressive connection to one another. Those who take pride in themselves could not be content with showing themselves to others as unkempt. More to the point, Garvey thinks the character of one's mind *always* expresses itself in one's bodily comportment. Accordingly, to take oneself as capable of self-rule means one must show others that one is capable of self-rule. Mark Christian Thompson summarizes Garvey's combination of hygiene and racial morality thusly: "If one is kempt, one is clean in every aspect of life. Proper racial thinking shapes outer appearance and situates the body within an intellectual racial economy that can be viscerally apprehended. To be in possession of a 'filthy' body means one is the owner of a dirty mind."[106] Despite the harshness of Garvey's language I think the most charitable interpretation of his thinking would see him as espousing the view that civic virtue must be cultivated and maintained, and this begins with concern over the state of the self. The mind must be continually cared for if black people are to become free subjects.

Garvey opens his lectures by telling his audience, "You must never stop learning."[107] He goes on to tell his audience to never stop reading in order to get information on human nature because "personal experience is not enough for a human to get all the useful knowledge of life, because the individual life is too short, so we must feed on the experience of others."[108] The focus on education and literacy is not unique to Garvey or Garveyism. Jarvis R. Givens shows that "teaching and learning continued to be 'a means of escape,' as Woodson[109] wrote. Education would guide black people in pursuit of a new world and a new way of being; it was a total critique of the current order."[110] Garvey

[105] Garvey, *Message*, 47.
[106] Thompson, *Black Fascisms*, 56.
[107] Garvey, *Message*, 3.
[108] Garvey, *Message*, 3.
[109] Carter G. Woodson (1875–1950) was an African-American historian, journalist, and founder of the Association for the Study of American Life and History who focused on creating institutions of education that focused on the history of African-Americans and the African diaspora. The second African-American to obtain a PhD from Harvard, after Du Bois, he is credited with laying the foundations for Black History Month with the creation of "Negro History Week."
[110] Jarvis R. Givens, *Fugitive Pedagogy: Carter G. Woodson and the Art of Black Teaching* (Cambridge, MA: Harvard University Press, 2021), 30.

was intent on constructing an ideological space that would allow his students to grasp how the space of reasons had been denied to them for so long. Garvey thought the cultivation of one's mind required educational institutions that could construct free subjectivity as well as protect black minds from the norms of servility and ignorance that comprise the white polity.[111]

The distrust of dominant institutions of knowledge production concerning truth and black capacity courses through these lectures. Garvey laments, "The educational system hides the truth as far as the Negro is concerned. Therefore, you must searchingly scan everything you read, particularly history, to see what you can pick out for the good of the race."[112] Garvey and Du Bois sound similar notes concerning racist propaganda and its effects on education. I would caution against overemphasizing their similarity on this score, however. For Garvey, black education not only extends outward to understand how things are in the world, but it also manifests the very activity of intelligence that connects the black person with God. Du Bois was always wary of religion and thought the role of ideas was to guide social science or uplift black people into healthier forms of cultural life. Garvey thinks that educating oneself is participation in one's godliness.

Garvey's metaphysics of God is not a form of personalism. He proclaims that God "is not a person, nor a physical being. He is spirit and He is *Universal Intelligence*."[113] Garvey goes on to offer a thoroughly idealist account of God and intelligence when he states, "It is intelligence that creates."[114] Education, for Garvey, does not only concern learning facts. It is the essential source of creativity for the black person. All creation and matter emerged from the Universal Intelligence that is God. What is important for Garvey here is that God does not have desires or wants. God is not even wrathful. For Garvey, God is fundamentally creative thought and order: "God is fair and just to everybody. He is no respecter of things or persons."[115] God

---

[111] Jagmohan, "Between Race and Nation," 281–284.
[112] Garvey, *Message*, 11.
[113] Garvey, *Message*, 34.
[114] Garvey, *Message*, 34.
[115] Garvey, *Message*, 35.

does not bring divine justice because God simply is the emanation of creative intellect from us as "a unitary particle of God's Universal Intelligence."[116]

Now Garvey does not deny that we, unlike Universal Intelligence, have bodies. He affirms that "Man is made of body and spirit" but "The spirit is God. It is intelligence."[117] Strikingly, for Garvey, this does not leave us in a state of alienation wrestling with our embodiment as an unnatural state contrary to our intelligence. Matter, or the body, is not the degraded or imperfect reflection of ideas. This could not be the case since matter proceeds from and testifies to the power of the intellect. He goes so far as to say, "*It is thought that created the Universe. It is thought that will master the Universe.* . . . If man can think most excellently, then he climbs in that excellence to the companionship of the *most excellent*."[118] More forthrightly, Garvey concludes, "*Mind is matter, mind is king, when it goes wrong, it loses its sceptre. It remains right and wields the sceptre and sits upon a throne.*"[119] Garvey will take this to mean that there cannot be anything shameful about having a black body because that very body is a manifestation of mind and intelligence. But, more to the point, the black body attains a distinctive reconceptualization in that it is not the site of shame or subjection. It is the evidence of intelligent creativity. Simply put, Garvey develops a new justification narrative for black people to individually and collective organize themselves as sovereign subjects.

Garvey attempts to yoke together this metaphysical idealism with his racialist politics. He argues, "The Negro should never completely surrender himself to the institutional life of other people, otherwise, ιe will not be original, but purely and merely a copyist."[120] We can see ɔw generative the space of black politics would be with the creation of nmunicative institutions that, themselves, reveal the creative power ʼack intellection. Throughout these metaphysical pronouncements ey offers a politics of black self-realization. This new institu- form of life is preceded by the awakened activity of intelligence.

ʼy, *Message*, 34.
ʼ, *Message*, 34.
Message, 80.
Message, 76.
ʼessage, 73.

He encourages them to see themselves as already the black nation they seek.

I think this emphasis on the capacity or "excellence" that already resides within the black body makes clear what would have been so attractive and invigorating in Garveyism. It counsels that one's potential has been right before one's very eyes. The black body is not an impediment, but proof positive that one is capable. I would conjecture that this is the most productive aspect of the legacy of Garveyism. Steven Hahn recounts in *The Political Worlds of Slavery and Freedom* that even after the dissolution of the UNIA and Garveyism political activity of members in chapters all over the South did not abate.[121] They redirected those organizational capacities and energies in other activities. I think this shows that emigration to Africa was rarely the motivating principle that was moving many of these black working-class folks, nor was it Garvey the individual. It was the ideological space that Garveyism opened up and the ideas it allowed to circulate.

I find that there are still serious problems in Garveyism. The emphasis on self-mastery goes as far as the very constitution of the black body. For Garvey, the black body is not a site of joy and excess. Instead, it must express the utmost discipline of the mind. In a lecture on "Elocution," Garvey goes so far as to say that one must evince absolute mastery of one's body if one is to succeed in giving speeches to others. He insists, "Your lungs must be sound. You must have a healthy chest. Your stomach must not be over full and you must not be hungry. Never try to make a speech on a hungry stomach.... You should eat eggs at least once a day, not hard but soft boiled or raw, if you can stand it."[122] The black body becomes a rigid site of absolute mastery and paranoia. It is hyper-regulated and constrained in the face of ongoing white supremacy. The very capacities Garvey's idealism bestows upon the black body are withdrawn in the service of a racialist political project.

My sense is that Garvey's politics can help explain this unfortunate tension. While Garvey argues, "Life is an important function. It was given for the purpose of expression," he warns that this expression for man's life cannot be anything whatsoever since "[m]an should have a

[121] Hahn, *Political Worlds*, 147.
[122] Garvey, *Message*, 31.

purpose and that purpose he should always keep in view.... How pitiful it is to see a man living without a program, not knowing how he is going to use his todays and tomorrows."[123] Garvey's political ambitions press his metaphysical idealism into a unitary mold that inhibits what could be genuinely emancipatory. He notes, "Nature never made anyone dually, but singly, therefore you have your single responsibility."[124] But why should this be so? Intelligence does not have a telos except the realization of its own creative capacities. Garvey opens life only to close it again. Life, like utopia, does not aim for borders, but seeks to shatter them.

Garvey wards off racial despair with a creative metaphysics, but the contradiction was that in his moment politics did not furnish much reason for hope. He lived in a moment when the world seemed to be opening and yet, at the same time, closing due to war at home and abroad. Garveyite black nationalism expresses the conflicting non-synchronicities of the political world. Garvey says of war that it is "the hellish passion of man let loose in opposition to man. It sums up the cruelty of man towards man.... [It is] the failure to use human reason."[125] Metaphysical norms and political forms of life find themselves at cross-purposes and reveal what is truly tragic in this world. However, I want to conclude with this reference to human reason in Garvey because it shows that utopia is not the abandonment of reason, but its critical partner. I would assert that the abandonment of utopia is the dereliction of whatever reason we can bring to black social life.

I maintain that we should hold onto the aspect of Garveyism that expresses the essential creativity of things and their capacities. We should allow Garveyism to open up new problem-spaces for black politics that will strip away its racialism while upholding its remarkable effectiveness at base-building. What we can retain from this analysis of Garvey and Garveyism is that the concept of utopia need not be constrained to a vision of a fantastic and impossible elsewhere. Utopia is comprised of the institutional work to carve out ideological space for fresh political visions. It is what Adom Gotachew might call

[123] Garvey, *Message*, 112, 113.
[124] Garvey, *Message*, 82.
[125] Garvey, *Message*, 95.

"worldmaking."[126] Utopia is a mode of communication in the service of world building. Garveyism communicates a conception of the black body that challenges some of our contemporary problem-spaces and turns us toward the work of building institutions that would sustain black life and allow it flourish under its own reason.

Black Nationalism Reconsidered

Black nationalism, from Delany to Garvey, endeavors to make black people full subjects in a space of reasons. The nation is transformed from a passive site of subjection, into a web of justificatory narratives that endow black people with powers of citizenship. By approaching the nation as an anchoring practice that structures the social practices of the polity, black nationalists attempted to create autonomous ideological spaces where black people could imagine themselves as a self-cultivating community. However, the struggle for autonomy proves to be ambivalent as black nationalism must always attempt to reappropriate historically salient values of the dominating polity. Rather than transcend the racial polity by transforming its anchoring practices, black nationalism lives non-synchronously within it, inside and out of its norms of subjection. The ensuing paranoia over racial identification becomes paramount lest the black nation risk reabsorption by the white polity. In other words, the problem of non-synchronicity remains.

We can appreciate the crystallization of a new problem-space *and* the depths of danger in utopian nationalism. The black body becomes the object and subject of absolute mastery, absolute control, in the effort of racial emancipation. The black nation expands into the state and compresses itself into the body. The body politic and the racialized body become a corporate entity such that no sphere of social life is left untouched. Race becomes *fetishized* as an abstraction that has real life rather than what becomes real because of our social practices. By collapsing race and nation, black nationalism attempts to win a form of

---

[126] Adom Getachew, *Worldmaking after Empire: The Rise and Fall of Self-Determination* (Princeton, NJ: Princeton University Press, 2019).

sovereignty from the white polity at the price of becoming enmeshed in concerns of purity and identity. Furthermore, I think that black nationalism misdiagnoses the nation as the anchoring practice for racial subjection rather than our economic form of life. I will elaborate on this point in chapter 5 when I discuss the ideas of James Boggs.

Nevertheless, black nationalism inaugurated an epochal shift in black political discourses and cultures. The public sphere of the UNIA opened up new pathways of organization in international struggles against exploitation and racial domination. Black nationalism militates against being integrated into a form of life that is judged to be not only unjust, but incapable of reform. The importance of black nationalism, I think, is that it expresses an important tendency in black political thought: the yearning for *separation*. Indeed, what I hope to have shown is that the ideal of separation is a necessary and fruitful aspect to any concept of utopia. All utopias develop a narrative for the necessity of separation from the world as it is.

To refuse the polity of the United States, to say that its national character is irrevocably broken, is an act that finds little acknowledgment in the justification narratives of the American nation. Steven Hahn suggests that it is because of the "powerful influence that a liberal integrationist framework [has] had on American history writing for at least the past half century" that Garveyism and black nationalism have been so marginalized as political tendencies worthy of discussion.[127] The supposition that integration must be a value worth fighting for tends to foreclose normative inquiries into whether our present form of life is all that is possible. The utopian kernel I have sought to rescue from black nationalism was the struggle to develop a separate space of reasons from which such a normative inquiry would have been possible. The ideal of opening the space of reasons to allow for self-activity, freedom, and non-domination should guide critical theory and social practices. Accomplishing this task may require affirming a separation from life as it is currently lived. The question, to which I turn in the following chapter, is how can we effect this separation from social practices that unduly constrain the space of reasons?

---

[127] Hahn, *Political Worlds*, 159–160.

4
Racial Fetishism and the Alienation of Time
A Fanonian Critical Theory of Utopia

Introduction

Throughout this book I have sought to develop a critical theory of utopia that emerges from the real tensions between the temporalities of political freedom and social emancipation. I have aimed to show that we ought to understand the effectiveness of racial emancipation through a critical analysis of how well social practices cohere across forms of life in a given polity. In the next chapter, we will see how social practices decohere in a class society where the temporality of economic life far outpaces the temporality of the political sphere or "the State." In the previous chapter, I demonstrated how emancipation remains unsecured when political freedom outstrips the anchoring practices of the nation. In both cases we see how the achievement of civil rights does not necessarily guarantee permanent emancipation from racial domination. This *Ungleichzeitigkeit* or non-contemporaneity of racist societies has been the subject of this book thus far. This chapter is a mediating link between the objective analyses of black nationalism in chapter 3 and of black power in chapter 5. It is important not to forget that the subjective moments of racial domination are integral to any critical theory of utopia.

In this chapter, I want to explicitly analyze what these objective tensions between forms of life mean for the "lived experience" of racial injustice. Lived experience has long been a central concept in the phenomenological tradition, from Edmund Husserl to Martin

Heidegger and Maurice Merleau-Ponty to Jean-Paul Sartre.[1] A critical theory of utopia cannot neglect the evidence of experience if we are going to map the terrain between social practices and social transformation. We must be able to offer some plausible explanation for why and how agents experience what I have called *crisis consciousness* and pass into a socially effective *utopian consciousness* (see chapter 1). Building on what I demonstrated earlier we can now stipulate that "lived experience" has its own sedimented temporal structure that is neither reducible to nor extricable from the temporal structures of the sphere of politics and the sphere of the economy. The legislation of rights and duties alongside the rise and fall of economic development shape forms of social consciousness that agents inhabit in order to make sense of their world and their conduct. Thus, lived experience will not refer solely to the "inner" life of individuals, but the social conditions of cognition and reason that attend our social practices.

My thesis will be that racial domination ossifies social forms of consciousness such that lived experience will "lag" behind transformations in the form of life of politics and the form of life of economics. What does it mean for a form of consciousness to be social? Following Vincent Descombes, we can analyze a social form of consciousness along the lines of an "objectified mind" where "I can confront someone with a law that is his law, not necessarily because he knows it explicitly, but because *all are presumed to know the law*."[2] A social form of consciousness always attends the institutions and customs that comprise a given form of life. The complex coordination of various social practices into a stable formation requires subjects to act *as if* certain rules and norms are taken for granted given that we

---

[1] See Edmund Husserl, *Logical Investigations*, trans. J. N. Findlay (1900; London: Routledge and Kegan Paul, 1970); Martin Heidegger, *Being and Time*, trans. Joan Stambaugh, revis. Dennis J. Schmidt (1927; Albany: State University of New York Press, 2010); Maurice Merleau-Ponty, *Phenomenology of Perception*, trans. Donald A. Landes (1945; London: Routledge, 2012); and Jean-Paul Sartre, *Being and Nothingness: An Essay in Phenomenological Ontology*, trans. Hazel Barnes (1943; New York: Washington Square Press, 1983).

[2] Vincent Descombes, *The Institutions of Meaning: A Defense of Anthropological Holism*, trans. Stephen Adam Schwartz (Cambridge, MA: Harvard University Press, 2014), 75.

lack direct access to thoughts of others. A social form of consciousness synchronizes the actions of diverse agents into a shared form of time such that the idea that "this is what one does" acquires the appearance of a natural state of affairs.[3] Racial injustice has the effect of fetishizing social forms of consciousness whereby relationships of hierarchy and domination become sedimented not because every individual believes them to be justified, but because agents presume that *others* take them to be so. The impersonal imposition of this social form of consciousness is diagnosed by Fanon, as I will argue below, as a problem of *racial fetishism*.

Memories, habits, and justifications of racial domination and hierarchy are neither easily forgotten nor undone. They do not evaporate simply because a given polity decrees that all citizens are equal or because capitalist dynamics are (supposedly) blind to social identities in their drive for the accumulation of surplus value. This does not mean that every individual in fact thinks and believes the same thing. It is always possible for an individual to have the *lived experience* of the discrepancy between "what *one* does" and "what *I* in fact do." Thus, agents can experience a painful type of temporal alienation where their personal future of meaning creation is blocked by sedimented past meanings. Racial fetishism is not a form of mind control or collective delusion as if all white people and black people are tricked into believing race is real. It is an objectified set of justifications that appear unassailable. However, these justifications are liable to conflict with the justifications that emerge in the sphere of politics and economics.

---

[3] Carter G. Woodson captured this dynamic in *The Mis-education of the Negro* (Trenton: Africa World Press, [1933] 1990) where he observes, "Negroes daily educated in the tenets of such a religion of the strong have accepted the status of the weak as divinely ordained, and during the last three generations of their nominal freedom they have done practically nothing to change it.... No systematic effort toward change has been possible, for, taught the same economics, history, philosophy, literature and religion which have established the present code of morals, the Negro's mind has been brought under control of his oppressor" (4). What Woodson calls "the Negro mind" is better understood as a social form of consciousness that obtains within a black form of life rather than a description of what every black person thinks or believes. Woodson criticizes the taken-for-granted justifications that black people must act and think against. Indeed, it is implausible that Woodson could think that the "mis-education" he describes is an affliction for every individual black mind given that it would mean he could not explain his own insight into the social mis-education he describes.

These temporal misalignments create the conditions where utopian consciousness may begin to crystallize precisely because of the endemic failures of being able to integrate social practices into the various rhythms of social life.

The work of the philosopher and psychologist Frantz Fanon elucidates helpfully, but problematically, the sociopathology of inertia in the lived experience of colonial societies as well as the intrinsic capacity for action to break free from this inertia. For Fanon, racism was a cultural phenomenon that prevented human action from reinventing itself in the future. Accordingly, racial emancipation is not reducible to political rights and duties that are conferred by states, but the attainment of social forms of consciousness that can shake free from the determinations of history and allow agents to self-consciously reinvent themselves. While Fanon's descriptions of this temporal movement are limited insofar as he seems to think that one can simply cut oneself free from history, he is useful for filling out a theory of emancipation that is adequate to the temporal distinction I have made between political freedom and social emancipation. I will argue that racial justice must go beyond claims for political reparations and turn toward a utopian analysis of the futural temporality of social freedom.

To prevent any misunderstanding: my claim is not that people are irremediably racist or that they will inevitably engage in racist social practices in racist societies. To argue this would mean disavowing the social theory of temporal sedimentation that I have defended thus far. Our social practices are anchored in conflictual forms of life and thus adhere to disparate ethico-functional norms. What I aim to explain is how racially unjust societies produce pathological forms of social consciousness and *why we have good reason to think that it is possible to overcome these pathologies*. The insight I hope to offer is that the barrier to racial emancipation has less to do with prejudicial beliefs than the conflictual form of time that obtains in contemporary societies.[4]

---

[4] See the Introduction and chapter 5 for a detailed explanation of what I am calling the "conflictual form of time" that exists in modern societies.

Freedom and Justification

We should begin from the end and work our way back. To understand Fanon's critique of racism and what his account could contribute to the project of racial emancipation it is important to see that his criticisms are offered from the standpoint of what he takes to be the necessary conditions for a free society. His analyses of the pathologies of racism take their shape from his social theory of freedom. Fanon does not begin from the fact of racism and work his way through this negative experience to an account of freedom. My interpretation of Fanon departs from those that approach his account of freedom *via negativa*. For better or worse, Fanon posits an account of freedom and works his way back into the vicissitudes of colonial society. Thus, Fanon does not offer a universal theory of racism that is applicable to all societies. Fanon in *Black Skin, White Masks* explicitly claims that his analyses are specific to the "French Antilles." He develops a specific social diagnosis of racism as a pathology of freedom.[5] However, all he means by this is that freedom must be understood as the effort to transcend historical conditions because for him freedom is a historical achievement.

Theoretical accounts of racism generally take two forms. On one account racism is analyzed as a series of more or less coherent beliefs that individuals hold about the supposed inferiority of another social group.[6] On another account racism is identified as institutional biases that occur independently of the thoughts of individuals.[7] These two accounts can be distinguished as either *epistemic* or *political*. We can understand the structure of racism as a chain of beliefs or values that are either empirically false or justify treating others unequally.

---

[5] Frantz Fanon, *Black Skin, White Masks*, trans. Richard Philcox (1952; New York: Grove Press, 2008); Frantz Fanon, *Œuvres*, ed. Jean Khalfa and Robert Young (Paris: La Découverte, 2011).

[6] Tommie Shelby, "Is Racism in the 'Heart'?," *Journal of Social Philosophy* 33, no. 3 (2002): 411–420; Charles W. Mills, *The Racial Contract* (Ithaca, NY: Cornell University Press, 1997) and "Kant's Untermenschen," in *Black Rights/White Wrongs* (New York: Oxford University Press, 2017); Sally Haslanger, *Resisting Reality: Social Construction and Social Critique* (New York: Oxford University Press, 2012), ch. 17.

[7] Ian Haney López, *White by Law: The Legal Construction of Race* (New York: New York University Press, 2006); Eduardo Bonilla-Silva, *Racism without Racists*, 3rd ed. (Lanham, MD: Rowman & Littlefield, 2009); Michael Omi and Howard Winant, *Racial Formation in the United States*, 3rd ed. (New York: Routledge, 2015).

Alternatively, racism may have less to do with the beliefs agents form than the inertia of institutional rules that persist because we lack the necessary political will to develop a more egalitarian society.[8]

Fanon does not deny that racism has epistemic and political dimensions. *Black Skin, White Masks* is replete with analyses and examples of black and white people making false inferences on the basis of race.[9] What is important for Fanon, however, is that the epistemic and political effects of racism are anchored by its temporal dimension. The social form of consciousness that is racism conditions the space of reasons that agents take to be publicly available. Nowhere is this clearer than when Fanon analyzes the sexual anxieties and fantasies that swirl around the black body: "Is the black man's sexual superiority real? Everyone *knows* it isn't. But that is beside the point. The prelogical thought of the phobic has decided it is."[10] What Fanon calls "pre-logical" is most fruitfully understood as the background norms that permeate French society. Our development as rational agents is never wholly self-determined. We come into a world where certain meanings and reasons have already been decided before we have had the chance to evaluate them according to our individual powers of judgment. Eventually we can attain a critical disposition to what has been pre-decided; however, in societies as we currently know them it seems near impossible that we could ever achieve full self-transparency and control over the "pre-logical" social conditions we have inherited. The problem here is that what a subject "knows" in the present is practically disarmed by what has been decided upon in

---

[8] An alternative account of racism that I find more illuminating focuses on the mundane and everyday interactions of capitalist social relations that are premised upon neither individual attitudes nor written laws or rules, but how our society organizes and produces value. See Vanessa Wills, "What Could It Mean to Say, 'Capitalism Causes Sexism and Racism?,'" *Philosophical Topics* 46, no. 2 (2018): 229–246.2.; Keeanga-Yamahtta Taylor, *Race for Profit: How Banks and the Real Estate Industry Undermined Black Homeownership* (Chapel Hill: University of North Carolina Press, 2021); Michael McCarthy, "Alternatives: Silent Compulsions: Capitalist Markets and Race," *Studies in Political Economy*, 97, no. 2 (2016): 195–205; David Camfield, "Elements of a Historical-Materialist Theory of Racism," *Historical Materialism*, 24, no. 1 (2016): 31–70; Edna Bonacich, "A Theory of Ethnic Antagonism: The Split Labor Market," *American Sociological Review* 37 (1972): 547–559.

[9] See especially Fanon, *Black Skin, White Masks*, ch. 6.

[10] Fanon, *Black Skin, White Masks*, 137; Fanon, *Œuvres*, 192.

the past, thus inculcating a temporal diremption between lived experience and social forms of consciousness. Below I argue that this is the core insight of Fanon's theory of *racial fetishism*.[11]

A racist society is a society that is mired in the past. For racism to make sense there must be some practical commitment to the idea that the intelligibility of individuals is preceded by their membership in some "race." The interpretation of an agent's actions takes place against a sedimented backdrop of racial meanings. Fanon calls this backdrop the "historical-racial schema" which produces a situation where the recognition of one's actions are "woven ... out of a thousand details, anecdotes, and stories."[12] Fanon gives the example of "phobogenesis" wherein the visual apprehension of black people tends to evoke anxieties and aggression.[13] The rightness or wrongness of such an interpretation is beside the point for Fanon because what he wants to criticize is how this social disposition prioritizes the past over futurity. Between one's present and one's not-yet defined future sits the weight of a past over which one can have no power. Both the dominant and the dominated are conditioned by an unreasonable form of social consciousness.

Alia Al-Saji describes Fanon's phenomenological description of racism as "*colonial glueing*" whereby racialized subjects are synchronized "not with the present but a constructed, colonized, and already sticky past. Rather than coexistence in the present, we find ourselves fastened to the past in backward projection, rendering us perpetually late."[14] The world of intersubjectivity where agents present themselves to one another in their practices becomes affixed to the horizon

---

[11] Rainer Forst interprets Marx's critique of commodity fetishism as a critique of the "lack of transparency and control" that typifies capitalist social relations. Rainer Forst, *Normativity and Power: Analyzing Social Orders of Justification*, trans. Ciaran Cronin (New York: Oxford University Press, 2017), 127.

[12] Fanon, *Black Skin, White Masks*, 61; Fanon, *Œuvres*, 154–155.

[13] Fanon, *Black Skin, White Masks*, 132–136; Fanon, *Œuvres*, 189–191. For an analysis of Fanon's controversial use of psychoanalysis, see Nicole Yokum, "A Call for Psychoaffective Change: Fanon, Feminism, and White Negrophobic Femininity," *Philosophy & Social Criticism* 50, no. 2 (2022): 1–26; Tommy J. Curry, *The Man-Not: Race, Class, Genre, and the Dilemmas of Black Manhood* (Philadelphia: Temple University Press, 2017), 88–93; David Marriott, *Whither Fanon? Studies in the Blackness of Being* (Stanford: Stanford University Press, 2018), ch. 3.

[14] Alia Al-Saji, "Glued to the Image: A Critical Phenomenology of Racialization through Works of Art," *Journal of Aesthetics and Art Criticism* 77, no. 4 (2019): 478.

of past meanings. Al-Saji argues that our perceptions and apprehension of ourselves and our shared social world become stuck in the long process of racialization that has preceded us. Social forms of consciousness do not emerge out of thin air, but are the concretion of traditions, habits, and meanings that have accumulated over generations. This does not mean that change and novelty are not possible. After all, traditions, meanings, and habits are not anchored in a static environment. Changing conditions and social problems will test the viability of historical practices in the present. But this would still mean that the transformation of social forms of consciousness is often a long and arduous process.

As I will discuss in the following chapter, Fanon differs from James Boggs in his emphasis on what he takes to be the anchoring mechanism of racial domination. Boggs considers the rapidity of economic development within capitalist social relations to be the explanation, while Fanon insists that it is the inertia of cultural forms of consciousness. There is no reason to say that either Boggs or Fanon is more correct since we can bring them together in order to highlight the extraordinary strain racially unjust societies put on the coherence of our practices. When Fanon describes the "lived experience" of the colonized he is dramatizing social forms of consciousness that are out of sync with both agents and their environment. Fanon's thesis is that the slowness of social consciousness prevents agents from unburdening themselves to take action in the future. Instead their practices are continually conscripted into being reactions against the past. Fanon thinks that racially unjust societies introduce social pathologies because they systematically prevent agents from being the foundations of their own actions.

What Fanon understands as freedom is the capacity for being recognized as the source of my actions. The necessary condition of my freedom is that another (whether an individual or a society) can hold me as responsible for my conduct by asking me to give reasons for why I do what I do. An action will have been free insofar as I can justify it to another. When I justify an action of mine, I acknowledge that the other person can assess the appropriateness of my conduct and thus I could potentially come to see I was wrong. But for such a situation to take place there must already be shared norms of interpretation that would allow my actions to appear in the first place. Becoming agential does not take place outside socio-historical processes of subject formation. Free agency, for Fanon, is not an undetermined space of action. Freedom is an outcome of reciprocal patterns of exchanging reasons. This means that whether an action will qualify as free is not completely up to the actor. There is a retroactive element to freedom insofar as the action must be socially recognized as, at least, *potentially* coherent with our shared norms of interpretation.

Fanon's account of freedom as justification contextualizes his relationship to the discourses of psychoanalysis and psychopathology. Racist societies inhibit social freedom by distorting the link between action and justification. When Fanon analyzes the diremption between *knowing* that black people do not possess distinctive sexual capacities and *acting* as if they do, he is not criticizing some cognitive failure on the part of white people. He is diagnosing the collapse of practical reason. If my normal disposition toward the world takes the form of what Slavoj Žižek calls the fetishistic disavowal of "I know very well *x*, but nevertheless," then I refuse the power of reasons (whether mine or others) to bind my conduct.[15] We need not have an overly rationalistic conception of agency to glean why a lack of reciprocity between my reasons and my conduct would be pathological for my psyche.[16] In effect, it would mean that I would have to make peace with the reality that my freedom of self-direction and self-explication will always be abrogated by "pre-logical" forces that can never be justified because they can never offer reasons that can be interrogated. I would be condemned to being a mere bystander to my own life.

Rainer Forst argues that if we are to understand ourselves as creatures of reasons this must mean that we take ourselves to be *"justifying beings"* who are "free to choose their reasons but ... are bound by the reasons that are available to them."[17] Social freedom that would be appropriate to the creatures of reason must consist in

---

[15] Slavoj Žižek, *The Sublime Object of Ideology* (New York: Verso, 2008); Lucas Ballestín, "Žižek's Politics of Fetishism," *Philosophy Today* 67, no. 3 (2023): 1–19.
[16] See Michael Rosen, *On Voluntary Servitude: False Consciousness and the Theory of Ideology* (Cambridge, UK: Polity, 1996), 243–251 for a critique of critical theory's overreliance on rationalism and control as the ideal of agency.
[17] Forst, *Normativity and Power*, 55.

being able to justify and take responsibility for my form of life. Fanon sees colonial life as permeated by a social form of consciousness that is constitutively impaired from binding agency to universally justifiable norms. The injustice of racism, for Fanon, is that it generates a social form of consciousness where reasons cannot hook into actions. Put another way, racism is intrinsically *unjustifiable* because it erodes the very possibility of anchoring our agency in historically evolving reasons. Without this anchor the freedom of justification and critique becomes degraded. It is for this reason that Fanon ends *Black Skin* with his prayer that his body "make me a man who questions!" because the capacity to interrogate and contest unjustifiable norms is a central condition for freedom.[18]

Intersubjectivity and the Colonization of Language

In *Black Skin, White Masks*, Fanon announces the fundamental importance of language because it provides us with the possibility for "understanding the black man's dimension of being-for-others."[19] The linguistification of social action opens Fanon to the charge that he is an idealist who thinks language and intersubjectivity can be divorced from the material matrices of social and economic power.[20] Such a charge would be overly hasty since Fanon does not think that if black and white people only learned to listen to one another and exchange reasons with one another that would be sufficient for overcoming the pathologies of colonial society. Instead Fanon's claim is that we can look at how language operates in the French colonial context and find evidence that racism has already pathologized this dimension of reciprocity.

Fanon thinks that to speak a language is more than the enunciation of this or that sentence; it is the social practice of taking on a whole culture.[21] The best way to understand this claim is to see that

---

[18] Fanon, *Black Skin, White Masks*, 206; Fanon, *Œuvres*, 251.
[19] Fanon, *Black Skin, White Masks*, 1; Fanon, *Œuvres*, 72.
[20] See Michael J. Thompson, *The Domestication of Critical Theory* (London: Rowman & Littlefield, 2016), ch. 1.
[21] Fanon, *Black Skin, White Masks*, 2; Fanon, *Œuvres*, 72.

Fanon endorses a species of holism when analyzing language use.[22] The speaking of any language takes place against the backdrop of social practices and values that are implicit rather than explicit in any particular sentence. When an actor steps onto a stage and claims to be "Othello" I do not wonder if their mother really named them "Othello." I understand they are playing a part. But if I were at a party and someone introduced themselves as "Othello" I may assume that this person is not playing a part, but really is someone named "Othello." If they were playing a part this would introduce a deep conflict between our normative expectations for action in this context. Potentially, this conflict could be resolved, but the point of the example is that I am not confused about the literal meaning of the other person's sentence. The source of the conflict is that I do not understand what they are trying to do with that sentence or the claim that sentence makes on my action.

In the colonial context, such conflicts are intrinsic to social life given that the background social practices and values really are divided. Fanon notes that the Martinican "possesses two dimensions: one with his fellow Blacks, the other with the Whites. A black man behaves differently with a white man than he does with another black man. There is no doubt whatsoever that this fissiparousness is a direct consequence of the colonial undertaking."[23] There are two aspects to Fanon's observation that are worth nothing. First, when Fanon analyzes language he means something more capacious than the words one chooses. Instead, it seems that what he means by "speaking a language" is the assumption of distinct dispositions toward another subject. So a black Martinican may speak French to another black Martinican and a black Martinican may speak French with a white French person, but that does not mean the black Martinican is speaking the same language in both contexts. Second, language expresses the social divide that is immanent to colonial domination. Language does not exist apart from this background context.

---

[22] Vincent Descombes, following Ludwig Wittgenstein, develops what he calls "anthropological holism" for his philosophy of mind. He insists, "We must understand something of a being's form of life before we can understand the meaning of its statements. The expression 'form of life' here should call to mind at one and the same time a psychological core of needs, desires, and natural reactions as well as a historical core of institutions and customs." Descombes, *The Institutions of Meaning*, 90.

[23] Fanon, *Black Skin, White Masks*, 1; Fanon, *Œuvres*, 71.

Fanon seems to think that when we take up a language, we also take up socially sanctioned relationships to one another. When I speak, I not only have in mind what I want to say, but how I expect the other person will receive what I say.[24] Speaking is one mode for me to make my action publicly available for another person so that I can link up with their action to accomplish some end. What this means is that I will have to take into account not only what I mean to say, but the social roles that mediate our interactions. Imagine a professor who wants to let a student of theirs know that they have done good work. Perhaps the professors usually communicates with their friends through sarcasm or irony, but they understand that given the relationship that obtains between them and their student it is better to be forthright and clear. The "language" (or linguistic context) of the academy shapes what actions will likely be intelligible in certain relationships.

We might even consider the case of a police officer pulling a driver over. We can understand why the driver might not respond to the police officer with sarcasm, but deference. The socially legitimated power the police officer has over the civilian plausibly constrains how behaviors are expressed in language. Now Fanon thinks that what sets colonial society apart from non-colonial, nominally democratic societies is that social roles of racial subordination and domination are not only exercised, but legitimated. The language that Fanon describes is not literally the French language, but the social dispositions that appear in the use of the French language by concrete speakers.

For instance, Fanon describes what he calls a "universally familiar experience" where a white priest reflexively begins talking to a black teacher in "pidgin [*petit-nègre*]."[25] To speak to a black person in *petit-nègre* is to "behave like a grown-up with a kid."[26] How does Fanon characterize the wrong here? No doubt it is demeaning and disrespectful. But not all instances of disrespect should be described as situations of unfreedom. The nature of the wrong consists in the fact that these speech acts trap black Martinicans in social roles of subordination that

---

[24] Vincent Descombes discusses Sartre's theory of language in respect to this (*The Institutions of Meaning*, 271–285).
[25] Fanon, *Black Skin, White Masks*, 14; Fanon, *Œuvres*, 84.
[26] Fanon, *Black Skin, White Masks*, 14; Fanon, *Œuvres*, 81.

are not of their choosing. The meaningfulness of their actions lack creativity and instead become retreads of the image that the powerful project onto black subjects. Fanon goes so far as to say that being made to speak *petit-nègre* is tantamount to "tying [the black person] to an image, snaring him, imprisoning him as the eternal victim of his own essence, of a *visible appearance* for which he is not responsible."[27] In other words, black subjectivity becomes reified by how black people appear without any recourse to justifying themselves.

One might think that the critique of racism that Fanon offers is how the preconceptions of racial ideology collapse the distinction between essence and appearance. Who black people *really are* (human individuals) is supplanted by what they *appear to be* (black) and thus the task is to strip away our reliance on judging people by their appearance and see them in their humanity. Fanon, indeed, is disquieted by the fact that "the black man has to wear the livery the white man has fabricated for him."[28] However, what Fanon calls "livery" is just another way of describing a social role that one takes up in language. It is only through language that my freedom can appear as publicly available for others to recognize. The problem of the "livery" that racism imposes on black people is not that it obscures their true essence, but that it prohibits them from taking on social roles for which they can claim responsibility.

Let's return to the first example of speaking *petit-nègre*. When Fanon criticizes the white priest for addressing the black teacher as a child he does so because the priest does not acknowledge the black man *as* a teacher. The priest effectively disregards the livery of teacher and imposes his own speech-situation onto the black man. I think it is important to draw the conclusion that Fanon does not expect the priest to treat the black man as an abstract human being; what he thinks is essential is that the priest draw the right inference of the black man presenting himself as a teacher and address him as is appropriate for a teacher to be addressed. Fanon's account of freedom analyzes how well our behavior fits with our background norms of interpretation.

---

[27] Fanon, *Black Skin, White Masks*, 18; Fanon, *Œuvres*, 84.
[28] Fanon, *Black Skin, White Masks*, 17; Fanon, *Œuvres*, 84.

Freedom, for Fanon, is irrevocably tied to the nexus of social roles that we share. Addressing another in their freedom means acknowledging the social roles they choose to adopt.[29]

The example of language allows Fanon to make the point that the essence of our freedom is in the socially validated form of appearance it takes. Fanon resists overly psychological accounts of freedom that posit a separation between what I do (appearance) and what I think (essence). In other words, he thinks it is untenable to believe that black people can act servilely across many interactions with white people, but on the inside remain psychologically free. Preserving the divide between essence and appearance risks assuming that the racist practices of colonial society do not mutilate and deform the consciousness of its inhabitants. The speech-acts of *petit-nègre* allow Fanon to analyze how language not only traps black people in social roles not of their choosing but "perpetuate[s] a conflictual situation where the white man infects the black man with extremely toxic foreign bodies."[30] The practice of servility really does deform the character of black people and thus the form of their freedom.

We now reach the heart of what Fanon takes freedom to be. It is not to be free from social roles in favor of some humanity we already possess, but to have the freedom to innovate and take responsibility for how we appear before others. Fanon emphasizes that freedom is the ability to "*choose* action."[31] The social role of black people in

---

[29] Fanon makes this point when describing how he acts when meeting a German or Russian who cannot speak French well: "I try to indicate through gestures the information he is asking for, but in doing so I am careful not to forget that he has a language of his own, a country, and that perhaps he is a lawyer or an engineer back home" (*Black Skin, White Masks*, 17; *Œuvres*, 83). Here we see Fanon take up the importance of addressing people in their proper social roles even when one does not have the information to know what roles they are trying to take up in language.

[30] Fanon, *Black Skin, White Masks*, 17–18; Fanon, *Œuvres*, 85.

[31] Fanon, *Black Skin, White Masks*, 80; Fanon, *Œuvres*, 142. See also Fanon (*Black Skin, White Masks*, 132; *Œuvres*, 189) where he writes, "[W]hen Blacks make contact with the white world a certain sensitizing action takes place. If the psychic structure is fragile, we observe a collapse of the ego. The black man stops behaving as an *actional* person. His actions are destined for 'the Other' (in the guise of the white man), since only 'the Other' can enhance his status and give him self-esteem at the ethical level." Compare this to Jean-Jacques Rousseau's analysis of *amour-propre* in the development of civilization with private property and the division of labor: "We find here all the natural qualities put into action, the rank and fate of each man established not only on the basis of the quantity of goods and the power to serve or harm, but also on the basis of intelligence,

colonial society is not only a passive one, but more importantly a *reactive* role. The problem of *petit-nègre* is that it imposes a social role upon black subjects whose space for innovation is quite narrow. It does not challenge the social structure of colonial life and, hence, reduces black Martinicans to repeating machines.[32] Within a colonial form of life Fanon argues that "[i]t is understandable that the black man's first action is a *reaction*" because the conditions for human freedom have been vitiated by the fact that the social roles that obtain have been reduced to mechanisms rather than free appropriations of social activity.[33]

Critics of Fanon's humanism misunderstand the account of freedom that underwrites his attachment to this ideology.[34] There is no abstract, non-phenomenal essence that Fanon seeks to liberate and have recognized. For Fanon, *appearance and essence are one*. However, this unity is conflict-ridden in colonial societies with racial domination. The problem is that racism constrains the space of appearance such that new acts cannot appear.[35] Attempts to introduce novelty

---

beauty, strength, or skill, on the basis of merit or talents. And since these qualities were the only ones that could attract consideration, he was soon forced to have them or affect them. It was necessary, for his advantage, to show himself to be something other than what he in fact was. Being something and appearing to be something became to completely different things; and from this distinction there arose grandiose ostentation, deceptive cunning, and all the vices that follow in their wake" (*Basic Political Writings*, 2nd ed., trans. Donald A. Cress, intro. David Wootton [Indianapolis: Hackett, 2011], 77). See also Rosen, *On Voluntary Servitude*: "The Society that lives under the auspices of *amour-propre* is one in which each individual does not merely *desire* the opinion of others (and, hence, is led to strive for those goods—luxury and status—that bring opinion with them) but *needs* it ... *Amour-propre*, for Rousseau, has a double aspect: it is at one and the same time a *turning-outwards*—a socialization of desire that makes individuals become dependent for their sense of themselves and their own worth on how others see them—and a *turning-inwards*—a process involving the increasing isolation and privatization of the self and its ends and feelings" (83–84).

[32] Fanon, *Black Skin, White Masks*, 6, 206; Fanon, *Œuvres*, 75, 251.
[33] Fanon, *Black Skin, White Masks*, 19; Fanon, *Œuvres*, 85.
[34] Frank B. Wilderson, *Red, White and Black: Cinema and the Structure of U.S. Antagonisms* (Durham, NC: Duke University Press, 2010); Calvin L. Warren, *Ontological Terror: Blackness, Nihilism, and Emancipation* (Durham, NC: Duke University Press, 2018).
[35] Fanon's characterization of the space of appearance tracks closely with how Forst conceives of the relationship between power and the space of reasons: "the true phenomenon of power is noumenal or intellectual in nature: having power means being able to influence, determine, occupy, or even close off the space of reasons and justifications

are misrecognized or not taken up by the addressees. Both black and white members of the colonial polity merely repeat and continue "the inhuman voices of their respective ancestors" and thus prevent the possibility of "genuine communication."[36] If our social roles can only express our freedom insofar as they are appropriately validated by others, then freedom can only obtain in a society where we not only share norms of interpretation, but are able to challenge and transform our social structures when our norms of interpretation prevent communication. Fanon claims that the purpose of *Black Skin, White Masks* is to "get my brother, black or white, to shake off the dust from that lamentable livery built up over centuries of incomprehension."[37] And this can only be accomplished in a disalienated society where "things, in their most materialist sense, have resumed their rightful place."[38] But if appearance and essence are one in a racist society then what could the source of new action be? It would seem that both black and white people are trapped in infernal circles of reaction. I will develop Fanon's answer to this problem near the end of the chapter, but to anticipate my arguments there, the conclusion Fanon comes to is that the future or the not-yet determined in lived experience can potentially break apart the reification of social forms of consciousness. For now, I want to unpack the theory of *racial fetishism*.

Racial Fetishism and the Alienation of Social Action

Near the end of *Black Skin* Fanon offers the puzzling conclusion, "Before embarking on a positive voice, freedom needs to make an effort at disalienation."[39] In the previous section, I reconstructed Fanon's account of freedom as requiring two conditions to be met. First, there

---

of other subjects.... This can occur in a single case, through a good speech or through deception; but the locus of power can also be a social structure that rests on specific justifications or condensed justification narratives" (*Normativity and Power*, 63).

[36] Fanon, *Black Skin, White Masks*, 206; Fanon, *Œuvres*, 251.
[37] Fanon, *Black Skin, White Masks*, xvi; Fanon, *Œuvres*, 67.
[38] Fanon, *Black Skin, White Masks*, xv; Fanon, *Œuvres*, 66.
[39] Fanon, *Black Skin, White Masks*, 206; Fanon, *Œuvres*, 251.

must be the socially validated recognition of the appropriate social roles internal to a given context. Second, agents ought to be receptive to the manner in which agents take up and innovate their social roles. Fanon develops what Karen Ng calls "a historically sensitive formal anthropology."[40] Human freedom is always historically situated, but never automatically determined by its given situation.[41] For Fanon there is no human being that transcends the historical situations in which we appear. That is to say that there is no acontextual or ahistorical *essence* that is hidden behind the various appearances of our social actions. If I am right that Fanon collapses the distinction between appearance and essence in his account of freedom, then what are we to make of his use of the concept of "disalienation"? If there is no essence that is independent of social reality, then what is being alienated?

The critical theory of utopia that I have set out to construct must have an answer for how the concept of alienation can remain a necessary source of social critique without relying upon an essentialist presupposition of humanity. The normative justification of utopia rests upon some claim that social life distorts our capacities for freedom, but thus far I have yet to make clear how we can describe this distortion without appeal to some account of undistorted freedom. In other words, how can we be sure that utopia is not yet another ideological distortion that arises from the pathologies of our social life?[42]

Critical theory, thankfully, does not require an essentialist conception of humanity or freedom in order to diagnose social pathology. Having a historically developed conception of humanity and freedom does not mean that we are condemned to the problem of relativism wherein what humanity or freedom means is whatever human creatures happen to be doing at any given time. Instead we can follow the insight from Günther Anders that "in order to be at home,

---

[40] Karen Ng, "Ideology Critique from Hegel and Marx to Critical Theory," *Constellations* 22, no. 3 (2015): 401.

[41] In *Being and Nothingness*, 653, Jean-Paul Sartre notes that agents are "never free except *in condition*." See Thomas Busch for an account of Sartre's changing conception of freedom from *Being and Nothingness* to *Critique of Dialectical Reason*. Thomas Busch, "Sartre on Surpassing the Given," *Philosophy Today* 35, no. 1 (1991): 26–31.

[42] Axel Honneth, *Pathologies of Reason*, trans. James Hebbeler (New York: Columbia University Press, 2009), ch. 2..

man is forced to superimpose on the natural world an artificial world, arrested and constructed by him—that is, the social and economic world with its customs and laws—he shows undoubtedly that he is not cut out for the natural world."[43] We develop forms of life not because they are natural, but because the type of creatures we are could not endure in a *purely* natural world. For our freedom and reason to become actual, for us to be able to recognize our actions as springing from our social agency, we must give a social form to our time. The distinct temporalities I have been tracking between political freedom and social emancipation are not in themselves pathologies but become so once we act as if they are natural. Naturalizing our forms of life produces social pathologies of alienation insofar as we prevent ourselves from self-consciously appropriating our conduct as our own.[44] Utopia need not be a vision of a perfect form of life for it to do its critical work. Instead, utopia emerges from the historically contextualized need to estrange us from forms of life that we have taken to be natural.

Thus, racist societies, Fanon repeatedly insists, essentialize social action and social practices through what he calls "cultural impositions" or "cultural crystallization."[45] Fanon argues this happens through "a constellation of the given [*une constellation de données*] and a series of propositions slowly and stealthily work[ing] their way through books, newspapers, school texts, advertisements, movies, and radio... shap[ing] his community's vision of the world."[46] What Fanon

---

[43] Günther Anders, "The Pathology of Freedom: An Essay on Non-identification," *Deleuze and Guattari Studies* 3, no. 2 (2009): 303. Fanon references this article in the conclusion of *Black Skin* in order to make the point that racist societies distort human subjectivity along two lines (200; Fanon, *Œuvres*: 247). First, they tend to draw their normative justifications from past practices or "being" rather than the future disclosing capacity of action of "non-being." Second, they mystify these past practices as *natural* rather than *artificial* and thus frame the interrogation of our freedom and social practices as questions of essence or authenticity rather than invention. What I take from Fanon is the idea that struggles for racial emancipation ought to avoid these two confusions. For a summary of Fanon's appropriation of Günther Anders, see Robert Bernasconi, *Critical Philosophy of Race* (New York: Oxford University Press, 2023), 196–197.

[44] Rahel Jaeggi, *Alienation*, trans. Alan E. Smith (New York: Columbia University Press, 2014), 157–164. On reification, see also György Lukács, *History and Class Consciousness: Studies in Marxist Dialectics*, trans. Rodney Livingstone (Cambridge, MA: MIT Press, 1971), 83–110.

[45] Fanon, *Black Skin, White Masks*, 167–171, 179; Fanon, *Œuvres*, 216–219, 225.

[46] Fanon, *Black Skin, White Masks*, 131; Fanon, *Œuvres*, 187, translation modified.

calls "a constellation of the given" is a reflection of his indebtedness to the phenomenology of Sartre and Merleau-Ponty. Racist societies impose pre-made and objective meanings upon the consciousness of the dominated. Contrary to what the Sartre of *Being and Nothingness* seems to claim, Fanon does not think that agents can arbitrarily divest themselves from these naturalized practices.[47]

Fanon is clear that under conditions of racial domination the racially dominated suffer because the given practices of forms of life distort the very fabric of their subjectivity. The spontaneous consciousness, desires, and reflexes of the dominated have been determined by their form of life. This means that there is not some untouched reserve of consciousness that transcends historical conditions. Unequivocally, Fanon supposes the arrow of causality runs from objective conditions to subjective life. He proclaims that "the true disalienation of the black man implies a brutal awareness of the social and economic realities. The inferiority complex can be ascribed to a double process: First, economic. Then, internalization or rather epidermalization of this inferiority."[48] Elsewhere, Fanon concludes, "The racist in a culture with racism is therefore normal. He has achieved a perfect harmony of economic relations and ideology."[49] What Fanon calls "normal" is not simply a reference to what merely appears to be the case for a majority of the dominant group.[50] Fanon supposes that racism is the objectively correct disposition for subjects to hold in racially unjust societies. This produces the rather uncomfortable conclusion that black people are normal insofar as they accord with relations of subjection and are abnormal insofar as they resist.

---

[47] Sartre understands the freedom of consciousness in terms of its ability to surpass the given or "nihilate" it. He seems to think that consciousness may be dependent on the objective world which precedes but is in no way conditioned by it: "It would be vain to imagine that consciousness can exist without a given . . . but if consciousness exists in terms of the given, this does not mean that the given conditions consciousness; consciousness is pure and simple negation of this given, and it exists as the disengagement toward a certain existing given, and as an engagement toward a certain not yet existing end" (*Being and Nothingness*, 615).
[48] Fanon, *Black Skin, White Masks*, xv; Fanon, *Œuvres*, 66.
[49] Frantz Fanon, *Toward the African Revolution: Political Essays* (New York: Monthly Review Press, 1967), 40; Fanon, *Œuvres*, 721.
[50] Fanon observes, "An ever greater number of members belonging to racist societies are taking a position. They are dedicating themselves to a world in which racism

The Fanonian challenge is that distortion and normality are not antithetical. The utopian moment of freedom, according to Fanon, cannot but appear as an instance of abnormality and misrecognition. The task of freedom, then, is not to make recourse to some prior form of social being that has been distorted by processes of racialization. Instead, Fanon intimates that colonialism indelibly transformed both colonizer and colonized. The very foundations of social reason have been transformed by the economic relations that crystallized under colonialism. It is for this reason that Fanon resists the theorization of racism as a mere "psychological flaw" that mars an otherwise healthy reasoning subject.[51] Racism is not an alien element that has yet to be eradicated by setting reason on its feet. Its fundamental problem is not that it obscures how life really is, but that it is in fact contiguous with the present state of reality.[52] In other words, Fanon develops a theory of *racial fetishism*.

A theory of racial fetishism is necessary for comprehending how Fanon understands racism to be both a distortion and normal. Fanon begins all his analyses from the economic relations that comprise a form of life and then traces how these relationships pattern social action and value orientations. What this means is that racial fetishism is not primarily a set of prejudicial ascriptions pertaining to some social group that we may judge to be empirically false. Racial fetishism is a social form of consciousness that mediates and legitimizes exploitative economic relations. Fanon argues that any society that "draws its substance from the exploitation of other peoples, makes those people inferior. Race prejudice applied to those people is normal."[53] Race becomes

---

would be impossible" (*Toward the African Revolution*, 40; Fanon, *Œuvres*, 723). Cf. Charles Mills, *The Racial Contract* (Ithaca, NY: Cornell University Press, 1997); José Medina, "Epistemic Injustice and Epistemologies of Ignorance," in *The Routledge Companion to Philosophy of Race*, ed. Paul Taylor, Linda Alcoff, and Luvell Anderson (New York: Routledge, 2017), 247–260.

[51] Fanon, *Toward the African Revolution*, 39: Fanon, *Œuvres*, 721.
[52] See Fanon: "Racism bloats and disfigures the face of the culture that practices it. Literature, the plastic arts, songs for shopgirls, proverbs, habits, patterns, whether they set out to attack it or to vulgarize it, restore racism.... Racism stares one in the face for it so happens that it belongs in a characteristic whole" (*Toward the African Revolution*, 37: *Œuvres*, 721).
[53] Fanon, *Toward the African Revolution*, 41: Fanon, *Œuvres*, 724.

real not because people believe it to be so, but because whether they believe it or not, their conduct reproduces a society that is sustained through the exploitation of one class of people by another class.

I understand Fanon as holding a heterodox theory of racism that refuses to define it as the distorted *perception* of social reality. Racial fetishism, instead, is the objective fact that social reality *is* distorted and our conduct is fused into this form of life. Fanon analyzes racial fetishism as a systemic-functional problematic rather than a problem of belief and knowledge. Fanon describes racial fetishism as "a disposition fitting into a well-defined system [*un système déterminé*]."[54] We can think of race as a "constitutive rule"[55] that constrains patterns of social action and value orientation. Fanon's basic hypothesis is that those racialized as non-white do not *appear* to be inferior, but that within the pattern of system functions that are internal to capitalist economic relation they *really are* inferior. The challenge is not to change how we think about or perceive *x* social group but to overturn "the worm-eaten foundations" that anchor our social actions and value orientations.[56]

The theoretical structure beneath Fanon's theory of racial fetishism is innovative, but not unprecedented when compared with Marx's description of *commodity fetishism*.[57] Marx notes that the social character of labor under capitalism necessarily produces the appearance of commodities having a life of their own while people are mere mechanisms for the production and consumption of commodities. On the one hand, this is clearly false since commodities do not bring

---

[54] Fanon, *Toward the African Revolution*, 41: Fanon, *Œuvres*, 724.
[55] John Searle, *The Construction of Social Reality* (London: Penguin, 1996); John Searle, *Making the Social World: The Structure of Human Civilization* (New York: Oxford University Press, 2010); and John Searle, *Freedom and Neurobiology: Reflections on Free Will, Language, and Political Power* (New York: Columbia University Press, 2008); Haslanger, *Resisting Reality*, 183–218. Also see chapter 3.
[56] Fanon, *Black Skin, White Masks*, xv; Fanon, *Œuvres*, 66.
[57] Karl Marx, *Capital: A Critique of Political Economy*, vol. 1, trans. Ben Fowkes, intro. Ernest Mandel (New York: Penguin Classics, 1990), 163–178. For differing interpretations of whether commodity fetishism is an ideological inversion or a practical inversion, see Søren Mau, *Mute Compulsion: A Marxist Theory of the Economic Power of Capital* (London: Verso, 2023), 188–194; Michael Heinrich, *An Introduction to the Three Volumes of Karl Marx's* Capital (New York: Monthly Review Press, 2012), 179–199 and *How to Read Marx's Capital: Commentary and Explanations on the Beginning Chapters* (New York: Monthly Review Press, 2021), 143–170; as well as Massimilano Tomba, *Marx's Temporalities* (Leiden: Brill, 2012), 110–113.

themselves into being and they are nothing but objects where our own social activities congeal. On the other hand, there is some truth to the perception that we are not in control of the effects that the value of commodities can have on our lives. Michael Heinrich sums this idea up well: "It is the social practice of capitalist society that constantly enacts a process whereby the 'factors of production' take on a life of their own and social cohesion is constituted as an objective necessity that individuals can only escape on pain of ruin. To that extent, personified things absolutely possess a material force."[58]

Similarly, the appearance of racism as a state of affairs or set of ascriptive beliefs over which we have little control is both false and true. False because racism does not do anything independently of our shared social practices, however mediated. True because we are alienated from the capacity to direct our social action beyond a society that reproduces itself through the exploitation of one class by another. This is why Fanon inveighs against "[c]ampaigns of deintoxification"; they mischaracterize racism as a cause rather than a consequence of our economic relations and the forms of thought they tend to reproduce.[59] Much like Marx's commodity fetishism, Fanon contends that the problem of racial fetishism is not overcome by demystifying racial prejudices because these strategies evade the truth of living in a racist society: our actions remain anchored in a form of life that we cannot self-consciously direct.[60]

Fanon does not think that the ideas we come to have are directly caused by our economic relations or else he could not explain how people come to abhor racist ideologies and commit themselves to their eradication.[61] There is a distinction between economic relations producing the conditions in which we come to have ideas and economic phenomena controlling what ideas we come to have. Put another way, Fanon thinks we can explain what ideas have justificatory

---

[58] Heinrich, *An Introduction to the Three Volumes of Karl Marx's Capital*, 185.
[59] Fanon, *Toward the African Revolution*, 38: Fanon, *Œuvres*, 723–724.
[60] Karen E. Fields and Barbara Jeanne Fields, *Racecraft: The Soul of Inequality in American Life* (London: Verso, 2012), 111–149; David Calnitsky and Michael Billeaux Martinez, "A Class Functionalist Theory of Race," *Du Bois Review* 20, no. 2 (2023): 239–267.
[61] Fanon, *Toward the African Revolution*, 40: Fanon, *Œuvres*, 723.

power in a social form of consciousness by examining the economic structure of a given form of life. Fanon's point is that racism does not admit of degrees if we accept that its anchor is in the form our social actions tend to take and not our moral values. In other words, we will not find out how racist a society is by polling individuals on their beliefs or even attempting to ascertain whether they have unconscious biases. Fanon remains resolutely focused on the range of objective outcomes for our social action in this determined social system: "One cannot say that a given society is racist but that lynchings or extermination camps are not to be found there. The truth is that all that and still other things exist on the horizon. These virtualities, these latencies circulate, carried by the life-stream of psycho-affective, economic relations."[62] So long as our form of life is primarily characterized by actions that reproduce exploitation, scarcity, and hierarchy we can expect outcomes that lead to populations being treated as surplus or disposable.

Our social actions or practices reproduce racial injustice partially because we are trapped within an "unreflected [*irréfléchie*] cultural imposition."[63] Fanon intends for his critical analyses to offer "a mirror with a progressive infrastructure where the black man can find a path to disalienation."[64] The cognition of the forms of life we have inherited would induce a normative-epistemic transformation of social consciousness that would allow for the critical appraisal of how "the actual organization of society falls short of the standards of rationality that are already embodied in the forces of production."[65] Fanon diagnoses the lack of utopian consciousness that would bring together the epistemic and normative insight of how racial fetishism continues to entrap social forms of consciousness.

What is compelling in Fanon's analysis is that he allows us to see that talk about the progress a society has made as it concerns racial attitudes is both true and false. True insofar as it is the case that fewer people now explicitly take themselves to believe in racial theories of inferiority and superiority. False insofar as we remain welded to a structure

---

[62] Fanon, *Toward the African Revolution*, 41: Fanon, *Œuvres*, 724.
[63] Fanon, *Black Skin, White Masks*, 167; Fanon, *Œuvres*, 216, translation modified.
[64] Fanon, *Black Skin, White Masks*, 161; Fanon, *Œuvres*, 211.
[65] Honneth, "A Social Pathology of Reason," 24.

of social action that reproduces the reality of precarity and exploitation for a subset of humanity. And so we are now in a position to summarize what Fanon means when he claims that freedom must "make an effort at disalienation."[66] The normal distortion that Fanon diagnoses is our separation from the self-conscious control over the effects of our actions. So long as we remain fused with the functional roles and dispositions that reproduce and stabilize our form of life we will lack the required self-consciousness of human action that can create a free society based upon mutual recognition. Disalienation requires "self-consciousness and renunciation [*dépouillement*] ... a permanent tension of... freedom" in order to "create the ideal conditions of existence for a human world."[67]

What Fanon calls *dépouillement* is the metaphorical equivalent of a snake shedding its skin.[68] Fanon calls for a freedom that negates the roles we have come to adopt in our relations with one another. Critique aims to shed the objective determinations of our actions so that we can finally take them over as our own. For Fanon this is essentially a question of what disposition agents adopt toward their social form of time. The critical and utopian agency that could catalyze a transformation of our social form of consciousness, he will argue, can only emerge by breaking with the past rather than trying to repair it.

Beyond Reparations

The value of Fanon's theory of racial fetishism and alienation as I have described it is that it places the utopian function of racial emancipation on new terrain. To be free, according to Fanon, is to be able to take responsibility for the new meanings I choose to bring into the world and have those meanings taken up by other agents. There is an irreducibly temporal character to Fanon's theory of freedom. The social conditions for communication and understanding must always remain

---

[66] Fanon, *Black Skin, White Masks*, 206; Fanon, *Œuvres*, 251.
[67] Fanon, *Black Skin, White Masks*, 206; Fanon, *Œuvres*, 251.
[68] See Robert Bernasconi, "Casting the Slough: Fanon's New Humanism for a New Humanity," in *Fanon: A Critical Reader*, eds. Lewis R. Gordon, T. Denean Sharpley-Whiting, and Renée T. White (Oxford: Blackwell, 1996), 113–121.

consciously revisable so that free actions can genuinely confront one another. Fanon's theory opens up the possibility of conceptualizing racial justice as the effort to disclose the not-yet-seen future rather than correcting the injustices of the past.

Fanon forthrightly rejects calls for reparations as commensurate to the task of disalienation.[69] What he understands as reparations is the demand that white people acknowledge or recognize the harms that have been done to black people in the past. The problem with these recognitive efforts is that they do not shed the racial dispositions that are anchored in an antagonistic social structure. Indeed, efforts at psychological reparations may have the unintended effect of solidifying racial roles as speakers come to identify as descendants of oppressors and oppressed.[70] Fanon's concern is that the discourse of reparations fuses agents into the pathological structure of race that blocks the possibility of free activity.

To demand reparations means that one must identify as the wronged party and appropriate for oneself the capacity to speak on behalf of those who have been wronged in the past. Returning to Fanon's analysis of language as the practice of giving reasons via socially validated roles, we can ask: What roles are being adopted in the reparative speech situation? Can these agents truly take responsibility for the historical conduct of others? What counts as reason-giving in this context? When Fanon contends, "I have not the right to become mired by the determinations of the past. . . . I am not a slave to slavery that dehumanized my ancestors" he recenters the idea that the aim of freedom is not reconciliation with the past, but unbinding oneself as far as possible from its determining force on our conduct.[71] Fanon takes history to task because he understands it as being too full of "being." It is dead and ossified action that predetermines our conduct and represses discovery and development. If for Fanon all human

---

[69] Fanon, *Black Skin, White Masks*, 201, 203; Fanon, *Œuvres*, 247, 249.
[70] For a different view of reparations, see Olúfẹ́mi Táíwò, *Reconsidering Reparations* (New York: Oxford University Press, 2022) and Catherine Lu, *Justice and Reconciliation in World Politics* (Cambridge: Cambridge University Press, 2017), ch. 6. For critiques of the reparations paradigm, see Jeremy Waldron, "Superseding Historic Injustice," *Ethics* 103 (October 1992): 4–28 and Janna Thompson, "Historical Injustice and Reparation: Justifying Claims of Descendants," *Ethics* 112 (October 2001): 114–135.
[71] Fanon, *Black Skin, White Masks*, 205; Fanon, *Œuvres*, 250.

problems must be resolved on the "basis of time" then reparative discourse appears to him as continuous with the pathological temporality of the colonial form of life.[72] The past encircles the present and locks these agents in a semantic and material universe where blackness and whiteness are inescapable roles that one must play.

No doubt Fanon is too harsh in his rejection of history. He tends to look at his Martinican ancestors as purely passive agents which historically was not the case.[73] It might even seem as if Fanon is simply claiming that we ought to stop thinking about race and become either colorblind or post-racial. I think Fanon would respond that the spontaneous reaction to his claims that can only think in terms of colorblindness is evidence of how limiting the ideological universe of race is. The problem is not primarily how we think or talk about one another; it is how we are enabled to live with one another. Are we able to freely appropriate our actions creatively? Or are our actions already captured and predetermined?

Fanon brings together the prospect of free action and utopian temporality in his concept of the "zone of non-being" which is "an incline stripped bare [*dépouillée*] of every essential from which a genuine new departure can emerge."[74] What Fanon calls "non-being" should be counterposed to his understanding of history as filled with "being" or ossified action. The openness of every action to what is not-yet means that our activity can either reproduce the present or go beyond it. The pathology Fanon seeks to remove through his critique of racial fetishism and alienation is the petrification of social time. If the past determines my action, it is only the future, what is not-yet, that can liberate my actions from the petrification of history. For Fanon there must be a transformation of one's subjective disposition toward time in order for the subject to actualize the virtual possibilities that exist in the moment.

I think Fanon is at his least convincing when he outright rejects reparations, but there is a key insight that we can glean from his

---

[72] Fanon, *Black Skin, White Masks*, xvi; Fanon, *Œuvres*, 67.
[73] Dale W. Tomich, *Slavery in the Circuit of Sugar: Martinique and the World Economy, 1830–1848*, 2nd ed. (Albany: State University of New York Press, 2016), ch. 7 and David Macey, *Frantz Fanon: A Biography*, 2nd ed. (New York: Verso, 2012).
[74] Fanon, *Black Skin, White Masks*, xii; Fanon, *Œuvres*, 64.

remarks. The utility of reparations ought to be analyzed in tandem with the social form of time that obtains within a given form of life. History, as Fanon well understood, is nothing but a matrix of objectified social practices. It does not stand outside our form of life as if it were immune to the pathologies of reason we have developed. History is appropriated, narrated, deciphered, and interpreted through socially validated practices.[75] Walter Benjamin had a similar understanding, noting, "In every era the attempt must be made anew to wrest tradition away from a conformism that is about to overpower it."[76] A racist society tends to shape history as a source of social honor or shame as well as justification for one's present actions. History is not only evaluated, but taken as *the source of value* from which we learn how to make proper inferences concerning what is appropriate or just conduct. Fanon insists that so long as history takes this social form our capacity to bring reason and freedom together will be vitiated.

Fanon points to the corrosive power of history on social action through the use of examples of Martinican children in school citing the "Gauls" as their ancestors or the sexual desires of black men and women who misunderstand whiteness as an intrinsic source of value and validation.[77] The sense of dishonor that flows from the practice of history habituates black subjects into acting as if values such as liberty and justice have an implicit racial content.[78] Fanon is of course aware that the counter-movement against this racial appropriation of history

---

[75] Reinhart Koselleck makes this point in reference to the relationship between singularity and repetition in history. We can only apprehend events as singular against a backdrop of temporal regularity: "Take the banal case of the mail carrier who comes in the morning and brings you the message of a close relative's death. You might be shocked or perhaps even pleased. In any case, this is a singular occurrence mediated to you via the mail carrier. But the fact that the mail carrier comes each morning at a specific time is a recurrent process, which is made possible, in turn, by a regulated postal administration and its budget that is renewed on a yearly basis." Reinhart Koselleck, *Sediments of Time: On Possible Histories*, trans. Sean Franzel and Stefan Ludwig-Hoffmann (Stanford: Stanford University Press, 2018), 5. The idea is that even an invention or singularity must take place against historical patterns of an inherited form of life if the invention will be intelligible and thus recognizable to others. See also Hortense Spillers, "Ellison's 'Usable Past': Toward a Theory of Myth," *Interpretations* 9, no. 1 (1977): 53–69 and Tomba, *Marx's Temporalities*.
[76] Walter Benjamin, *Illuminations: Essays and Reflections*, trans. Harry Zohn, ed. Hannah Arendt (New York: Schocken Books, 2007), 255.
[77] Fanon, *Black Skin, White Masks*, 126; Fanon, *Œuvres*, 184.
[78] Fanon, *Black Skin, White Masks*, 195; Fanon, *Œuvres*, 241.

is to search for authentically "black" values that will be a source of honor and justification.[79] The limitations of this strategy are apparent for Fanon. It traps black subjects in the conceptual vise of "race" and blocks out of consciousness that free action does not emerge from the restitution of history, but the transformation of one's form of life toward self-transparency and collective justification.

Reparations, Fanon thinks, misconstrue the relationships between action, freedom, and reason. The source of value for concepts such as "justice" ought to be the disclosive and transformative capacities of our living actions. Our ability to shed the weight of the past and bring value into social life that was not there before is the only way we can remain self-conscious and responsible for the freedom we must share with others. Of course the problem is that we do not live in a form of life where our actions can take full advantage of these capacities. Humanity has not taken its rightful place in social life.[80] Value appears as separate from our actions, imposed from the outside, and put to uses beyond the control of most subjects. In other words, we live in an alienating form of life where our actions are fused with the imperium of history. Thus it can seem as if justice can only be won insofar as history is "set right." Fanon's thesis is that history can only be set right once action, freedom, and reason have assumed their proper relationships in a disalienated form of life and not before. Justice will only emerge from the utopian temporality of action that dissolves our pathological relationship to history.

Even if we accept Fanon's argument that reparations are not sufficient for attaining the conditions of justice we need not think reparations have no part to play. Reparations can be a vital source of understanding the historical genesis of our form of life. It seems to me this is a critical aspect of reparative practices for the simple reason that while history may not absolutely determine our social actions it most certainly conditions them. It is here that we can see the limitations of Fanon's analyses as they are constructed in *Black Skin, White Masks*. He envisions the possibility that action can finally cut ties with the conditioning effects of history and "introduce invention into life

---

[79] See Fanon, *Toward the African Revolution*, 42; Fanon, *Œuvres*, 724.
[80] Fanon, *Black Skin, White Masks*, xv; Fanon, *Œuvres*, 66.

[*l'existence*]."[81] But our existence will always remain a historical existence rather than a purely inventive one.

Nevertheless, Fanon is surely right that our existence is not purely historical, but also futural. Non-being or what is not-yet also conditions our actions and thus makes possible that what we do will produce "misfires" where ossified actions break down in the face of changing contexts.[82] We can develop this insight along subjective and objective lines. Subjectively, I cannot engage any action without anticipating the future effects it will bring about and therefore action can become fetishized for me when I can no longer recognize or justify the effects of what I do. Objectively, the effects of any given action cannot remain confined to the historical context of its genesis because every action, in some way, modifies the world. Thus, even under conditions of extreme reification it is never possible to strip away the future opening element of social action. The ineradicable condition of the future is no guarantee for emancipation, of course. Developing the requisite social consciousness and institutions that can take advantage of these breakdowns takes time. It is Fanon's attunement to this immanent utopian temporality that critical theory ought to counterpose to the historical disposition of reparations.

Utopian temporality is not a promised heaven of perfection that resides just beyond our horizons. It is the restless and necessarily unmastered aspect of social time that "appears" within the gaps and breakdowns between forms of life. Racial domination is a disorder of social temporality that fragments the relationship between lived experience and social forms of consciousness by entrapping agents in a space of reasons that they cannot justify. However, the yearning for justification, the experience that one does not yet live in a world whose reasons they can justify, can be a critical resource for grasping the utopian temporalities that are suppressed in our form of life. Utopian temporality does not lie outside our form of life, but emerges from within it. Critical theory attempts to cognize the disjointed appearance of time in our form of life and by doing so also grasps the necessity of the emancipation of social life as a whole. In this way, we can see utopian

[81] Fanon, *Black Skin, White Masks*, 204; Fanon, *Œuvres*, 250.
[82] Fanon, *Black Skin, White Masks*, 7; Fanon, *Œuvres*, 75.

temporality as not only a motivational framework for social action, but a critical-diagnostic concept of how we share and live our time in this form of life. Fanon's call for invention, then, is not a voluntaristic *creation ex nihilo*. Rather it is the demand for a world where agents can transparently bind themselves to the norms and justifications of their choosing.

Fanon's Lesson: Racial Fetishism and the Time of Emancipation

In this chapter, I have drawn upon the work of Frantz Fanon in order to round out my analysis of the non-synchronicity of racial domination. Fanon's attention to "lived experience" and what I have called social forms of consciousness reveals the differential time scales upon which racial domination plays out. Our social practices tend to lag behind our professed political ideologies. A narrow focus on political freedom distorts our critical apprehension of these diverse temporalities. The critical-evaluative function of utopia brings into relief that racially unjust societies are anchored in a pathological or crisis-prone social form of time. The need to surpass our current form of time for future forms of life where we can self-consciously and inventively appropriate the time we share with one another is the normative basis of utopia as I have defended it.

Racial fetishism generates distinct *cognitive* and *practical* pathologies. Cognitively, it distorts our shared space of reasons in such a way that it appears as if "race" determines who counts as a reasonable subject rather than seeing that it is our practical activity and norms of justification that constitute our space of reasons. However, as Fanon well understood, this cognitive pathology could not persist over time if it were not anchored in the practical pathologies of a historically distinct economic form of life. The specificity of this anchor in capitalist social relations distinguishes *racism* which may be found in non-capitalist societies from *racial fetishism*. Capitalism, as an economic form of life, not only mediates access to vital social needs such as food and shelter, but it is insensitive to the new justifications and practices agents may develop. Instead, it tends to bend justificatory practices toward the ends of exploitation and surplus-value. In this way, practically, we really do lack control over our time insofar as the future is weighed down by the imperative of past accumulation.

Time is the fundamental basis of our social existence. Our social practices are irreducibly temporal insofar as their intelligibility is due in no small part to how we judge them appropriate to a current form of life. It is to Fanon's credit that he asks whether emancipation may be where we least expect it. Racial emancipation may emerge in those untimely moments when our social practices fail to hook into our present forms of life. We might think of when protest movements disrupt social consciousness, when revolution breaks with the rhythm of state governments, or when striking workers withdraw their time from the dominion of capitalist production. In all three instances, utopia can clarify the sedimentation of time that is being challenged rather than see these actions as momentary interruptions in the flow of time that must be returned to "normal."

I would venture that the task of racial justice must include the reordering of social time. Perhaps even the self-conscious control of our time. But accomplishing this would require that we overcome the cognitive and practical pathologies that constitute racial fetishism. Political freedom will not be sufficient so long as the temporality of social unfreedom persists. What account of justice could meet the challenge of transcending racial fetishism? Unfortunately, Fanon does not offer a robust account of how we can transform the practical anchor of racial fetishism and thereby also remove its cognitive pathologies. We should not be content with an account that calls on the powers of individual creativity or invention. We want to know what anchors these new powers of invention. In the next chapter, I turn to the work of the African-American intellectual and autoworker James Boggs to argue that an account of racial justice that is commensurate to the task of overcoming racial fetishism must anchor economic life in the space of reasons and the power of justification that belong to the dominated. In other words, the capitalist form of life that conditions our various political, social, and cultural forms of life would have to be made transparent and brought under collective control. Fanon's lesson remains, however: racial justice won't be found in repairing the past, but in disclosing the temporality of the not-yet.

5
Justifying Freedom
James Boggs and the Utopia of Black Power

Introduction

In the previous chapter we saw that racial fetishism limits social freedom by welding the space of reasons to past practices of racial domination. Race *appears* as a fundamental social reality which agents can neither take responsibility for nor break free from. The inverted world of racial fetishism is one where history dominates the present and represses the utopian temporality of the "not-yet" by reifying racial categories and relationships of domination. Given that we experience ourselves as not only historical creatures, but also futural creatures of creativity and anticipation, this repression of the "not-yet" reproduces agents who are temporally ill at ease with themselves and their world. This nonsynchronicity (*Ungleichzeitigkeit*), as I discussed it in chapter 2, is an impediment to freedom. Lacking the power to invent new justifications for one's social practices, forms of life lose their dynamic relationship to practical reason. Race *appears* to have a life of its own that subjects agents to its own imperatives that are insensitive to reason.

However, it bears repeating that race only appears to have a fundamental reality. The theory of racial fetishism that I developed in the previous chapter has a *cognitive* condition and a *practical* condition. Cognitively, racial fetishism systematically distorts our perception of the relationship of cause and effect between race and social practices. It seems as if social practices are the *effect* of "race" instead of "race" being an *effect* of our social practices. Practically, racial fetishism persists because our social practices *really are* anchored in the conflictual dynamics of capitalist social relations. Thus, control over the direction of our social practices is meaningfully constrained in such a way that I really cannot recognize myself as the source of my actions. Racial fetishism, in my account, is not reducible to individual prejudices or unfair laws. It is a form of life that is anchored in and mediates the contradictory tendencies of capitalist social relations. Truly incorporating the future into our social actions will require having the power to uproot *both* the cognitive and the practical conditions of racial fetishism.

In this chapter, I turn to the work of James Boggs in order to develop an account of racial justice that adequately theorizes emancipation from racial fetishism. A black autoworker and social theorist who lived in Detroit and worked in the automobile industry and autoworkers unions in the 1970s, Boggs articulates a conception of black power that explicitly contests the picture of justice that is solely concerned with the just distribution of good and benefits, or what Rainer Forst calls the "*recipient-oriented*" view of justice.[1] Bearing witness to the effects of deindustrialization and lack of stable access to the labor market on black workers, Boggs did not think the form of economic production could be taken for granted. Who he called "the outsiders" were a disproportionately racial minority who could not be integrated into civil society and thus had to make their living from inconsistent work, crime, or charity. For Boggs these "outsiders" were systematically produced by irrational capitalist social relations rather than a "culture of poverty."[2] Theorizing from the socially condemned "no place" of these outsiders Boggs insists that the root of racial injustice is not in the failure to equitably divide the social pie, but in how the pie is made.[3]

In Boggs's writings I find a compelling utopian alternative to accounts of racial justice that implicitly or explicitly assume that racial justice can be achieved absent the supersession of the capitalist form of life that anchors our social practices. In what follows, I develop Boggs's critique of the state as sufficient for achieving social freedom. Next, I reconstruct Boggs's notion of black power as a critique of the justifications that underpin contemporary class society. Here it will become clear that for Boggs power is not reducible to physical force.

---

[1] Rainer Forst, *Justification and Critique: Towards a Critical Theory of Politics*, trans. Ciaran Cronin (New York: Polity, 2014), 18.
[2] See Oscar Lewis, "The Culture of Poverty," *Society* 35, no. 2 (1998): 7–9 and Thomas Sowell, "Culture—Not Discrimination—Decides Who Gets Ahead: A Conversation with Thomas Sowell," *U.S. News & World Report*, Oct. 12, 1981.
[3] Forst, *Justification and Critique*, 23.

Instead, it is a measure of which norms are capable of shaping our conduct. In other words, power is intertwined with ideology and reasons. I connect this problematic back to my theory of racial fetishism and its relationship to economic disempowerment. I do this in order to describe the practical distortion I take to be the anchor of racial fetishism. From this I develop Boggs's critique of civil rights as leaving the social relations of fetishism in place and thus, inadvertently, justifying the exclusion of "the outsiders" from social life. Finally, I conclude by spelling out Boggs's utopia of racial emancipation as a society freed from the domination of class power and white power and thus capable of governing itself according to its own transparent justifications.

Black Power and the Critique of the State

Most often associated with the writings of Kwame Ture and Charles V. Hamilton, black power emerged in the post–civil rights era of the United States.[4] The proscription of legally enforced racial discrimination radically reshaped the political life of the United States. Elevating and respecting the rights and duties of citizenship became a focal point of the political discourse surrounding race. Nevertheless, for some, the achievement of civil rights is an ambivalent or paradoxical victory.[5]

---

[4] Kwame Ture and Charles V. Hamilton, *Black Power: Politics of Liberation in America* (1967; New York: Vintage, 1992).
[5] See Wendy Brown, "Suffering the Paradox of Human Rights," in *Left Legalism/Left Critique*, ed. Wendy Brown and Janet Halley (Durham, NC: Duke University Press, 2002), 420–434; Duncan Kennedy, "The Critique of Rights in Critical Legal Studies," in *Left Legalism/Left Critique*, ed. Wendy Brown and Janet Halley (Durham, NC: Duke University Press, 2002), 178–228; Christoph Menke, *Critique of Rights*, trans. Christopher Turner (New York: Polity, 2020); Radha D'Souza, *What's Wrong with Rights? Social Movements, Law, and Liberal Imaginations* (London: Pluto Press, 2018); István Mészáros, *Beyond Leviathan: Critique of the State*, ed. John Bellamy Foster (New York: Monthly Review Press, 2022); Steven Lukes, "Can a Marxist Believe in Human Rights?," *Praxis International* 4 (1982): 81–92; Frederick Neuhouser, "Marx and Hegel on the Value of 'Bourgeois' Ideals," in *Reassessing Marx's Social and Political Philosophy*, ed. Jan Kandiyali (New York: Routledge, 2018), 149–162; Tony Smith, *Beyond Liberal Egalitarianism: Marx and Normative Social Theory in the Twenty-First Century* (Leiden: Brill, 2017). For defenses of the role of rights and the progress of social freedom, see Megan Ming Francis, *Civil Rights and the Making of the Modern American State* (New York: Cambridge University Press, 2014); Christine Sypnowich, *The Socialist Concept of Law* (Oxford: Oxford University Press, 1990); G. A. Cohen, *Rescuing Justice*

Black power rearticulated strands of the black nationalist analysis that I discussed in chapter 3 by critiquing reliance on the supposedly neutral state for securing the conditions of freedom. After all, disadvantage and inequality persisted for broad swaths of black people in urban centers. This allowed resentment and disenchantment with the promise of legal equality to fester.[6]

This story should be familiar enough to most. The explanations for why the passage of these laws were not enough to establish full equality for black citizens vary.[7] As we saw in chapter 3, the black nationalist argument would suggest civil rights belong to the form of life of the state, and the state is anchored in the racial sedimentation of white nationhood. However, we need not accept this race-reifying analysis in order to question the relationship between civil rights and social emancipation. A critique of civil rights can begin from the black nationalist insight that the state is anchored in more fundamental social practices that limit its efficacy without presuming that "race" is the sole explanation. The task of this chapter is to analyze how racial domination persists when the state is anchored in capitalist social relations.

A defining feature of black power is a critical posture toward the state. The network of concepts and practices that typified black power increasingly shifted away from the assumption that the problems of

---

and Equality (Cambridge, MA: Harvard University Press, 2008); Ernst Bloch, *Natural Law and Human Dignity*, trans. Dennis J. Schmidt (Cambridge, MA: MIT Press, 1996); Axel Honneth, *Freedom's Right: The Social Foundations of Democratic Life*, trans. Joseph Ganahl (New York: Columbia University Press, 2014).

[6] Cedric Johnson aptly summarizes the social conditions for the emergence of black power as unfolding "within a context of class fragmentation; the decline of the left-labor militancy of the Depression, wartime, and the post–World War II years; and the transformation of metropolitan space after the 1949 Housing Act, which produced suburban homeownership and upward mobility for many whites and inner-city ghettoization and exploitation for the black poor." Cedric Johnson, *The Panthers Can't Save Us Now: Debating Left Politics and Black Lives Matter* (London: Verso, 2022), 17.

[7] See Michelle Alexander, *The New Jim Crow: Mass Incarceration in the Age of Colorblindness* (New York: New Press, 2010); Frank Wilderson, "Gramsci's Black Marx: Whither the Slave in Civil Society?," *Social Identities* 9, no. 2 (2003): 225–240 and *Red, White and Black: Cinema and the Structure of U.S. Antagonisms* (Durham, NC: Duke University Press, 2010); Calvin L Warren, "Black Nihilism and the Politics of Hope," *CR* (East Lansing, MI) 15, no. 1 (2015): 215–248; Isabel Wilkerson, *Caste: The Origins of Our Discontents* (New York: Random House, 2020); Touré F. Reed, *Toward Freedom: The Case against Race Reductionism* (New York: Verso, 2020).

inequality could be resolved within the juridical framework of liberal democracies.[8] James Boggs offered his own distinct analysis of how black power could be counterposed against state-centric theories of freedom.[9] What theories of black power share, however, is the claim that without independent bases of social power the state will tend to reconfigure relations of domination and dependence rather than abolish them. There are two forms of dependency that can be parsed from their analyses.

Appeals to the state establish a *cognitive dependence* on the discourses and ideas of the liberal state such that black citizens habituate themselves to only thinking of equality and freedom in terms that are legible to the state. Ellen Meiksins Wood describes this shift as the move "away from the active exercise of popular power to the passive enjoyment of constitutional and procedural safeguards and rights, and away from the collective power of subordinate classes to the privacy and isolation of the individual citizen."[10] Much like how the cognitive condition of racial fetishism distorts how the social world appears to us, the state also promulgates definite ways of apprehending the "natural" relationship between rights and freedom.

Boggs caustically claims, "The radical groups have been pushing welfare rights and confusing the struggle for rights with making a revolution. People on welfare are not automatically revolutionary; in

---

[8] For analyses of the state and its functions, see Bob Jessop, *The State: Past, Present, Future* (New York: Polity, 2016); Bob Jessop, "State," in *The Marx Revival: Key Concepts and New Interpretations*, ed. Marcello Musto (Cambridge: Cambridge University Press, 2020), 266–285; Nicos Poulantzas, *State, Power, Socialism*, trans. Patrick Camiller (New York: Verso, 1980); Philip Pettit, *The State* (Princeton, NJ: Princeton University Press, 2023); David Harvey, *Seventeen Contradictions and the End of Capitalism* (New York: Oxford University Press, 2014), esp. 38–53; Theda Skopcol, *States and Social Revolutions* (Cambridge: Cambridge University Press, 2015); Louis Althusser, "Ideology and Ideological States Apparatuses (Notes towards an Investigation)," in *Lenin and Philosophy and Other Essays*, trans. Ben Brewster (New York: Monthly Review Press, 2001), 85–127; Vladimir I. Lenin, *State and Revolution* (Mansfield, CT: Martino, 2011); Karl Marx and Friedrich Engels, *The Communist Manifesto* (1848; New York: Monthly Review Press, 1998); Karl Marx, *Critique of the Gotha Program*, trans. Kevin B. Anderson (Oakland, CA: PM Press, 2023); Friedrich Engels, *The Origin of the Family, Private Property, and the State* (New York: Penguin Classics, 2010).

[9] James Boggs, *Pages from a Black Radical's Notebook: A James Boggs Reader* (Detroit, MI: Wayne State University Press, 2011).

[10] Ellen Meiksins Wood, *Democracy against Capitalism: Renewing Historical Materialism* (Cambridge: Cambridge University Press, 1995), 227.

fact, the more welfare they get, the more they begin to act like subjects. Subjects don't make revolution. Revolutionists make revolution."[11] Now why does Boggs disavow the efficacy of so-called welfare rights? One reason could be that Boggs endorses the ideology of self-help that we find in black political traditions like Garveyism, as discussed in chapter 3. The focus on welfare may ameliorate social conditions of deprivation at the cost of increasing dependency on the powers of the state. It may even lead recipients of state welfare into thinking that the state is the *only* legitimate social power. If this is all that Boggs meant, then there would be little to distinguish him from the black conservative political tradition.

A more accurate interpretation of Boggs's separation of "welfare rights" from revolutionary practice would place the problem of *domination* at the center of his social analysis. His *primary* critique is not the receipt of welfare, but the intellectual confusion of state-sanctioned rights with revolutionary power. In other words, welfare rights are downstream from the more general category of rights as such. Therefore, Boggs contests confining the struggle for social freedom to the limited domain of rights anchored by the state. A similar position can be found in Vladimir Lenin's *State and Revolution* where he critiques confining the ends of the Russian Revolution to the mere takeover of the state rather than its supersession and thereby remaining trapped in the "narrow horizon of bourgeois right."[12] The thought is that the state shapes and constrains *horizons of normative expectations* by producing habitual patterns of identifying what constitutes a legitimate form of life. Boggs thinks reliance on the state for freedom closes off alternative justifications for the legitimate and liberatory exercise of power given the asymmetrical relations of force that obtain between the state and its citizens.[13]

In other words, rights tend to induce the systematic misrecognition that social freedom is granted by the state rather than through the self-conscious activity of agents. Recall that racial fetishism tends to endow

---

[11] Boggs, *Pages from a Black Radical's Notebook*, 262.
[12] Lenin, *State and Revolution*, 80–81.
[13] See Forst on "domination" as the closure of the space of reasons: *Normativity and Power*, trans. Ciaran Cronin (New York: Oxford University Press, 2017), 49; *Justification and Critique*, 10–11.

the abstraction of "race" with powers that truly belong to, and emerge from, our practical conduct. By misrecognizing the state as independent of our social practices, Boggs worries that our conceptions of freedom and progress will be hamstrung by the naturalization of forms of reasoning that reproduce social domination. Revolutionists, for Boggs, are those who adopt the perspective that they are responsible for advancing society in the interest of all rather than limiting themselves to securing their private interests against the interests of others. He distinguishes these two mentalities as socialist thought and bourgeois thought.[14] In sum, Boggs wants to induce a paradigm shift of how we *think* about power. Lucio Colletti aptly summarizes this point in reference to Lenin: "The essential point of the revolution, the *destruction* it cannot forgo ... is rather the destruction of the bourgeois State as a power *separate* from and *counterposed* to the masses, and its replacement by a power of a new type."[15] Describing what Boggs thinks this new type of power that he calls black power is will be the subject of the next section. For now, we can say that for Boggs power is not only the capacity to do *x*, but it is also the capacity to constrain what counts as the legitimate justification of power.

If cognitive dependency were all that were at stake in Boggs's critique of state power, then his solution would be that agents should recognize themselves as active participants in the state rather than passive recipients of its protection. But as with racial fetishism there is also a practical problem that must be diagnosed as well. The *practical dependence* on the state for rights must mean that the state really does have the apparatus for enforcing these rights by recourse to coercion or violence.[16] The concern for advocates of black power is that black people will no longer know how to govern themselves. Politics will be subsumed by electoral contests and the delegation of responsibility to officeholders. The practical problem is twofold: black people will actually not have power insofar as the state retains its monopoly on violence *and* they will lose the requisite

---

[14] Boggs, *Pages from a Black Radical's Notebook*, 261.
[15] Lucio Colletti, *From Rousseau to Lenin: Studies in Ideology and Society*, trans. John Merrington and Judith White (New York: Monthly Review Press, 1972), 220.
[16] Lenin, *State and Revolution*, 82.

ethical character for governing themselves amid disagreement and conflict.

Without the habit of self-governance citizens will have to rely on some instrument to mediate social conflicts. Boggs never denies that some instrument of mediation is necessary in our complex and diverse societies. What he questions is whether *this* form of the state is the only form of legitimate governance. The fact that it is scarcely questionable is what prompts his critical reevaluation of how the state mediates the problem of racial domination. From his perspective, the form that rights take under the state reproduce rather than mitigate egoism and social atomism.[17] Thus, dependence on the state tends to sap the potential for new forms of social power rather than enhance it.

These critiques are neither necessarily revolutionary nor even progressive. We can see these ideas as constituting a long thread of black conservatism from Booker T. Washington to Marcus Garvey and Clarence Thomas.[18] Distrust of the state can be explained by recourse to the supposedly essential racial character of the state or the putatively essential effects of statecraft. So, if Boggs is not conservative, then we must ask what is the difference that makes a difference? Why does he think that his critique of the state is both revolutionary and socialist rather than conservative and nationalist? The answer is that his account of black power is nested within a wider analysis of the state as itself dependent on the dynamics of capitalist accumulation. This dependency is a historical relationship rather than an essential relationship. If this holds, then black power, for Boggs, is an account of self-emancipation through the emancipation of society from what he takes to be a stultifying relationship of "political underdevelopment."[19]

---

[17] Boggs's position closely hews to Marx's "On the Jewish Question," in *The Marx-Engels Reader*, ed. Robert Tucker (New York: Norton, 1978), 45: "But the consummation of the idealism of the state was at the same time the consummation of the materialism of civil society. The bonds which had restrained the egoistic spirit of civil society were removed along with the political yoke. Political emancipation was at the same time an emancipation of civil society from politics and from even the *semblance* of a general content.... Thus man was not liberated from religion; he received religious liberty. He was not liberated from property; he received the liberty to own property. He was not liberated from the egoism of business; he received the liberty to engage in business."
[18] See Corey Robin, *The Enigma of Clarence Thomas* (New York: Metropolitan Books, 2019).
[19] Boggs, *Pages from a Black Radical's Notebook*, 233.

Boggs develops an ambivalent account of rights that aims to show why anchoring rights in the form of life of the state will produce incoherence and fragmentation for working-class black people so long as they continue to live in a class society. Nevertheless, Boggs does not completely do away with the language of rights insofar as they are anchored in the self-activity of "revolutionists." This transition from civil rights to black power leads him to claim, "Rights are what you make and what you take."[20] What I will show is that black power for Boggs is at base an account of racial justice that centers what Forst calls "relations of justification in a given society" rather than the state-mandated distributions of good.[21]

Black Power as Justificatory Critique

From the end of the civil rights movement to the beginning of the 1980s James Boggs set about the task of investigating black power as a *scientific* concept. Boggs was an autoworker for the Chrysler corporation in Detroit. His theory of black power emerges from his experiences of the impact of automation and deindustrialization on black urban communities as workers lost their jobs. Furthermore, Boggs was well-acquainted with the reality of racism within both unions and social life, more generally. Boggs bore witness to the systematic production of people he called "the outsiders," or what Marx called "surplus populations."[22] They are a segment of the population who lack regular access to work and develop forms of life outside the formal economy. Black power is developed from the objective analysis of these social patterns in capitalist economies.

Boggs's designation of black power as scientific was meant to signal a departure from the account of black power as developed by Kwame

---

[20] James Boggs, "The American Revolution," in *Pages from a Black Radical's Notebook* (1963; Detroit, MI: Wayne State University Press, 2011), 85.
[21] Forst, *Justification and Critique*, 35.
[22] Johnson, *The Panthers Can't Save Us* Now, 21–22. See also Marx and Engels, *The Communist Manifesto*; Karl Marx, *Capital: A Critique of Political Economy*, vol. 1, trans. Ben Fowkes, intro. Ernest Mandel (New York: Penguin Classics, 1990); Michael C. Dawson, "Hidden in Plain Sight: A Note on Legitimation Crises and the Racial Order," *Critical Historical Studies* 3, no. 1 (2016): 143–161.

Ture and Charles Hamilton in their book *Black Power: The Politics of Liberation*.[23] He based his understanding of power on his social analysis of the separation between the political form of life of *the state* and the form of life of *civil society* or the economy. For Boggs, black power must begin from the problem of racial domination in civil society where individuals are free to buy and sell commodities. Boggs was not convinced that equality actually obtained in capitalist markets or "that very Eden of the innate rights of man . . . the exclusive realm of Freedom, Equality, Property, and Bentham," as Marx described it.[24] In fact, and this cuts to the very heart of what makes black power scientific for Boggs, civil society did not contingently reproduce racial domination, but did so systematically. If this is so, then the form of rights that guarantees participation in civil society further entrenches racial fetishism rather than dissolves it. In this section I will elaborate on how Boggs understands "power" and why he thinks it is necessary to focus on the form of life of civil society rather than only the state to achieve emancipation.

The emergence of black power was a response to the hegemony of civil rights as the horizon of political contestation. In other words, the ethico-functional norms that constitute the form of life of the state construed the achievement of racial justice as primarily a question of integration. Black power advocates aim to critique these norms on the basis that they obfuscate how the market relations of civil society both reproduce and naturalize inequalities. One way of understanding the ideological aim of Boggs's theory of black power is that it was a struggle to unseat the justificatory force of what C. B. Macpherson called "possessive individualism" wherein "man is free and human by virtue of his sole proprietorship of his own person, and that human society is

---

[23] Boggs, in reference to SNCC and the Black Panther Party, criticizes their reliance on the emotive content of "Black Power": "Having neglected to make the necessary analysis, the easiest thing for black militants was to use Black Power as a slogan to keep the masses in a high state of excitement and expectation. This concept of keeping the masses in a high state of agitation is itself based on the erroneous belief that the masses in themselves are revolutionists, and that if they are constantly urged on by revolutionary rhetoric, they will be able to lead the revolutionary struggle to success" (*Pages from a Black Radical's Notebook*, 242).

[24] Marx, *Capital*, 280.

essentially a series of market relations."[25] The power of this justification narrative is evident in the black nationalism of Garvey, for instance, who assumed the appropriateness of capitalism as a given, but insisted it should be organized nationally.[26] Boggs, for his part, thought black people needed the resources to resist the ideology of possessive individualism, and that integration into the state as citizens would not be sufficient for emancipation. Black power was, first and foremost, the construction of an alternative ideological space or a "counterpublic" where new justifications and reasons could anchor social life.[27]

The invocation of "ideology" here invites a number of confusions and debates concerning the analytical usefulness of the concept.[28] What I hope to have shown in the preceding chapters is that a social theoretical account of ideology should not be reduced to a set of ideas or beliefs held by individuals, nor should we reserve the concept of ideology only for the pejorative designation of ideas and beliefs that do not accord with the objective facts of social life. I endorse a neutral account of ideology that relates social practices to their justifications. In this way, I will argue that ideologies always obtain within a space of reasons. Every social practice can be reconstructed ideologically

---

[25] C. B. Macpherson, *The Political Theory of Possessive Individualism: Hobbes to Locke* (New York: Oxford University Press), 270.

[26] See Marcus Garvey, "6," in *Philosophy and Opinions of Marcus Garvey or Africa for the Africans*, Vol. 2, ed. Amy Jacques-Garvey (Mansfield Centre, CT: Martino, 2014), 69–72; Garvey, "Capitalism and the State," in *Philosophy and Opinions of Marcus Garvey or Africa for the Africans*, Vol. 2, 72–74.

[27] See Andrew J. Douglas and Jared A. Loggins, *Prophet of Discontent: Martin Luther King Jr. and the Critique of Racial Capitalism* (Athens: University of Georgia Press, 2021), 55–74; Michael Warner, "Publics and Counterpublics," *Public Culture* 14, no. 1 (2002): 49–90.

[28] See Sally Haslanger, "Racism, Ideology, and Social Movements," *Res Philosophica* 94, no. 1 (2017): 1–22; Karen Ng, "Ideology Critique from Hegel and Marx to Critical Theory," *Constellations* 22, no. 3 (2015): 393–404; Tommie Shelby, "Ideology, Racism, and Critical Social Theory," *Philosophical Forum* 34, no. 2 (2003): 153–188 and "Racism, Moralism, and Social Criticism," *Du Bois Review* 11, no. 1 (2014): 57–74; Louis Althusser, *On the Reproduction of Capitalism: Ideology and Ideological State Apparatuses*, trans. G. M. Goshgarian, intro. Jacques Bidet (1970; London: Verso, 2014); István Mészáros, *The Power of Ideology* (New York: Harvester Wheatsheaf, 1989); Maeve Cooke, "Resurrecting the Rationality of Ideology Critique: Reflection on Laclau on Ideology," *Constellations* 13, no. 1 (2006): 4–20; Theodor Adorno, *Aspects of Sociology*, trans. John Viertel (Boston: Beacon Press, 1972), 182–206; Raymond Guess, *The Idea of a Critical Theory: Habermas and the Frankfurt School* (Cambridge: Cambridge University Press, 1989).

from the perspective of critical theory because social practices are not random, but purposive. Social practices are intelligible insofar as they cohere within shared horizons of normative expectations. So, to say that black power ought to be understood as the struggle to construct an ideological space autonomous from the state is to claim that we can reconstruct Boggs's account of black power not only in terms of its stated ideas, but the basic rules and norms that would make these social practices coherent.

Boggs insisted that black power attained salience in the aftermath of the successes of the civil rights movement because it was only with formal integration into the circuits of American democracy and capitalism that the limitations of civic recognition become apparent. Boggs's thesis was that civil rights and social power were analytically distinct. His account of power entails more than the capacity to x or y.[29] Power for Boggs is never neutral, as if the ability to pick up a cup were an adequate account of power. All exercises of social power cohere around ethico-functional norms. Unlike the passive permission signaled by rights, power accomplishes some purpose in light of implicit or explicit ends. As I understand Boggs, he sees power as the capacity to bind subjects to particular justifications and reasons that shape a form of life. It is not possible to simply take over a form of power without also taking on its justificatory force. For this reason Boggs concludes, "Just as Marx's concept of worker's power did not

---

[29] For instance, Steven Lukes describes three dimensions to a sociological account of power. First, we can say that power is defined by who can exercise the required force in decision-making contexts. In other words, whose preferences win out? In the historical example of Reconstruction, we can say that the preferences of the northern capitalists won out when presented with the choice between black redistribution and white accumulation. Second, we can say that power is defined by who shapes what choices are taken to be salient in a given context. In the U.S., the fact that major political decisions are often broken down into a choice between two political parties is not a natural occurrence, but an effect of powerful constraints. And third, power is defined by one party being able to extract the consent of another party. What is key for Lukes here is that we are able to evaluate whether the dominated party would have chosen differently if they knew there were other options. Steven Lukes, *Power: A Radical View*, 3rd ed. (London: Red Globe Press, 2021), 113–157. See also Thomas E. Wartenberg, "The Situated Conception of Social Power," *Social Theory and Practice* 14, no. 3 (1988): 317–343 and *The Forms of Power: From Domination to Transformation* (Philadelphia: Temple University Press, 1990); Jeffrey C. Isaac, "Beyond the Three Faces of Power: A Realist Critique." *Polity* 20, no. 1 (1987): 4–31.

mean workers becoming a part of or integrating themselves into capitalist power, so black power does not mean black people becoming a part of or integrating themselves into white power."[30] The comparison between black power/worker power and white power/capitalist power is complex, but central for understanding Boggs's transition from civil rights to black power.

At first blush, it seems that what Boggs understands power to be is the zero-sum contest over who has the capacity to rule or, at the very least, direct the imperatives of social life. He acknowledges that the emergence of the slogan "black power" has provoked whites into recognizing "that once the issue of power is raised it means one set of people who are powerless replacing another set of people who have the power."[31] This claim immediately precedes the comparison with "Marx's concept of worker's power" cited above. Read in isolation we might infer that Boggs is making two sorts of claims about black power. First, that *all* power, irrespective of historical forms of life, reduces to struggles between ruler and ruled. Second, that Boggs advocates for black people to rule over white people rather than vice versa. If this were the case, then the ideology of black power is nothing more than the social practice of having *power over* others. In other words, Boggs would seem to be advocating some form of race war whereby society will always be ruled by some racial contingent and the question to be resolved is "Which race?" Boggs would certainly be breaking with the liberal paradigm of civil rights and individual liberty with the regrettable conclusion that society ought to be organized around the principle of "might makes right."[32]

Boggs does indeed break with liberal justifications of civil rights, but not with rights as such. What black power contests is the *social form* these rights take.[33] The argument Boggs makes is that when

[30] Boggs, "The American Revolution," 172.
[31] Boggs, "The American Revolution," 172.
[32] Versions of this argument can be found in political theories that are concerned with struggles over hegemony. See Michel Foucault, *Society Must Be Defended: Lectures at the Collège de France, 1975–1976*, ed. Mauro Bertani and Alessandro Fontana, trans. David Macey (New York: Picador, 2003); Carl Schmitt, *The Concept of the Political*, trans. George Schwab (Chicago: University of Chicago Press, 2007); Chantal Mouffe, *On the Political* (New York: Routledge, 2005).
[33] Igor Shoikhedbrod argues alongside Marx that "different standards of right apply in different modes of production" and thus a different organization of our time and how we

whites react to black power with the recognition that it means the replacement of those with power by those currently without power, they accurately understand what is at stake, but misrecognize why black power eschews integration as embodied by civil rights. It is not that Boggs thinks power struggles between ruler and ruled are intrinsic to every conceivable form of political life. His point is that *our* society, or what he calls "class society," is shaped by antagonistic relationships wherein the necessary form of appearance for power is *power over*. Boggs takes Marx's insight that a society shaped by capitalist power will necessarily be a society shaped by competition and exploitation and brings it to bear on the racial dynamics of the United States. Civil rights may blunt these effects, but only at the price of legitimating class society as the only viable form society could take. The ideological aim of black power is to denaturalize the justification of class society and in so doing make another form of life intelligible.

Nevertheless, even if Boggs means to highlight the historical specificity of class society, he does seem to endorse an account of power as intrinsically *power over* and thus it would seem as if he remains committed to carrying over the formal characteristics of class society into whatever form of life emerges from the activity of black power. This conclusion would be unavoidable without analyzing the justificatory critique that black power offers. Rainer Forst's concept of "noumenal power" is instructive here. He argues, "Power is not only exercised by and over free agents; it is also the term for what is going on when someone acts for certain reasons for which others are responsible.... To be a subject of power is to be moved by reasons that others have given me and that motivate me to think or act in a certain way intended by that reason-giver."[34] For Boggs the black power critique of white power does not stop at the question of whether some have power over others, but interrogates *how white power is justified to black agents in order to reproduce class society*. Boggs counterposes

---

use it to meet our needs will generate different conceptions of objective right and subjective rights. Igor Shoikhedbrod, *Revisiting Marx's Critique of Liberalism: Rethinking Justice, Legality and Rights* (Cham: Palgrave Macmillan, 2019), 35. See also Christoph Menke, *Critique of Rights* (Cambridge, UK: Polity, 2020), 267–292.

[34] Forst, *Normativity and Power*, 38.

black power as a justificatory narrative for black people to attain power over the economic infrastructure of civil society *in order to overcome class society*. This would require the capacity for ethico-functional self-development and as such rights could not be anything other than "what you make."[35]

The comparison of black power to worker power and white power to capitalist power is suggestive in another way. Capitalist power is qualitatively distinct from worker power in terms of the forms of consciousness, social skills, and justifications it tends to produce. Let's consider the ideological space of a workplace via the work of Göran Therborn. For Therborn, we should understand ideological formation along the axes of "subjection-qualification."[36] Subjection designates the dispositions and drives that are favored in distinct contexts. For instance, the manager of a firm will be disposed toward increasing efficiency and keeping pace with competitors while their employees will subjected to the disposition toward executing tasks and respecting the chain of command. However, being disposed to accomplish some purpose does not guarantee that one knows how to do so. Qualifications, understood as skills and practices, must be developed. An employee may love their job and deeply believe in the ethos of the workplace, but lack the knowledge or creativity to keep pace with the specific demands that are commensurate with their role in the workplace and thus is fired from the firm. Therborn concludes, "The reproduction of any social organization, be it an exploitative society or a revolutionary party, entails a basic correspondence between subjection and qualification. . . . But there is always an inherent possibility that a contradiction may develop between the two."[37] A coherent ideological space must achieve a relatively stable unity of subjection and qualification or, in my language, fulfill both the *cognitive condition* and the *practical condition*.

What Boggs understands as worker power is a fundamentally distinct ideological space from capitalist power. It is composed of

---

[35] Boggs, "The American Revolution," 85.
[36] Göran Therborn, *The Ideology of Power and the Power of Ideology* (London: Verso Classics, 1999), 17.
[37] Therborn, *The Ideology of Power and the Power of Ideology*, 17.

potential justifications for a form of life that is not reconcilable with the form of life that is conducive to the reproduction of capitalist social relations.[38] Capitalist power attempts to subject worker power to dispositions that are congenial for ever-increasing accumulation by controlling what skills and practices link together in the workplace. Worker power, for its part, seeks to dispose workers toward horizontal solidarity and the foundation of an economy oriented around democratic control over one's time rather than capital accumulation by developing skills for self-emancipation and democratic governance.[39]

Any attempt to integrate worker power into capitalist power will mystify the justificatory dynamics of class society and legitimize the idea that capitalist power is the only form power can take. Boggs's point is that the idea that worker power could be integrated into capitalist power is practically incoherent. Boggs understands emancipation as

---

[38] Michael A. Lebowitz, *Beyond Capital: Marx's Political Economy of the Working Class*, 2nd ed. (New York: Palgrave Macmillan, 2003).

[39] Boggs clearly assumes that democratic control over one's time would entail a society that is organized around human *needs*. Boggs means more than developing a society that meets the bare necessities of food, water, and shelter. The category of "need" is extraordinarily thorny given that needs become ever more complex as our social relations become more complex. Both Hegel and Marx, from different perspectives, have analyzed the dynamic transformation of needs throughout history. For instance, before the development of the internet we could not say that access to broadband was a need, but now that entire sections of world economies depend on the internet for work the internet has become a need. Moreover, it is not possible to say that capitalist social relations do not produce and satisfy certain needs. Commodities are produced, distributed, and sold with incredible speed every day. I interpret Boggs as claiming that *how* needs are produced and met in capitalist societies is *obscure* and *needlessly divisive*. His critique of capitalist class society follows Kate Soper's reconstruction of Marx where the irrational organization of social time is anchored in "the exchangeability of products, and that in turn by its specific relations of distributions of social wealth." Kate Soper, *On Human Needs: Open and Closed Theories in a Marxist Perspective* (Sussex: Harvester Press, 1981), 58. I think the strongest interpretation of Boggs would see him as claiming that democratic control over one's time is a *need* for social emancipation insofar as we would have the power to organize our needs in a *transparent* and *solidaristic* manner. See also G. W. F. Hegel, *Hegel: Elements of the Philosophy of Right*, ed. Allen Wood, trans. H. B. Nisbet (Cambridge: Cambridge University Press, 1991); Karl Marx, *Grundrisse: Foundations of the Critique of Political Economy*, trans. Martin Nicolaus (London: Penguin Books, 1993), 88–89, 91–92; Mark Neocleous, "Policing the System of Needs: Hegel, Political Economy, and the Police of the Market," *History of European Ideas* 24, no. 1 (1998): 43–58; David Merrill, "Hegel's System of Needs: The Elementary Relations of Economic Justice," *Hegel Bulletin* 19, nos. 1–2 (1998): 51–72; Ian Fraser, *Hegel and Marx: The Concept of Need* (Edinburgh: Edinburgh University Press, 1998); Paul Cobben, *Value in Capitalist Society: Rethinking Marx's Criticism of Capitalism* (Leiden: Brill, 2015), ch. 5. I thank Jacob Singer for pushing me on this point.

political relations of justification that are in principle equal and generalizable. The power of capital justifies an inequality between those who own the means of production and those who are compelled to sell their labor. For Boggs this is not only a question of who gets what, but how social time is organized and justified.

If the analogy holds, then Boggs's claim is that a similar practical incoherence emerges when black power is integrated into white power via the ideological space of civil rights. Black agents would be subjecting themselves to a standpoint they cannot occupy in a class-stratified society. Boggs's insight here is that race is anchored in a class dynamic that justifies relations of domination. Thus, it can only be dealt with by altering the structure of class society as a whole. Boggs argues that civil rights advocates who are "sponsored, supported, and dependent upon the white power structure" are "simply asking to be given the same rights whites have had and blacks have been denied. By equality they mean just that and no more: being equal to white Americans."[40] This is precisely the problem of whose justifications bind our actions. If the ideological space of white power is practically shaped by social patterns of domination, then the equality of civil rights would amount to being equal with those qualified to dominate apart from those qualified to be dominated. To avoid this practical conclusion, Boggs formulates black power as the ideological struggle against this order of justification by developing an alternative unity of subjection-qualification.

To avoid any misunderstanding, I think it is important to understand that what makes black power *black* for Boggs has little to do with ethnicity or racial identity. His comparison of black power to Marx's concept of worker power should tell us that he thinks black power is a product of distinct social relations in institutional life: "The uniqueness of Black power stems from the specific historical development of the United States. It has nothing to do with any special moral virtue in being black, as some black nationalists seem to think.... The chief virtue in being black at this juncture in history stems from the fact that

---

[40] James Boggs, "Black Power: A Scientific Concept Whose Time Has Come," in *Pages from a Black Radical's Notebook: A James Boggs Reader*, ed. Stephen M. Ward (1970; Detroit, MI: Wayne State University Press, 2011), 176–177.

the vast majority of the people in the world who have been deprived of the right of self-government and self-determination are people of color."[41] And this is what makes black power *scientific* for Boggs. It is not about a pre-constituted identity or emotion, but it must base itself on "a scientific evaluation of the American system and of revolution, knowing that black power cannot come from the masses doing what they do when they feel like doing it but must come from the painstaking, systematic building of an organization to lead the masses to power."[42] Power, for Boggs, would mean the political establishment of a new space of justifications for a wholly different form of life. Unbinding black agents from the justificatory dynamics of white/capitalist power would stimulate the utopian movement beyond class society.

Racial Fetishism and Economic Disempowerment

Thus far I have mostly focused on the cognitive condition for black power, but now I will turn to its practical condition. Describing the practical condition of success for black power requires a theoretical analysis of the functional purpose of institutions. Social life as we know it is only possible by virtue of the many institutions that have been embedded in the daily life of our practices and expectations. Institutions are structures of rules and customs that establish equilibria between our various social practices.[43] The normative function of institutions is to provide a stable order for the justifications that enable our social practices.

In other words, institutions ought to provide the conditions for coherent social practices. For Boggs, we need coherent social practices in order to flourish as human beings. But not just any social practices will do. In a text he co-authored with Grace Lee Boggs, he outlines a

---

[41] Boggs, "Black Power," 176.
[42] Boggs, "Black Power," 177.
[43] Rahel Jaeggi describes institutions as "constituted by social practices and characterized by habit. They represent more or less complex systems of lasting expectations placed on behavior, which establish more or less stable positions of status and which achieve particular public effectiveness and recognition." Rahel Jaeggi, "Was ist eine (gute) Institution?," in *Sozialphilosophie und Kritik*, ed. Rainer Forst, Martin Hartmann, Rahel Jaeggi, and Martin Saar (Frankfurt: Suhrkamp, 2009), 531.

normative anthropology of human nature as revolutionary and evolutionary. He declaims the tendency of "militant activists [to] usually disregard the evolution of man/womankind [because] they fail to recognize that what we are today is the result of a long and continuing process of evolution, and that this process of evolution is still going on and will go on as long as there are men and women on this planet."[44] James and Grace Lee Boggs are not concerned with biological evolution per se, but political evolution. They provide a formal, historically sensitive, philosophical anthropology that I gestured toward in chapter 4. As our social needs and expectations change we require coherent social practices to accord with our malleable nature.

It is because we are not purely biological creatures driven by unreflective instincts that we need institutions.[45] Boggs advocates a distinctly political basis for humanism that centers the historical mediation of our reason-giving practices in transforming our social conduct. Contrary to dominant understandings of institutions as conservative, Boggs develops an account of institutions as necessary for engaging our capacities for political evolution and revolution. Social problems arise when our forms of life are no longer responsive to reasons and do not address our reasons as politically dynamic.

Boggs explains the ongoing domination and exploitation of black people as symptomatic of a more general crisis of the form of life of the United States. He proclaims, "The essential, the key, contradiction in the United States that must be resolved if this country is to survive is the contradiction between economic overdevelopment and political underdevelopment."[46] Here Boggs diagnoses the non-synchronicity between our economic form of life and our political form of life. The speed of development that one finds in politics cannot keep up the temporal dynamics of the economy. Boggs saw the seemingly irresistible drive toward automation as inaugurating a wholly new form of life where increasingly workers will be rendered obsolete.[47] Here Boggs's

---

[44] James Boggs and Grace Lee Boggs, *Revolution and Evolution in the Twentieth Century* (New York: Monthly Review Press, 1974), 13.
[45] Günther Anders, "The Pathology of Freedom: An Essay on Non-identification," *Deleuze and Guattari Studies* 3, no. 2 (2009): 303
[46] Boggs, *Pages from a Black Radical's Notebook*, 232–233.
[47] "One of the major aims of the Kennedy administration is to encourage automation by granting subsidies to companies who go full speed ahead on it, both directly and in

notion of black power as a scientific concept comes into full view: either black people develop politics such that control over economic dynamics becomes justifiable or the force of technological development will push them to the margins of social life irrespective of what civil rights they may have.

The "silent compulsion of economic relations" that Marx describes takes on a different gloss once we understand power as the capacity to bind others to given justifications for their social practices since, from one perspective, these economic relations do not speak, do not have to give justifications for the form that they take.[48] Boggs takes this to mean that black workers are forced to act as if technological development in capitalist societies are beyond question or akin to a law of nature. When Boggs analyzes the lack of power of "the outsiders" he is not primarily focused on the fact that society does distribute enough good to them fairly, but that they live in a society that feels no obligation to justify itself to them. What is worse is that their immiseration will be justified as either evidence of their lack of talent to compete in civil society or the price to be paid for the productive dynamism of capitalism. Either way "economic development" *appears* as the dominant form of time against which all other forms of life must synchronize themselves.[49]

Civil society is defined by the practical expectations and imperatives of technical production or creativity toward the end of accumulation. The domination of these values over the rest of social life subsumes political values to the dictates of economic values. Boggs criticizes how economic overdevelopment tended to ideologically invert the categories of political life as well as practically distort our capacity

---

the form of tax write-offs. Therefore, when workers fight the introduction of automation, they are taking on not only private capitalism but the federal government itself. Yet so great is the contradiction generated by automation that the government, while giving it such encouragement, must at the very same time set up a new committee to study what is going to happen to the millions of displaced workers" (Boggs, "The American Revolution," 104).

[48] Marx, *Capital*, 899.
[49] Sylvia Wynter, "Is Development a Purely Empirical Concept, or Also Teleological? A Perspective from 'We the Underdeveloped,'" in *Prospects for Recovery and Sustainable Development in Africa*, ed. Aguibou Y. Yansané (Westport, CT: Greenwood, Press, 1996), 299–316.

to cooperate and deliberate. As it concerns ideological inversion, he claims, "Liberty has turned into license. Equality has become the homogenization of everybody at the lowest common denominator of the faceless anybody. Fraternity has become mass-man cheering and groaning at the various modern spectacles—sports, lotteries, and television give-aways."[50] Our social practices are reason-giving. The reasons they can offer will depend on the power of the institutions that underwrite our social practices. Given the political underdevelopment of our institutions vis-à-vis the overdevelopment of economic institutions we are led into a situation of "social anarchy" due to the lack of "human values or *qualitative* standards imposed by human beings on the *quantitative* cancerous growth of production for the sake of production or the expansive virulence of quantitative expansion which by its very nature cannot limit its own growth."[51] The domination of economic quantity over political qualification bodes ill for the ideological coherence of the newly won civil rights. If in class society economic power is what has *power over* the practices of social life, then domination can obtain despite the achievement of formal equality in civil status.[52]

Overcoming racial fetishism requires an account of racial justice that unmasks technological development as reified social relations rather than a form of progress over which there can be no democratic control. Boggs deftly weaves together economic, political, and psychological relations when he argues that there are only a limited number of workers that "capitalism can continue to employ in

---

[50] Boggs and Boggs, *Revolution and Evolution in the Twentieth Century*, 181.
[51] Boggs and Boggs, *Revolution and Evolution in the Twentieth Century*, 182. See all the critiques of modernity found in Max Horkheimer and Theodor Adorno, *Dialectic of Enlightenment: Philosophical Fragments*, ed. Gunselin Schmid Noerr, trans. E. F. N. Jephcott (Stanford: Stanford University Press, 2002), 4–5.
[52] "In capitalist democracy, the separation between civic status and class position operates in both directions: socio-economic position does not determine the right to citizenship—and this is what is *democratic* in capitalist democracy—but, since the power of the capitalist to appropriate the surplus labor of workers is not dependent on a privileged juridical or civic status, civic equality does not directly affect or significantly modify class inequality—and that is what limits democracy in capitalism. Class relations between capital and labor can survive even with juridical equality and universal suffrage. In that sense, political equality in capitalist democracy not only coexists with socio-economic inequality, but leaves it fundamentally intact" (Wood, *Democracy against Capitalism*, 213).

production at a pace killing enough to be profitable. The rest are like refugees or displaced persons. . . . There is no way for capitalism to employ them profitably, yet it can't just kill them off. It must feed them rather than be fed by them. . . . This antagonism in the population between those who have to be supported and those who have to support them is one of the inevitable antagonisms of capitalism." He goes on to say that this antagonism is "brought to a climax by automation. . . . In this crisis one section of population will be pitted against another, not only the employed against the unemployed but those who propose that the unemployed be allowed to starve to death rather than continue as such a drain on the public against those who cannot stand by and see society degenerate into such barbarism."[53] Given the overrepresentation of the racially dominated in the surplus populations generated by economic progress, Boggs thinks class society will become fertile ground for the reemergence of *racist* ideas and justifications. However, as I have been arguing, racial fetishism and not racism is the problem because it is the specific dynamics of capitalist relations that must be transformed. The utopian moment of black power emerges as the contestation of the justifications that support a society that reproduces barbarism against those who attempt to rationalize barbarism.

However, the problem is not only that social values are distorted by economic drives, but our capacity for social cooperation is distorted. Boggs thinks that the United States has "become a nation so dedicated to technological advancement that its citizens systematically evade any political decisions that might interfere with their personal economic interest."[54] Here we have a different claim than the one advanced above. The crisis that exists between the economic and political spheres weakens the capacity of the citizenry to engage in collective action. We not only misunderstand our values, but the values to which we do become committed systematically block the realization of social emancipation. From within the bind of this double mystification, the conditions are ripe for ongoing racial oppression amid *de jure* civil equality.

---

[53] Boggs, "The American Revolution," 102–103.
[54] Boggs, *Pages from a Black Radical's Notebook*, 233.

Struggling against the economic foundations of racial fetishism, for Boggs, goes beyond the concern of poverty and employment. By taking responsibility for economic development, the struggle becomes social by reopening the question of "the relations of man to man."[55] Boggs, perhaps overly optimistically, thought the sheer speed of the technological revolution created the conditions for us to begin asking what form of life we could create when the production of goods no longer needed to be the center of social life. Black power aims at opening up the space of reasons for envisioning a new rational structure for our social time. Boggs thinks that without this power we will have "no clear idea of what people would do with themselves, what would be their human role, or how society would be organized when work is no longer at the heart of society."[56] This is an unequivocally utopian line of inquiry insofar as the idea that there would no longer be any need to make whole populations superfluous to the organization of social life is at this moment far outside our settled horizons of normative expectations. I would add to Boggs's question this: What role would rights and the state have once we have delinked from the antagonistic and dispossessive tendencies of capitalist relations? What conflicts would it mediate? How would social problems appear to us once social life no longer seems to be imposed upon our conduct from the outside?

The point is not to have readymade answers to these questions, but to clear the ideological space for these questions to be posed and answers freely formed. After all, there is a choice contained within Boggs's title "The American Revolution." The revolution will either be the technological revolution of social obsolescence that will further entrench racial fetishism, or it will be a social revolution of appropriating our technological capacities within our space of reasons. Black power, Boggs hoped to show, emerges at this precise historical juncture where those who have been cast into the "no place" of social life can emancipate society and consciously take it to where it has never been before: the realm of freedom.

Before moving on, I want to summarize the argument thus far. Civil rights are an insufficient guarantee of social freedom within a class

---

[55] Boggs, "The American Revolution," 103.
[56] Boggs, "The American Revolution," 106.

society since agents can be formally equal in political life, but substantively unequal in economic life. The social relations of a market society can reproduce racial domination in the absence of legal discrimination. Racial justice, thus, should not be confined to the question of how to distribute goods more fairly in this economic form of life, but instead should aim at establishing a space of reasons where our economic form of life can be critiqued or justified. Such a critical transformation requires the development of a counter-power that provides alternative justifications for how social life can be organized. For Boggs, this was black power, and its goal was to overcome the cognitive and practical dependence of black subjects on a narrow focus on the state rather than social life as a whole. Thus, the argument is not against civil rights *per se*, but the role of civil rights in a class society.[57] These rights need to be enriched as an alternative form of power than what Boggs calls "capitalist power" or "white power." In what follows, I flesh out Boggs's utopian concern for a transformed social life by relating his justificatory critique to the problem of institutions.

The Functional Critique of Civil Rights

If Boggs is right that social life has become so distorted at the level of ideology and social practice, then how is it possible for him or anyone to develop a critique of our social norms? In this section, I will develop Boggs's resources for justificatory critique. There are two potential sources for this critique. First, there is the functional critique of civil rights as enabling a range of social practices that contravene the putative end of social emancipation. Second, there is the ethical critique of civil rights as legitimating a form of life that distorts our social character. My argument will be that black power criticizes how institutions in class societies anchor some practices of justification while delegitimating others. What Boggs shows is how racial fetishism is a structural problem of our form of life that frustrates building emancipatory learning processes.

---

[57] Shoikhedbrod, *Revisiting Marx's Critique of Liberalism*, 84–97.

There are two potential sources for the black power critique. First, a conflict arises between the cognitive and the practical condition of civil rights. For instance, the civic equality achieved by the civil rights movement for black citizens runs up against ongoing class inequality for a segment of that population. Formal equality and substantive subjection lead to the experience of disrespect. I take this to be a *functional* critique. Second, the practical pursuit of one's civil rights consistently contravenes expectations of success. Boggs came to the conclusion that integrating into class society, learning how to be a respectable bourgeois citizen, did not protect many black citizens from becoming "outsiders." Moreover, it encouraged the justification of the existence of "the outsiders" as an inevitable feature of modern life. I take this to be the *ethical* critique. Continued support for the state not only did not lead to greater stability, but actively reproduced the social conditions for dysfunction.[58] Black power is a critical response to these crises. But to make this claim we first must look at how institutions work.

Institutions have an ineradicable normativity that allows us to develop an immanent critique of how they function.[59] Institutions are thought to have some justification for why they ought to persist as resources for organizing our social practices with one another. An institution that did not provide such a justification would either be no institution or a dysfunctional institution.[60] Undoubtedly,

---

[58] In "Liberation or Revolution?" Boggs makes the case, "In essence, we, the American people, now have only two alternatives. Either we can continue to drift as most people are doing, continuing to hope, despite all evidence around us, that if capitalism continues its material and technological expansion, the benefits from this expansion will dribble down to us, hoping against hope that the politicians we elect will solve the problems of our society for us or that somehow things will get better for us even if they get worse for somebody else. This alternative means that our society will continue our present drift into barbarism. Hate, suspicion, and antagonism will continue to rule the relationships between classes, the races, the sexes, and the generations. Determined to remain free of our responsibilities to one another and to our nation as a whole, we will increasingly lose the freedom even to go outdoors at night" (in *Pages from a Black Radical's Notebook*, 303–304). Boggs explicitly argues that the current social practices we adopt as citizens of the state are also the practices that frustrate our expectations of equality and social freedom. He concludes that humanity must realize "a new concept of citizenship based on social and political responsibilities we assume for our communities, our nation, and our planet. On the basis of that new vision, we can create a new America" (304).

[59] Jaeggi, *Forms of Life*, 190–215 on immanent critique.

[60] For instance, see Johann Gottfried Herder, *Reflections on the Philosophy of History of Mankind*, ed. Frank E. Manuel (1787; Chicago: University of Chicago Press, 1968), 101: "Even [mankind's] most corrupt institutions cry aloud: 'had not a glimmering of

dysfunctional institutions exist, but their continued persistence is a fact to be explained rather than assumed. In other words, dysfunction is not sufficient for guaranteeing social transformation if new justifications for better institutions do not emerge.

Insofar as civil rights are a type of institution whose normative expectations are justified by the partial realization of respect and equality in social life, these normative expectations are regularly violated. The disproportionate vulnerability to joblessness and poverty experienced by many urban black people put into question how committed the United States was to equality.[61] Boggs lived in a situation where the integration into the institution of rights provided little stability against the impersonal flux of the market or shielding of black citizens from the experiences of disrespect that attend joblessness and precarity. Black people could continue to expect regular disadvantage and inequality that seemed unjustified. And it is from this contradiction that Boggs sees the *weakness* of civil rights when the market is the anchoring practice of social life. The values that emerge in class society contravene the values of "mutual respect, responsibility, and cooperation" that Boggs thinks are necessary for a stable form of life.[62]

The irony is that the market as an institution is often theorized as ineluctably leading to the dissipation of prejudice, and it is just this institution that Boggs will argue poses the greatest risk to the newly won civil rights by black citizens.[63] The argument in favor of the

---

equity and reasons been retained in us, we should have long ceased to be, nay we never should have existed.'" I thank Kwesi Thomas for pointing me toward this quote.

[61] See Axel Honneth, *Disrespect: The Normative Foundations of Critical Theory* (Malden, MA: Polity, 2007), ch. 3.

[62] Boggs, "Liberation or Revolution?," 304. See also "In the present period, however, legal recognitions of the civil rights of blacks has coincided with the separation of blacks from their traditional relationship to the economy. Rejected by the economic system, today's 'field hands' have also been freed to reject the system. Pushed out of the system by the system itself, they have become outlaws, at war with all the values and legalities of white America" (Boggs, *Pages from a Black Radical's Notebook*, 208).

[63] Arthur W. Lewis, *Racial Conflict and Economic Development* (Cambridge, MA: Harvard University Press, 1985), 120 concludes, "Racism is powerful, but market forces are powerful too; and, despite the reservations made, they work on the side of desegregation, when allowed full play." Thomas Sowell claimed in 1981, "If you look at the housing market before restrictive covenants were struck down in the 19th century, blacks had more housing integration than they have today. No civil-rights act caused that; it arose out of the normal functioning of the marketplace" ("Culture—Not

market institution goes: insofar as the market incentivizes us to engage in behaviors that will maximize our own personal gain by engaging in equal transactions, then norms that would prevent me from engaging in productive exchanges will be selected out over time. A further argument goes so far as to claim that the market "encourages the development of beliefs in equality."[64] This may be true insofar as we are thinking of the ideational content of *racism*, but it tells us nothing about the persistence of *racial fetishism*.

If upon being recognized as formally equal in civil society black people in urban centers still found themselves locked out of union participation, the first ones to be fired during economic downturns, selected to do the most dangerous jobs in factories, and returning to live in poor social conditions as capital and middle-class white people flee the city, then these disadvantages will have to be justified in order to remain socially legitimate.[65] The cognitive and practical experience of civil rights created the basis for critiquing the relationship between the state and capitalist social relations. Boggsian black power begins from a functionalist critique of how civil rights work when anchored in capitalist social relations and then proceeds to describe the vicious effects this form of rights tends to have on the body politic. The question for Boggs is to offer an account of why black citizens remain integrated into these institutions when such inequality introduces instability into black forms of life that, from his perspective, should delegitimize them in the eyes of many black citizens.[66]

Discrimination—Decides Who Gets Ahead," 74). See also Shaun P. Hargreaves Heap, "The Magic of the Market," *International Review of Economics* 58, no. 1 (2011): 113–114.

[64] Hargreaves Heap, "The Magic of the Market," 113.
[65] "That is the universal concept of Justice; according to this concept, the social inequality prevailing at any given time requires a rational justification. It ceases to be considered as a good, and becomes something that should be overcome." Max Horkheimer, "Materialism and Morality," in *Between Philosophy and Social Science: Selected Early Writings*, trans. G. Frederick Hunter, Matthew S. Kramer, and John Torpey (Cambridge, MA: MIT Press, 1993), 40.
[66] None of this is to imply that this will be successful or that it will happen automatically. Boggs writes, "Such an organization [of black power] must be clearly distinguished not only from the traditional civil rights organizations that have been organized and financed by white[s] to integrate blacks into the system, and thereby save it, but also from the ad hoc organizations that have sprung up in the course of the struggle, arousing the masses emotionally around a particular issue and relying primarily on the enthusiasm

The Ethical Critique of Civil Rights

Having established the sources of critique as arising from the experience of disrespect or dysfunction we can reconstruct black power as an ideological response to the lack of justification for the inequalities in social life. Boggs uproots the discourse of rights from the ideological space of the state and inserts them into the justificatory horizon of socialist black power. But such a shift cannot but change what would be entailed by the project of racial justice. In the previous section I outlined Boggs's functional critique of civil rights as a social practice that contravenes its own imputed ends insofar as it fails to address the economic conditions that maintain disadvantage and inequality. In this section I will detail the ethical critique he offers of civil rights that are anchored in class society. This ethical critique focuses on the type of character one tends to develop in a class society. Taken together, black power can be analyzed as the ideological struggle to produce new binding norms of justification.

The black struggle for rights normally has two components. First, there is the assertion of a moral claim or normative expectation. The enslaved or the racially dominated are saying, "I ought not be treated in such and such a manner and *you* ought to recognize that." So, to assert a right is to make a particular type of moral demand on another person that is institutionally enforceable.[67] When black people made the claim that they had a right to their bodily autonomy, to the security of their families, to the right to vote, they were drawing a border between themselves and what others may do to them. But a moral claim for recognition does not suffice for guaranteeing a truly effective right.

And so, second, black people who have struggled for their rights have also fought for a set of social relations that would institutionalize their moral claims. Fighting for the end of slavery in the United States was substantially more than a fight to get whites to agree that black

and good will of their members and supporters for their continuing activity" ("Black Power," 178).

[67] For the distinction between ethics and right (*Recht*), see Arthur Ripstein, *Force and Freedom: Kant's Legal and Political Philosophy* (Cambridge, MA: Harvard University Press, 2009), 14.

people were human beings. It was a fight to constrain what whites could do to black people by transforming their humanity into legally recognized personhood.[68]

Now we might think that the struggle for rights begins and ends as the struggle of integration into the institutions of the state. After all, rights can only be guaranteed insofar as some legitimate state justifies and enforces these rights. But this is where I believe Boggs notices a problem for black citizens: rights are not self-enforcing but require institutional life. What makes institutions effective? Or, to use Boggs's language, how do institutions mobilize their power? The power of institutions can be understood as the capacity to bind the social actions of agents by shaping "the space of reasons for B and/or C (etc.) such that they think and act in ways they would not have without . . . interference. . . . [M]oreover, the move by A must have a motivating force for B and/or C (etc.)."[69] In distinction from Forst, Boggs does not think agents must know how an institution is coordinating their conduct. It is enough that the institution shapes the cognitive and practical terrain of decision-making and appears justified.

Racial fetishism functions as a coordinating institution much like how the flows of capital coordinate and direct the activities of workers. If we understand racial fetishism not simply as cognitive prejudice against other social groups, but as a set of norms that shape the justificatory practices of individuals, then we can see how the reticence to enforce the civil rights of African-Americans can be explained by the assumed social costs of enforcing these rights rather than inborn hatred. For instance, agents may perceive enforcing the civil rights of the racially dominated as increasing competition in labor markets, decreasing efficiency in industries, or leading to a decline in housing values. Boggs seems to think as much when he says of the United States

---

[68] See Nicholas Knowles Bromell, *The Powers of Dignity: The Black Political Philosophy of Frederick Douglass* (Durham. NC: Duke University Press, 2021); Charles W. Mills, *Black Rights/White Wrongs: The Critique of Racial Liberalism* (New York: Oxford University Press, 2017); Glenda Elizabeth Gilmore, *Defying Dixie: The Radical Roots of Civil Rights, 1919–1950* (New York: W. W. Norton, 2008); Francis, *Civil Rights and the Making of the Modern American State*; and Aldon D. Morris, *The Origins of the Civil Rights Movement: Black Communities Organizing for Change* (New York: Free Press, 1986).

[69] Forst, *Normativity and Power*, 49.

that "fascism, or the naked oppression of a minority race not only by the state but by ordinary citizens of the master majority race, is the normal, natural way of life in this country."[70] It is a form of life that is not easily overcome for reasons that have to do with the power of ideology.[71]

Boggs conceives of racial fetishism as an ideological pathology that shapes social conduct. In *The American Revolution*, Boggs claims that

> inside each American, from top to bottom, in various degrees, has been accumulated all the *corruption* of a class society that has achieved its magnificent technological progress first and always by exploiting the Negro race, and then by exploiting the immigrants of all races. At the same time the class society has constantly encouraged the exploited to attempt to rise out of their class and themselves become the exploiters of other groupings and finally of their own people.[72]

Now there are two plausible interpretations of this passage that, at first blush, seem to be similar but will lead to very different conclusions. One interpretation could take Boggs as saying that spiritual "corruption" is the *explanans* of why black people have not attained the status of full moral and social equals. The other interpretation would take Boggs to hold the position that the "corruption" of racism is an *explanandum* and thus the formative cause of the persistent inequality found in black working-class life must be found elsewhere. I will argue that Boggs holds the latter position.

In the first interpretation Boggs would be claiming that racial fetishism is explained by the accumulation of racial fetishism. The circularity of this argument would imply that not only does racial fetishism have a life of its own (which would be a fall back into fetishism), but

---

[70] Boggs, "Black Power," 173.
[71] See Haslanger, "Racism, Ideology, and Social Movements"; Shelby, "Ideology, Racism, and Critical Social Theory" and "Racism, Moralism, and Social Criticism"; Mészáros, *The Power of Ideology*.
[72] Boggs, "The American Revolution," 108.

that the *idea* of race could be the primary mechanism for effecting social domination.[73] But if this were the case then the problem that black power is thought to solve would not be the problem of power at all, but the problem of cognitive defects. The solution would be to uproot or disprove the ideas of race so that our conduct could be guided by true ideas rather than false and pernicious ones.

One response to this conclusion could be that we need not think that debunking false ideas of race would be sufficient to change our social conduct because we could imagine a scenario where acting as if race were real was expedient or in an individual's interest. However, this response entails that racial fetishism could not be explained by the causal efficacy of racist ideas *solely*, but that we would have to examine the objective patterning of social life. If we do so, then we are closer to the second interpretation of the above passage, where the corruption that Boggs describes is explained by the anchoring practices of social life. Indeed, Boggs does not describe corruption *simpliciter*, but the "corruption *of* class society." It is the objective form of class society that explains both the spiritual corruption of the citizenry and the persistence of racial fetishism. It is in a class society that requires and naturalizes social differentiation between those who have control over the economic means of production and those who do not that empowers the efficacity of ideologies of social domination and weakens ideologies of solidarity.

Being clear on the logical priority of Boggs's social analysis matters because how we understand the status of racial fetishism will affect how we understand the putative goals of black power. There is no doubt that Boggs thought beliefs mattered. The crucial insight that he had was that beliefs must be analyzed in light of the anchoring practices of our form of life. In other words, we must discern what practices are accorded more justificatory power over our forms of life. The key for Boggs is that if black people are to free themselves of the social constraints and spiritual corruption of class society then ideas must be introduced into social life in such a way

---

[73] See David Calnitsky and Michael Billeaux Martinez, "A Class Functionalist Theory of Race," *Du Bois Review* 20, no. 2 (2023): 239–267 for an argument for why race is better conceived as an *explanandum* rather than *explanans*.

that they strengthen and reproduce the agential capacities of these new subjects.[74]

The problem, to which black power is the answer, is that agents in a class society are not absolutely incapacitated, but have taken on the qualities of power that are proper to the reproduction of class society. They bind themselves to the justifications that cohere capitalist power and white power. The spiritual corruption of which Boggs speaks is not merely privative, repressive, or distortive. In fact, the drive to exploit others rather than be exploited can enable one to become a subject with skills and attunements that qualify one as a legitimate member of society. Learning how to adapt to the impersonal demands of the markets and the continual revolution of production techniques can train one to see oneself as living up to one's responsibilities as an economic agent as well as feel that one is expressing a modicum of creativity and initiative. It can *appear* as if one if truly free.[75] In light of this problem description, the task of black power is to subvert and replace the ideological formations of class society on two fronts. First, black power will need to reshape the subjectivity or self-understandings of black agents who have been spiritually corrupted by class society. Second, the practice of black power will have to develop new skills for political decision-making.

This latter task is the sticking point for any alternative ideological formation. To merely desubjectify black agents by convincing them to see class society as unjustified or, at least, their position in class society as unjustified without the development of new skills will not be sufficient for overcoming the corruption of class society. We can imagine a scenario where an agent no longer sees their position in social life as

---

[74] Boggs seems to follow Marx and Engels from *The German Ideology*, in *Collected Works*, vol. 5 (New York: International Publishers, 1976), 53, where they conclude, "Both for the production on a mass scale of this communist consciousness, and for the success of the cause itself, the alteration of men on a mass scale is necessary, an alteration which can only take place in a practical movement, a *revolution*; the revolution is necessary, therefore, not only because the *ruling* class cannot be overthrown in any other way, but also because the class *overthrowing* it can only in a revolution succeed in ridding itself of all the muck of ages and become fitted to found society anew."

[75] "The market makes men free; it requires for its effective operation that all men be free and rational; yet the independent rational decisions of each man produce at every moment a configuration of forces which confronts each man compulsively" (Macpherson, *The Political Theory of Possessive Individualism*, 106).

legitimate, but does not have the social capacity to bring about a new state of affairs, so they continue on in the skills that they know.

Without this analysis of ideological formation as "subject-qualification" in a class society, black power can take many forms that Boggs would not consider revolutionary or progressive. In "The Myth of Black Capitalism" we can see Boggs attacking a form of black power that emphasizes self-determination at the point of subjectivity, but does not attempt to transform the skills or qualifications that would follow from this subjectivity.[76] Black empowerment becomes a call to become a more efficient and profitable member of class society rather than offering an alternative to class society as such. What makes black power "scientific" for Boggs is that it responds to the institutional life of racism as explained by class society and thus argues for a more thoroughgoing break from the corruption endemic to this social totality.

As thus outlined, Boggs's political thought appears to be caught on the horns of a dilemma. Either the civil rights that black people acquired will be ineffective because they are anchored in the form of life that is class society and thus continue their spiritual corruption, or the new rights of black power will be ineffective since they have no justificatory power in the dominant space of reasons.[77] The task, as Boggs sees it, is to make it such that black agents can emancipate themselves through their own self-activity. He would have to show how a utopian transformation could emerge from within the historical habits that have accumulated in class society.

Black Power as Ideological Self-Emancipation

Fundamentally, black power is the collective effort to resubjectify black agents *and* the rest of society as "revolutionists" rather than state subjects.[78] Becoming a "revolutionist" requires acquiring new

---

[76] James Boggs, *Racism and the Class Struggle: Further Pages from a Black Worker's Notebook* (New York: Monthly Review Press, 2020).
[77] Philip Pettit, *The State* (Princeton, NJ: Princeton University Press, 2023), 216.
[78] Sonja Buckel analyzes the tension between the hierarchical and differential subjectivations that occur in class societies and the need to reproduce some form of social cohesion through the law and legality in class societies: "Legal practices do not negate subjectivation and its isolating and hierarchising aspects, but they tie the subjects

habits of justifying our social practices. In *State and Revolution*, Lenin emphasizes that the withering away of the state has as much to do with its violent overthrow as it has to do with developing constitutive habits that will allow agents to develop new forms of life for governing themselves.[79] Moreover, whatever the gaps of the text, Lenin does not deny that overcoming the state means disavowing any representative institutions for governance.[80] Now it must be said that Boggs was responding to substantially different social conditions than Lenin was, and to novel historical problems. There was nothing like the mass movement to which Lenin responded, the state was anchored more deeply in the body politic than Lenin's state, and the reality of racial fetishism was far more salient. Boggs endeavored to conceptualize what a distinctly American revolution would be given the historical fragmentation of racial fetishism. He wanted to encourage the dominated to develop a self-conscious and transparent form of life that relied on the realization and satisfaction of human needs rather than accumulation of capital. Black power was a social *and* ideological revolution.

Therborn argues that ideologies relate subjects to questions of *what exists, what is good,* and *what is possible.*[81] The breakdown of justifications produces an ideological crisis concerning *what is taken to be good* (crisis consciousness, as discussed in chapter 1), but this does not mean that there will be an immediate apprehension of what ought to be done or what a reasonable society could look like (utopian consciousness). Most importantly, synchronizing these two forms of

---

together in an external unity. Concluding contracts, settling conflicts in court, as well as punitive and administrative acts are ways in which subjects practice their sociality. *The Legal form thus produces subjectivation and cohesion.*" Sonja Buckel, *Subjectivation and Cohesion: Towards the Reconstruction of a Materialist Theory of Law,* trans. Monika Vykoukal (Chicago: Haymarket Books, 2020), 232. See also Paul Hirst, *On Law and Ideology* (London: Macmillan Press, 1979) and Jan Rehmann, *Theories of Ideology: The Powers of Alienation and Subjection* (Chicago: Haymarket Books, 2013), 301–319.

[79] Lenin, *State and Revolution,* 68.
[80] "The way out of parliamentarism is to be found, of course, not in the abolition of the representative institutions and the elective principle, but in the conversion of the representative institutions from mere 'talking shops' into working bodies. . . . Without representative institutions we cannot imagine democracy, not even proletarian democracy; but we can and *must* think of democracy without parliamentarism" (Lenin, *State and Revolution,* 40–41).
[81] Therborn, *The Ideology of Power,* 18.

consciousness can transform what agents take to be *possible* and that is key for attaining the conditions of emancipation that will do away with racial fetishism.

Boggs believed that black power, sufficiently organized, can reshape the forms of life that have emerged in class society by opening spaces in social life for agents to bind themselves to new justifications in their conduct. Why Boggs would think this is premised on his observation that unemployed and working-class black people are systematically destabilized by the automation of work. He takes the unemployment and underemployment of black people to be an objective tendency within the class society of the United States that is not reducible to the overt or covert racist beliefs that white people may hold.[82] Countering this objective tendency will require more than a change in consciousness; it will require a transformation of the capacity for black people to act in concert.

Nevertheless, if black people are to act in concert they must do so self-consciously since the important problematic of racial fetishism is the tendency to misrepresent the effects of one's actions (i.e., race causes x, rather than race is an effect of our social practices) and to act according to justifications that one would not otherwise choose. This will require a critical transformation of black peoples' subjectivity away from the subjection of class society. Accomplishing the desubjectivation and consequent resubjectivation of black agents will require organizing a new form of life. Boggs differentiates his idea of a black power organization from "civil rights organizations that have been organized and financed by white citizens to integrate black citizens into the system."[83] It is not because Boggs is hostile to the idea of racial integration as such that he castigates civil rights organization. Rather the reason is that Boggs understands the subjective outcome of civil rights struggles as a commitment to "being equal to white Americans [but t]his is based on the assumption that the American

---

[82] Cf. Ture and Hamilton: "Institutional racism relies on the active and pervasive operation of anti-black attitudes and practices. A sense of superior group position prevails: whites are 'better' than blacks; therefore blacks should be subordinated to whites. This is a racist attitude and it permeates the society, on both the individual and institutional level, covertly and overtly" (*Black Power*, 5).

[83] Boggs, "Black Power," 178.

way of life (and American democracy) is itself a human way of life, an ideal worth striving for.... [T]he civil rights advocates evade the fact that the American way of life... has been achieved through systematic exploitation of others."[84] Once again, we see Boggs link the social practice of exploitation to a form of spiritual corruption that would stain the ideological formation of subjects. But there is something new in Boggs's formulation here: the standpoint for critiquing civil rights is the "human way of life." Boggs echoes Marx and Engels's 10th thesis from *Theses on Feuerbach* where they write, "The standpoint of the old materialism is civil society; the standpoint of the new is human society, or social humanity."[85]

Boggs takes his form of analysis from Marx's materialist writings and seeks to update it by confronting a situation where the working classes of highly developed capitalist countries have been "integrated into pillars of support for the capitalist system" and thus are ill-suited to play the role of revolutionary agents.[86] Insofar as society is arranged according to the drive of exploitation there is no reason to think that civil rights and civil society can remain autonomous from these productive relations. Boggs's key insight, presented perhaps hyperbolically, is that the struggle to attain the status of "equal" citizen takes for granted the exploitative relations of commodity exchange and thus forgoes the struggle to transcend the material basis of inequality.

The ideological foregrounding of citizenry, Boggs implies, naturalizes the current form of the state as the proper domain of rights rather than the self-activity of workers confronting a global market economy. The organization of black power aims to desubjectify

---

[84] Boggs, "Black Power," 177. Despite their differences Ture and Hamilton also insist against the assumption that integration is the sole imperative of black political action (*Black Power*, 40, 82).

[85] Karl Marx and Fredrick Engels, "Theses on Feuerbach," in *Collected Works*, vol. 5 (New York: International Publishers, 1976), 5. The humanism of Boggsian black power is explicit when he summarizes the end of black power revolutionizing "this society and human beings, liberating both society and man from the barbarism and the subjugation to inhuman forces into which they have been plunged by capitalism and racism. It aims to create new socially responsible, socially creative human beings" (*Pages from a Black Radical's Notebook*, 218). Also see Karen Ng, "Humanism: A Defense," *Philosophical Topics* 49, no. 1 (2021): 145–164.

[86] Boggs, "Black Power," 172.

unemployed and working-class black people from the standpoint of seeing themselves as citizens striving to become equal in American democracy and resubjectify these agents from the standpoint of a social humanity that transcends national borders. The task of identifying the source of social corruption in economic arrangements and cohering this new ideological standpoint falls to the "cadre-type organization whose members have ... no illusions about the necessities of a struggle for power."[87] What Boggs calls a cadre-organization is an autonomous political space where leaders attempt to bind and persuade unorganized black citizens to new norms of justification. Boggs thinks this is necessary because black agents developing new justifications does not happen spontaneously, but requires the formation of a counter-power. To repeat power, for Boggs, is a neutral concept. The basis of critique is not whether power is in play, but what sorts of justifications anchor social practices.

Boggs understands black power as the effort to accomplish ideological self-emancipation. The problem of spiritual "corruption" or "the muck of ages" is that it subjects agents to a matrix of practical illusions. In a class society, the world appears essentially as one cleaved between exploiter and exploited, winners and losers, the powerful and the dominated. It appears this way because of the actually existing forms of life required to reproduce class society.[88] Boggs's concern is that integration into class society via the ideology of civil rights will reconstitute the subjection of black people. Developing black power from within the counter-power of a cadre-organization dispels these illusions both cognitively and practically. The struggle for power that Boggs insists upon can only be understood as the power to take responsibility for one's ideas and the power to take responsibility for one's conduct rather than the struggle to attain state power. I will elaborate on each in turn.

Cognitively, black power is an exercise in political education insofar as it would allow black people to cognize the contradictory structure of their form of life rather than merely living it. Boggs points to the

---

[87] Boggs, "Black Power," 178.
[88] Charles W. Mills, "The Concept of Ideology in the Thought of Marx and Engels," *Owl of Minerva* 17, no. 2 (1986): 244–245.

continual reproduction of "the outsiders" in class society as evidence of its social contradiction. The promise of integration into the liberal polity runs up against the systematic exclusion of poor black citizens from the formal economy of waged life. The subjectivation of black power allows for the apprehension of these exclusions as intrinsic to the social logic of class society rather than an extrinsic anomaly. Boggs does not deny that many black people live these contradictions in their day-to-day lives, but what he thinks they lack is a coherent ideological explication of what their experiences mean. Political education enables blacks to emancipate their experience from the realm of abstraction and release it into concrete thought.[89]

The transition of experience to knowledge is not only epistemological on Boggs's account; it is normative. Grasping the corruptive tendencies of class society should also shift one's normative expectations. Boggs wants black people to ask: what should I want for myself? Hence the question "do I really want to integrate into a burning house?"[90] But this transformation of normative expectations are not arbitrary or moralistic. It emerges from the recognition that assent to class society would be unreasonable insofar as my conduct and my aim of self-determination are systematically rather than contingently at cross-purposes. I would be committing myself to a form of practical incoherence. Black power introduces a fork into black consciousness: either one commits to one's present conduct and forgoes self-determination or one commits to self-determination and forgoes one's present conduct. Boggs thought the current form of civil rights conceals this forced choice with the promise that one can reasonably unite one's conduct as a subject of class society and true self-determination. Boggs does not say as much but I think we can

---

[89] There is a relationship here between Boggs's ideology critique and feminist work on hermeneutic injustice and standpoint theory. See Nancy Hartsock, "The Feminist Standpoint: Developing the Ground for a Specifically Feminist Historical Materialism," in *Discovering Reality: Feminist Perspectives on Epistemology, Metaphysics, Methodology, and the Philosophy of Science*, ed. Sandra Harding and Merrill Hintikka (Dordrecht: D. Reidel, 1983), 283–310; Miranda Fricker, *Epistemic Injustice: Power and the Ethics of Knowing* (New York: Oxford University Press, 2007); Briana Toole, "From Standpoint Epistemology to Epistemic Oppression," *Hypatia* 34, no. 4 (2019): 598–618.

[90] James Baldwin, "The Fire Next Time," in *Collected Essays*, ed. Toni Morrison (1963; New York: The Library of America, 1998), 340.

conclude that he sees the state as a complex ideological formation that distorts our normative expectations.

Practically, black power should inspire black people to believe that they can effectively change society. Without a practical transformation of one's normative expectations the process of cognitive emancipation is liable to lapse into despair or cynicism. Boggs points to the practical transformation of the French Revolution, when ordinary people "became citizens rather than subjects" and instigated the end of feudalism.[91] He then claims that the Russian Revolution initiated another emancipatory movement when ordinary people recognized "the clear and conscious intent of going beyond capitalism and creating a socialist system."[92] Finally, in 1945, he argues there was the practical transformation of anticolonialism when "ordinary people all over the world unleashed a powerful struggle to rid themselves of the yoke of imperialism and colonialism."[93] Boggs cites these historical "turning points" because he understands black power as the movement of self-consciously inheriting these revolutionary moments when ordinary people changed the structures of social life. The self-conscious inheritance of this trans-ethnic revolutionary history is what makes black power a *revolutionary ideology* rather than an *ethnic ideology*.

Needless to say, the ethnic bases of all these historical revolutions are varied, and so it is not reasonable to think that black power refers to the ethnic consolidation of one's social group. The practical transformation that black power effects is to bring one's conduct in line with the conduct of past revolutionaries. Their conduct, as Boggs understands it, is a refusal to accept social integration into a contradictory form of life and thus develop the confidence in their capacity to emancipate themselves from a decaying society. To use Therborn's language, black power subjectifies and qualifies black people as revolutionaries rather than as liberal subjects dependent on the state: "People who are always calling upon others to free them from prison or from their miseries—people who have a victim mentality—don't make revolutions. They make liberals. Revolutionists make revolution."[94] The passage from

---

[91] Boggs, *Pages from a Black Radical's Notebook*, 255.
[92] Boggs, *Pages from a Black Radical's Notebook*, 256.
[93] Boggs, *Pages from a Black Radical's Notebook*, 256.
[94] Boggs, *Pages from a Black Radical's Notebook*, 261.

civil rights to black power is the crystallization of the power to emancipate oneself cognitively and practically from the normative expectations internal to the institutions of class society.

We are now in a position to definitively summarize the difference between the ethnic conception of black power as defended by Kwame Ture and Charles Hamilton and Boggsian black power. The former presumes that the cognitive and practical basis of black power is the understanding of oneself as part of an ethnic bloc within an ethnically segmented society.[95] If this is so, then black people ought to develop their conduct in accord with this analysis by engaging in ethnic self-defense or contestation. The latter understands itself as revolutionary rather than ethnic and thus forgoes a politics identified with blackness rather than the advancement of the whole society: "The black movement in the United States will not become a revolutionary movement until more of those who call themselves black revolutionaries are ready to accept the historical reality that, although our ancestors came from Africa, our future, like our past, is deeply rooted in the history of this country."[96] Boggs thinks ethnic valorization of any sort cannot help but become a form of particularist nationalism that disavows "the awesome responsibility for leading a revolution in the United States . . . [that] would require them to grapple with the real contradictions of this entire society because a revolutionist aims to change the political, social, and economic relations of everybody and for everybody in the particular society."[97] And it is this lesson that Boggs draws from prior revolutions.

Agency, for Boggs, is inescapably institutional. There is no question of being able to develop the agential capacities of black people as revolutionists without transforming the institutions of class society as whole. In this way, Boggs can bridge the tension between the seeming particularism of *black* power and *universal* freedom.

---

[95] "Black Power recognizes . . . the *ethnic* basis of American politics" (Ture and Hamilton, *Black Power*, 47).

[96] Boggs, *Pages from a Black Radical's Notebook*, 257.

[97] Boggs, *Pages from a Black Radical's Notebook*, 259. Boggs criticizes those who see the ideological aims of black power as finding evidence that there were once African kings and queens since this can only lead to the conclusion that there ought to be a type of society where the powerful dominate their subjects (257).

Self-emancipation is the emancipation of society. If I cannot be a self that is free to conduct myself according to the normative expectations of equality without institutions that make this a live possibility, then I will have to take responsibility for making institutions that will produce the coherence of conduct and norms. Boggs proclaims, "Socialist thought begins with the idea of advancing the society in which you have your roots so that all will benefit from the advance. Bourgeois thought begins with the idea of advancing some men and women at the expense of others. I take my stand with the advance of all men and women."[98] Boggs transcends the privative character of freedom that is reduced to *only* the non-interference of others in my goals and raises it up to the idea that emancipation is only realized through solidarity.[99]

Boggs's concept of black power enunciates the utopian kernel of self-emancipation. He does so despite concluding his co-authored book with Grace Lee Boggs with the proclamation that "there is no utopia, no final solution, no Promised Land.... [H]umankind will always be engaged in struggle, because struggle is in fact the highest expression of human creativity."[100] But if we set aside the "misplaced concreteness" of the idea that utopia is an actual place of perfection rather than the bursting asunder of ideological bonds of justification we can see that the conduct of revolutionists repeats the movement of utopian transformation.[101] Transparency of our justifications, democratic power over our economic form of time, and the concomitant withering away of racial fetishism are the necessary criteria of racial justice in our time. We cannot repeat the black power moment—we live in different historical conditions—but its ideal of self-emancipation remains as relevant as ever if utopia is to become a real source of power for social transformation.

---

[98] Boggs, *Pages from a Black Radical's Notebook*, 261.
[99] See Rochelle DuFord [Nathan DuFord], *Solidarity in Conflict: A Democratic Theory* (Stanford: Stanford University Press, 2022).
[100] Boggs and Boggs, *Revolution and Evolution in the Twentieth Century*, 266.
[101] A. N. Whitehead, *Science and the Modern World* (1953; New York: Free Press, 1925), ch. 3; Pettit, *The State*; Steven Gregory, "The 'Paradoxes' of Misplaced Concreteness: Thinking through the State," *Political Power and Social Theory* 15 (2002): 289–300.

Emancipation and the Standpoint of Utopia

I have aimed to show that Boggs provides important resources for formulating a critical theory of utopia by analyzing social life from the perspective of those who are systematically excluded from the power of justification. The analytic importance of "the outsiders" for Boggs is a social question concerning what happens to a society with growing ranks of men and women made obsolete by production. However, the outsiders are an ambivalent social group for him. They are a symptom of social disintegration and maladaptation as they often must resort to crime and antisocial behaviors since they cannot be integrated into society. But they are also the place of radical thinking since they "can only be absorbed into a totally new type of society."[102] There is an important parallel between Boggs and the Fanon of *The Wretched of the Earth*. The parallel is that for both Boggs and Fanon, the outsiders or lumpenproletariat, respectively, are the critical source for the total reorganization of society because "they have to find a new concept of how to live and let live among human beings.... [T]he outsiders, the workless people, now have to turn their thoughts away from trying to outwit the machines and instead toward the organization and reorganization of society and of human relations inside society."[103] Neither thinks this happens automatically or that they will inevitably succeed, but it is from their vantage point that the production of new rights through revolution becomes salient.

"The outsiders," insofar as they are banished to a non-place outside civil society and the formal labor market, challenge the coherence of racial justice as articulated from within the practices of class society. I have aimed to reconstruct a critical theory of utopia from the Boggsian account of black power. Boggs's ideology critique of class society attempts to re-anchor rights in a fundamentally different ideological space that demystifies capitalist power, white power, and even state power as the only horizon of normative expectations to which we can adhere.

---

[102] Boggs, "The American Revolution," 112.
[103] Boggs, "The American Revolution," 113.

In Boggs we find that rights are historically mediated by the social constraints of an era. While scarcity seemed to be permanent, the right to one's very life was connected to the duty to produce. But what becomes of rights once scarcity no longer obtains? Boggs calls for "a new Declaration of Human Rights to fit the New Age of Abundance."[104] Once rights are disarticulated from the necessities of production, we will discover that new values will have to emerge in our society. And so for Boggs rights, of necessity, must "fit" the existing forces of economic production. I think Boggs fruitfully outlines the interdependence of economy, social life, and political rights such that one cannot reasonably say that socialists/Marxists do not care about rights. Instead, thinkers like Boggs understand that rights must be anchored into the changing social practices of everyday life. It is not that we must do away with rights, but instead we should transform the conditions of life so that a new and more robust sense of right can be justified.

---

[104] Boggs, "The American Revolution," 109.

Conclusion

Marx famously includes in his analysis of commodity fetishism an invitation to "finally imagine, for a change, an association of free men, working with the means of production held in common, and expending their many different forms of labour-power in full self-awareness as one single social labour force."[1] This thought experiment emerges from Marx's analyses of different forms of life that allow him to demystify the "magic and necromancy" that tends to enshroud the social relations of capitalist societies.[2] Marx offers the "association of free men" as both a normative goal for a richer basis of social freedom *and* an imaginary juxtaposition that casts a critical light on the systemic dysfunctions that characterize capitalist forms of life. In other words, Marx is not only offering a prescription for what a future society should look like; he is, more importantly I think, generating conceptual resources for evaluating *this* life. This glimpse of an alternative form of life loosens the hold of the present on our subjectivity and thus allows our consciousness to hook into a different space of reasons from which transformative social practices may develop in "full self-awareness." There is what I would call a progressive "nonsynchronicity" in this image that opens the way for us to cast our anchor beyond the horizons of our fetishistic form of life.

The process of emancipation, I have argued, entails subjective emancipation. What I have called "utopian consciousness" in the first chapter is more comprehensive than wishes or hopes for a better world. One can wish for a better world and not believe that it is possible. Or one may have hopes for a better life, but find these hopes are premised upon the acceptance of, and integration into, existing

---

[1] Karl Marx, *Capital: A Critique of Political Economy*, vol. 1, trans. Ben Fowkes, intro. Ernest Mandel (New York: Penguin Classics, 1990), 171.
[2] Marx, *Capital*, 169.

relations of domination and unfreedom. What I have developed is an account of utopia as a historical tendency toward dissolving social relations of domination and unfreedom. Paul Ricœur's phenomenological analyses suggest that we should understand the "functional structure" of utopia as the subversion of the social roles that tend to integrate subjects into a definite form of life. Utopia casts a glance on our social relations from a "nowhere" that relativizes and estranges practical consciousness from the ideas it has inherited from the past.[3]

Sylvia Wynter offers a resonant account of utopia and emancipatory subjectivity in her analyses of the black aesthetics, black arts, and black studies movements of the 1960s and 1970s in the United States. She analyzes this "psychically emancipatory movement" that called into question the systemic racial denigration of black people, in particular, and non-white humanity, in general.[4] Wynter has two central aims in this essay. First, she wants to bring to the fore the territory of opaque social relations and values that induce black agents into experiences of self-alienation and submission. Much like Ricœur, Wynter argues that the revalorization of one's blackness aimed at contesting the legitimacy of social roles that enforced racial hierarchies of value. Second, and more importantly, Wynter implores us to see that these aesthetics movements were also movements of *self*-emancipation that attempted to uproot the social conditions that anchored and reproduced domination, dependency, and unfreedom. What Wynter calls "psychic emancipation" is the de-reifying movement of agents understanding themselves as the source of emancipation and refusing the social relations that have made opaque the role of human agencies in putting in place "allocations, divisions of labor, and structuring hierarchies."[5] What makes the moment of psychic emancipation necessary, but by no means sufficient, is that those who would be emancipated must know *themselves* to be the emancipators and, thus, preserve the experience

---

[3] Paul Ricœur, *Lectures on Ideology and Utopia*, ed. George H. Taylor (New York: Columbia University Press, 1986), 16–17.
[4] Sylvia Wynter, "On How We Mistook the Map for the Territory, and Re-imprisoned Ourselves in Our Unbearable Wrongness of Being, of *Désêtre*," in *Not Only the Master's Tools: African American Studies in Theory and Practice*, ed. Lewis R. Gordon and Jane Anna Gordon (New York: Routledge, 2006), 115.
[5] Wynter, "Map for the Territory," 134.

CONCLUSION 221

of self-transparent social autonomy so often denied under conditions of racial reification.

What Wynter preserves, and Ricœur neglects, is the *historical* basis of utopian processes of emancipation. Ricœur's focus on the phenomenological structure tends to place utopia in an unending relationship to the forces of ideological integration. The abstract dialectic of integration and subversion effaces the historical transmission of utopian consciousness that subtends *both* conditions of crisis and seeming stability so long as social relations of domination and unfreedom persist. Wynter attempts to rekindle for present-day consciousness the concrete memory of self-emancipation and universality that began to emerge in the black arts/aesthetics/studies movements before they were reabsorbed by the inertia of the academy and transformed into mere "ethnic" studies of particularity.

The process of emancipation is always a question of how to inherit these "failed" moments of social emancipation. The role of critical theory, as I understand it, is neither to mirror past struggles for emancipation as if nothing has changed nor to instruct present consciousness about what an emancipated future must look like.[6] The work of critical theory is to preserve and reconstruct what remains *unfinished* in the project of self-emancipation as a resource for elucidating the reifications of the present. This is precisely what I hope to have accomplished by returning to the, by no means exhaustive, historical contexts of the thinkers in the present volume. While Ricœur emphasizes the *subversive* tendencies of utopia, I prefer Ernst Bloch's description of the utopian function as historical reservoirs of *explosive* material that activate all-too-often blocked and suppressed tendencies toward self-emancipation.[7]

---

[6] See Dan Swain, *None So Fit to Break the Chains: Marx's Ethics of Self-Emancipation* (Boston: Brill, 2019), 55–63.

[7] Ernst Bloch, *The Principle of Hope*, vol. 1, trans. Neville Plaice, Stephen Plaice, and Paul Knight (Cambridge, MA: MIT Press, 1986), 146. See also Filippo Mennozi, "Inheriting Marx: Daniel Bensäid, Ernst Bloch and the Discordance of Time," *Historical Materialism* 28, no. 1 (2020): 150. Even Karl Mannheim describes utopia as only those practices that "when they pass over into conduct, tend *to shatter*, either partially or wholly, the order of things prevailing at the time." Karl Mannheim, *Ideology and Utopia: An Introduction to the Sociology of Knowledge* (Mansfield Centre, CT: Martino, 2015), 173.

I take this to be a key element of Wynter's thinking and follow her in this respect. Racial reification blocks the progressive role of reason in the activity of self-emancipation. The emotional intensity that often accompanies utopian consciousness is not, contrary to many critics of utopia, necessarily an abdication of reason, but the experience of reengaging it at the center of social practices. The demand and promise of self-emancipation as well as the defense of utopia's role in emancipatory processes has been the central argument of this book. Dictating how people will organize social life under conditions they themselves have emancipated is not the proper role of critical theory.

This is why I have had little to say about what the "utopia" of a racially just society would look like in day-to-day life. I have not done so for three reasons. First, I think a critical theory of utopia ought to be accompanied by a healthy amount of *epistemic humility* as it concerns the full content of a future form of life. There is no reason to think that the critical theorist can play the role of either fortune-teller or social engineer given that they, themselves, are a part of the very same historical processes that they aim to critique.[8] I think we overburden the "utopia" of utopian critical theory if we deem it is only legitimate insofar as it tells us what a fully resolved future looks like. Such a construal of utopia has led to its overly hasty dismissal by self-proclaimed "realists" and led proponents to overestimate the power of their own ideas.[9] Instead, the criteria for success of a critical theory of utopia are how cogently it diagnoses sources of unfreedom and how well it elaborates principles for expanding our horizons of normative expectation.

My second reason for refusing to offer a full picture of what a racially just society would look like is that it would be superfluous for the task at hand: enunciating *principles* of social emancipation vis-à-vis a specific problem in our social life. These principles have been

---

[8] Fredric Jameson insists that utopia at its most fruitful brings us into contact with "our constitutional inability to imagine Utopia itself, and this, not owing to any individual failure of imagination but as the result of systemic, cultural, and ideological closure of which we are all one way or another prisoners." Fredric Jameson, "Progress versus Utopia: Or, Can We Imagine the Future?," *Science Fiction Studies* 9, no. 2 (July 1982): 153.

[9] See Charles Mills, *Radical Theory, Caribbean Reality: Race, Class and Social Domination* (Kingston: University of West Indies Press, 2010), ch. 1.

1) transparency of social relations; 2) control over social time; and 3) equal and revisable justifications of power. I have developed my account of these principles from my analysis of "racial fetishism" that I take to be a problem that is specific to capitalist societies. Utopian principles for a transformed life are developed in a reciprocal relationship with historically salient problems. This means they are both immanent to historical forms of life and context-transcendent insofar as they point beyond a given form of life. If these principles center the importance of social conditions for creativity, autonomy, and collective determination, then the full content of a new form of life *must not* be up to the individual critical theorist, but the inventiveness of the newly free subjects. However, this does raise a complicated question concerning the temporality of critical theory itself: Do these principles emerge because the "problem" is already known, or does the "problem" only appear as a problem once the principles are selected?

My third reason for not engaging in traditional utopian theorizing is that I understand the temporal activity that is constitutive of a critical theory of utopia as foreclosing any reasonable conjecture about the concrete details of a new form of life. A critical theory of utopia is *both non-synchronous and synchronous* with our contemporary form of life. It is non-synchronous because its analyses and deployment of concepts are necessarily estranged from the common sense and fetishism of a given form of life. Nevertheless, a critical theory of utopia could only produce non-synchronous effects because it remains necessarily determined by the form of life being criticized. The problem spaces created by a critical theory of utopia can only desediment lines of inquiry into possible avenues for social transformation, but it cannot predict where those lines of inquiry may lead in practice. It is the dual temporalities of utopian critical theory that generates its creative reflexivity concerning our forms of life *and* constrains it from irresponsibly detailing what a new form of life will look like.

These three constraints on utopian critical theory (epistemic humility, formal principles, and non-synchronicity/synchronicity) might seem to make utopia simply another name for "reformism." I have tried to show why this is not the case. I began with an exploration of the relationship between "crisis consciousness" and "utopian consciousness" in order to show how struggles for racial justice periodically run up against the limits of our form of life in order to transcend them. The *experience* of breakdown in social norms may generate new *expectations* for how social life should be organized and toward what ends. What makes the relationship between the two forms of consciousness specific—what keeps crisis consciousness from reverting to the mere awareness that racial injustices exist—is precisely the critical experience that a form of life has limits, and these limits may be transcended. However, the confrontation of a limit is not the same as knowing what is on the other side. The peculiar temporality of utopian consciousness consists in the fact that it is not the experiential knowledge of a new form of life, but the critical experience of a lack of experience. Utopia is always "over there" or "not yet" and never where and when we are. Thus, it is a time and space that we have never directly experienced. We can only expect it.

Elucidating the structure of expectation responds to what Dan Swain has described as the "paradox" of self-emancipation given that "self-activity in the future must arise on the basis of self-activity in the present, within a society that consistently thwarts the possibility of self-activity."[10] Indeed, we have good reason to think that we are not yet free of the "muck of ages."[11] However, my central contention has been that history is not the accumulation of past modes of domination, but instead is the conflict *between* domination and utopian tendencies toward self-emancipation. Boggs understood that it was only by organizing and strengthening these implicit tendencies toward self-emancipation that transformed social creatures could emerge. All the thinkers I have discussed held the view that beneath the naturalized and eternalized relations of racial domination roiled conflictual tendencies always threatening to break in on the present. The reified life of capitalist societies requires a utopian critique that clarifies these already existing non-synchronous tendencies.

When these utopian tendencies do "appear" in our experience they appear as interruptions or disruptions of our recursive habits in everyday life by introducing new horizons of normative expectations for

---

[10] Swain, *None So Fit*, 37.
[11] Karl Marx and Friedrich Engels, *Collected Works*, vol. 5 (New York: International Publishers, 1976), 53.

how the world could be. Reinhart Koselleck insists that this gap, or non-synchronicity, between experience and expectation structures temporal life: "Past and future never coincide, or just as little as an expectation in its entirety can be deduced from experience.... The one cannot be transferred into the other without interruption. Even if one could formulate this as an irrefutable experiential statement, no precise expectations could be deduced from it."[12] What he is getting at is that experience is the accumulation of past expectations that have already occurred, while future expectations may or may not correspond to these past expectations. He continues:

> Whoever believes himself capable of deducing his expectations in their entirety from his experience is in error. If something happens in a way different from what was expected, one learns from it. On the other hand, whoever fails to base his expectations on experience is likewise in error. He should have known better. There is clearly an aporia here that is resolved in the course of time.... In history, what happens is always more or less than what is contained by the given conditions.[13]

Utopia, as a new horizon of normative expectations, confronts past experience with its own limit, with its own inability to deductively predict what will be. The simultaneity of experience and non-experience may induce people to demand and expect new forms of life. These new expectations will become a new sediment for experience that may provoke demands that exceed our current form of life.

Nothing guarantees that utopian consciousness will appear "on time," that the conditions will be ripe for social transformation. Indeed, I have been keen to show that a persistent feature of utopian consciousness is that it generates a sense of untimeliness. It demands too much, too soon or else it arrives much too late and misses its moment.[14] Struggles for racial emancipation, in every historical era, encounter

---

[12] Reinhart Koselleck, *Futures Past: On the Semantics of Historical Time*, trans. Keith Tribe (Cambridge, MA: MIT Press, 1985), 272, 274.
[13] Koselleck, *Futures Past*, 274.
[14] See Frantz Fanon, *Black Skin, White Masks*, trans. Richard Philcox (New York: Grove Press, 2008), xi; Frantz Fanon *Œuvres* (Paris: Éditions La Découverte, 2011), 63.

some form of rationalization that insists that the expectations of the dominated are premature or would require upending a form of life that is too historically entrenched. My point has been to show that the racial fetishism of our form of life tends to block out utopian consciousness by attenuating the social experience of new horizons of normative expectations. "Race" appears as a permanent feature of our world, as a seemingly unsurpassable horizon that continually binds us to the experiences of history rather than future expectations. The question I have been trying to answer throughout this book is whether the untimeliness of utopia or its seemingly inevitable failure can play any role in social emancipation.

I think it can. Whether we look at the "failure" of Du Bois's "Talented Tenth," Delany and Garvey's black nationalism, Fanon's inventive existentialism, or Boggs's black power we find counterprinciples that give us a glimpse of a new form of life. These counterprinciples achieve their salience in relation to a form of life that I have characterized as afflicted with racial fetishism. This means that if we were to achieve a wholly new form of life beyond capitalist social relations then the normative principles I have drawn from their thinking may no longer have the utopian function that I have imputed to them. But what Jean-Paul Sartre says of Marxism applies for any critical theory of utopia: the point is not to hold onto a critical theory, but to achieve a world where it becomes obsolete.[15] That there will be new problems that require new experiences is not an embarrassment for utopian critical theory, but its hope. Kathi Weeks argues that the function of utopia is twofold: 1) it aims to negate the hold of the present through the experience of estrangement, and 2) it provokes this estrangement by orienting us to a glimpse of a substantially different future.[16] These functions are always related to a determinate form of life, and if that form of life were to be overcome then new

---

[15] "As soon as there exists *for everyone* a margin of *real* freedom beyond the production of life, Marxism will have lived out its span; a philosophy of freedom will take its place. But we have no means, no intellectual instrument, no concrete experience which allows us to conceive of this freedom or of this philosophy." Jean-Paul Sartre, *Search for a Method*, trans. Hazel E. Barnes (New York: Vintage Books, 1968), 34.

[16] Kathi Weeks, *The Problem with Work: Feminism, Marxism, Antiwork Politics, and Postwork Imaginaries* (Durham, NC: Duke University Press, 2011), 205.

glimpses of new futures would have to emerge in relationship to new conflicts.

However, I think one question remains: If utopia names novel future expectations, then why have I focused solely on historical thinkers? One might think that to read and analyze figures from as far back as a century ago is to forestall contemporary questions of the future. I have turned to the past because these thinkers represent political ideas that have sedimented our present practices and thus shaped our experiences. The problem is that these ideas have been too easily absorbed into or excluded from the dominant justification narratives that support our form of life. If a critical theory of utopia cannot change the world it can at least elucidate the discordant temporalities buried in history in the hopes that utopian consciousness can learn from them in practice. I have insisted throughout this book that utopian temporality is immanent to our form of life, but often fetishisticly disavowed. I have hoped to mobilize these thinkers and their ideas so that we are confronted with the experience of utopia that will induce us to create new spaces of reason and justificatory power.

Without these new spaces of reason, social action will remain inhibited by the fragmentary experience that is immanent to capitalist social relations. I hope to have shown that even if they did not name it the figures covered in this book were struggling against a racial fetishism that forecloses new expectations and temporalities. My aim has been to reconstruct them in this light. We live lives that are temporally out of joint with any notion of a novel future that proceeds from reasonable and justifiable collective practices. Racial injustice compounds this condition by excluding or weakening the capacity of the dominated to bind others to free and equal norms of regard. Overcoming racial fetishism should lead us to expect a form of life that does not necessitate exclusion and domination. I have argued that capitalist social relations do, in fact, impose relations of domination. Here I hope that I have shown the critical usefulness of utopia for struggles against racial injustice. I cannot pretend to know what a new form of life will look like, but I hope to have raised a mirror to the problems of ours.[17]

---

[17] Fanon, *Black Skin, White Masks*, 161; Fanon, *Œuvres*, 211.

Bibliography

Aboulaifa, Mitchell. 2010. *Transcendence: On Self-Determination and Cosmopolitanism.* Stanford: Stanford University Press.
Adam, Barbara. 1995. *Timewatch: The Social Analysis of Time.* Cambridge, UK: Polity Press.
Adorno, Theodor. 1972. *Aspects of Sociology* translated by John Viertel. Boston: Beacon Press.
Adorno, Theodor. 2005. *Critical Models: Interventions and Catchwords,* translated by Henry W. Pickford, introduction by Lydia Goehr. New York: Columbia University Press.
Adorno, Theodor W. 2005. "Marginalia to Theory and Praxis." In *Critical Models: Interventions and Catchwords,* translated by Henry W. Pickford, 259–278. New York: Columbia University Press.
Akinnibi, Fola. 2021. "NYC's Violent Crime Is Up; So Is the City's Police Budget." *Bloomberg,* May 6. https://www.bloomberg.com/news/articles/2021-05-06/new-york-city-s-police-budget-is-increasing-again.
Alcoff, Linda Martín. 2007. "Epistemologies of Ignorance: Three Types." In *Race and Epistemologies of Ignorance,* edited by Shannon Sullivan and Nancy Tuana, 39–59. New York: SUNY Press.
Alexander, Michelle. 2010. *The New Jim Crow: Mass Incarceration in the Age of Colorblindness.* New York: New Press.
Allen, Robert Loring. 1969. *Black Awakening in Capitalist America: An Analytic History.* Garden City, NY: Doubleday.
Alridge, Derrick P. 2008. *The Educational Thought of W. E. B. Du Bois: An Intellectual History.* New York: Teachers College Press.
Althusser, Louis. (1970) 2014. *On the Reproduction of Capitalism: Ideology and Ideological State Apparatuses,* translated by G. M. Goshgarian, introduction by Jacques Bidet. London: Verso.
Althusser, Louis. 2001. "Ideology and Ideological State Apparatuses (Notes towards an Investigation)." In *Lenin and Philosophy and Other Essays,* translated by Ben Brewster, 85–127. New York: Monthly Review Press.
Anderson, Benedict. 2003. *Imagined Communities: Reflections on the Origin and Spread of Nationalism.* New York: Verso.
Appiah, Kwame Anthony. 1985. "The Uncompleted Argument: Du Bois and the Illusion of Race." *Critical Inquiry* 12, no. 1 (October): 21–37.
Appiah, Kwame Anthony. 2014. *Lines of Descent: W. E. B. Du Bois and the Emergence of Identity.* Cambridge, MA: Harvard University Press.
Arendt, Hannah. 1998. *The Human Condition.* 2nd edition, introduction by Margaret Canovan. Chicago: University of Chicago Press.
Baldwin, James. 1988. *Collected Essays,* edited by Toni Morrison. New York: Library of America.

Balibar, Étienne. 2007. *The Philosophy of Marx*, translated by Chris Turner. New York: Verso.
Ballestín, Lucas. 2023. "Žižek's Politics of Fetishism." *Philosophy Today* 67, no. 3: 1–19.
Bell, Derrick A., Jr. 1995. "Brown v. Board of Education and the Interest Convergence Dilemma." In *Critical Race Theory: The Key Writings That Formed the Movement*, edited by Kimberlé Crenshaw, Neil Gotanda, Gary Peller, and Kendall Thomas. 20–29. New York: New Press.
Benhabib, Seyla. 1986. *Critique, Norm, and Utopia: A Study of the Foundations of Critical Theory*. New York: Columbia University Press.
Bensaïd, Daniel. 2002. *Marx for Our Times: Adventures and Misadventures of a Critique*, translated by Gregory Elliott. New York: Verso.
Berman, Russell A. 1997. "Du Bois and Wagner: Race, Nation, and Culture between the United States and Germany." *German Quarterly* 70, no. 2: 123–135.
Bernasconi, Robert. 1996. "Casting the Slough: Fanon's New Humanism for a New Humanity." In *Fanon: A Critical Reader*, edited by Lewis R. Gordon, T. Denean Sharpley-Whiting, and Renée T. White. Oxford: Blackwell.
Bernasconi, Robert. 2009. "'Our Duty to Conserve': W. E. B. Du Bois's Philosophy of History in Context." *South Atlantic Quarterly* 108, no. 3 (Summer): 519–540.
Bernasconi, Robert. 2023. *Critical Philosophy of Race*. New York: Oxford University Press.
Bloch, Ernst. 1977. "Nonsynchronism and the Obligation to Dialectics," translated by Mark Ritter. *New German Critique* 11 (Spring): 22–38.
Bloch, Ernst. 1988. "Something's Missing: A Discussion between Ernst Bloch and Theodor W. Adorno on the Contradictions of Utopian Longing." In *The Utopian Function of Art and Literature: Selected Essays*, translated by Jack Zipes and Frank Mecklenburg. 1–18. Cambridge, MA: MIT Press.
Bloch, Ernst. 1988. *The Utopian Function of Art and Literature: Selected Essays*, translated by Jack Zipes and Frank Mecklenburg. Cambridge, MA: MIT Press.
Bloch, Ernst. 1991. *Heritage of Our Times*, translated by Neville Plaice and Stephen Plaice. Cambridge, UK: Polity Press.
Bloch, Ernst. 1995. *The Principle of Hope*. Vol. 1, translated by Neville Plaice, Stephen Plaice, and Paul Knight. Cambridge, MA: MIT Press.
Bloch, Ernst. 1996. *Natural Law and Human Dignity*, translated by Dennis J. Schmidt. Cambridge, MA: MIT Press.
Bloch, Ernst. 2006. *Traces*, translated by Anthony A. Nassar. Stanford: Stanford University Press.
Bloch, Ernst. 2009. *Atheism in Christianity*, translated by J. T. Swann, introduction by Peter Thompson. New York: Verso.
Blumenfeld, Jacob. 2023. "Climate Barbarism: Adapting to a Wrong World." *Constellations* 30, no. 2: 162–178.
Boggs, James. 2011. *Pages from a Black Radical's Notebook: A James Boggs Reader*, edited by Stephen M. Ward. Detroit, MI: Wayne State University Press.
Boggs, James. 2011. "The American Revolution." In *Pages from a Black Radical's Notebook: A James Boggs Reader*, edited by Stephen M. Ward, 83–174. Detroit, MI: Wayne State University Press.

Boggs, James. 2011. "Black Power: A Scientific Concept Whose Time Has Come." In *Pages from a Black Radical's Notebook: A James Boggs Reader*, edited by Stephen M. Ward, 171–180. Detroit, MI: Wayne State University Press.

Boggs, James. 2011. "Liberation or Revolution." In *Pages from a Black Radical's Notebook: A James Boggs Reader*, edited by Stephen M. Ward, 293–306. Detroit, MI: Wayne State University Press.

Boggs, James. 2020. *Racism and the Class Struggle: Further Pages from a Black Worker's Notebook*. New York: Monthly Review Press.

Boggs, James, and Grace Lee Boggs. 1974. *Revolution and Evolution in the Twentieth Century*. New York: Monthly Review Press.

Bonacich, Edna. 1972. "A Theory of Ethnic Antagonism: The Split Labor Market." *American Sociological Review* 37: 547–559.

Bonilla-Silva, Eduardo. 2009. *Racism without Racists*. 3rd edition. Lanham, MD: Rowman & Littlefield.

Boxill, Bernard. 1992. *Blacks and Social Justice*. Revised edition. Lanham, MD: Rowman & Littlefield.

Bromell, Nick. 2021. *The Powers of Dignity: The Black Political Philosophy of Frederick Douglass*. Durham, NC: Duke University Press.

Brown, Cliff. 1998. "Racial Conflict and Split Labor Markets: The AFL Campaign to Organize Steel Workers, 1918–1919." *Social Science History* 22, no. 3: 319–347.

Brown, Jayna. 2021. *Black Utopias: Speculative Life and the Music of Other Worlds*. Durham, NC: Duke University Press.

Brown, Robert A., and Todd C. Shaw. 2002. "Separate Nations: Two Attitudinal Dimensions of Black Nationalism." *Journal of Politics* 64, no. 1: 22–44. https://doi.org/10.1111/1468-2508.00116.

Brown, Wendy. 2002. "Suffering the Paradox of Human Rights." In *Left Legalism/Left Critique*, edited by Wendy Brown and Janet Halley, 420–434. Durham, NC: Duke University Press.

Buckel, Sonja. 2020. *Subjectivation and Cohesion: Towards the Reconstruction of a Materialist Theory of Law*, translated by Monika Vykoukal. Chicago: Haymarket Books.

Burke, Edmund. 2003. *Reflections on the Revolution in France*, edited by Frank M. Turner. New Haven, CT: Yale University Press.

Byerman, Keith Eldon. 1994. *Seizing the Word: History, Art, and Self in the Work of W. E. B. Du Bois*. Athens: University of Georgia Press.

Caldwell, Bruce. 2005. *Hayek's Challenge: An Intellectual biography of F. A. Hayek*. Chicago: University of Chicago Press.

Callinicos, Alex. 1988. *Making History: Agency, Structure, and Change in Social Theory*. Ithaca, NY: Cornell University Press.

Calnitsky, David, and Michael Billeaux Martinez. 2023. "A Class Functionalist Theory of Race." *Du Bois Review* 20, no. 2: 239–267. https://doi.org/10.1017/S1742058X22000224.

Camfield, David. 2016. "Elements of a Historical-Materialist Theory of Racism." *Historical Materialism* 24, no. 1: 31–70.

Celikates, Robin. 2018. *Critique as Social Practice: Critical Theory and Social Self-Understanding*, translated by Naomi van Steenbergen. New York: Rowman & Littlefield.

Césaire, Aimé. 2000. *Discourse on Colonialism*, translated by Joan Pinkham. New York: Monthly Review Press.

Chandler, Nahum Dimitri. 2014. *X—The Problem of the Negro as a Problem for Thought*. New York: Fordham University Press.

Claeys, Gregory, and Lyman Tower Sargent. 2017. "Preface." In *The Utopia Reader*, edited by Gregory Claeys and Lyman Tower Sargent, xiii–xv. New York: New York University Press.

Clegg, John. 2015. "Capitalism and Slavery." *Critical Historical Studies* 2, no. 2: 281–304.

Clegg, John. 2020. "A Theory of Capitalist Slavery." *Journal of Historical Sociology* 33, no. 1: 74–98.

Cobben, Paul. 2015. *Value in Capitalist Society: Rethinking Marx's Criticism of Capitalism*. Leiden: Brill.

Cohen, G. A. 2008. *Rescuing Justice and Equality*. Cambridge, MA: Harvard University Press.

Colletti, Lucio. 1974. *From Rousseau to Lenin: Studies in Ideology and Society*, translated by John Merrington and Judith White. New York: Monthly Review Press.

Cooke, Maeve. 2006. "Resurrecting the Rationality of Ideology Critique: Reflection on Laclau on Ideology." *Constellations* 13, no. 1: 4–20.

Costa, M. Victoria. 2009. "Neo-republicanism, Freedom as Non-domination, and Citizen Virtue." *Politics, Philosophy & Economics* 8, no. 4: 401–419. https://doi.org/10.1177/1470594X09343079.

Cowherd, Carrie. 2003. "The Wings of Atalanta: Classical Influences in *The Souls of Black Folk*." In *The Souls of Black Folk: One Hundred Years Later*, edited by Dolan Hubbard, 284–298. Columbia: University of Missouri Press.

Cruse, Harold. 1984. *The Crisis of the Negro Intellectual*. New York: Quill.

Curry, Tommy J. 2017. *The Man-Not: Race, Class, Genre, and the Dilemmas of Black Manhood*. Philadelphia: Temple University Press.

Darby, Derrick. 2001. "Two Conceptions of Rights Possession." *Social Theory and Practice* 27, no. 3: 387–417. https://doi.org/10.5840/soctheorpract20012732.

Darby, Derrick. 2003. "Unnatural Rights." *Canadian Journal of Philosophy* 33, no. 1: 49–82.

Darby, Derrick. 2009. *Race, Rights, and Recognition*. Cambridge, UK: Cambridge University Press.

Darby, Derrick. 2020. "XI—Rights Externalism and Racial Injustice." *Proceedings of the Aristotelian Society* 120, no. 3: 253–276. https://doi.org/10.1093/arisoc/aoaa014.

Davis, Angela Y. 1998. "Black Nationalism: The Sixties and the Nineties." In *The Angela Y. Davis Reader*, edited by Joy James 289–293. Cambridge, MA: Blackwell.

Davis, Angela Y. 2003. *Are Prisons Obsolete?* New York: Seven Stories Press.

Davis, Brandon R. 2023. "The Politics of Racial Abjection." *Du Bois Review* 20, no. 1: 143–162.

Dawson, Michael C. 2001. *Black Visions: The Roots of Contemporary African-American Political Ideologies*. Chicago: University of Chicago Press.

Dawson, Michael. 2021. "Marcus Garvey: The Black Prince?" In *African American Political Thought: A Collected History*, edited by Melvin L. Rogers and Jack Turner. 260–290. Chicago: University of Chicago Press.

BIBLIOGRAPHY   233

Delany, Martin Robison, and Robert S. Levine. 2003. *Martin R. Delany: A Documentary Reader*. Chapel Hill: University of North Carolina Press.

Descombes, Vincent. 2014. *The Institutions of Meaning: A Defense of Anthropological Holism*, translated by Stephen Adam Schwartz. Cambridge, MA: Harvard University Press.

Dings, Roy. 2021. "Meaningful Affordances." *Synthese* 199: 1855–1875.

Douglas, Andrew J., and Jared A. Loggins. 2021. *Prophet of Discontent: Martin Luther King Jr. and the Critique of Racial Capitalism*. Athens: University of Georgia Press.

Douglass, Frederick. (1852) 2020. "What to the Slave Is the Fourth of July?" In *My Bondage and My Freedom*, 368–373. New Haven, CT: Yale University Press. https://doi.org/10.12987/9780300199338-035.

Draper, Theodore. 1970. *The Rediscovery of Black Nationalism*. New York: Viking Press.

D'Souza, Radha. 2018. *What's Wrong with Rights? Social Movements, Law and Liberal Imaginations*. London: Pluto Press.

Du Bois, W. E. B. 1897. Review of "Race Traits and Tendencies of the American Negro, by Frederick Hoffman." In *Annals of the American Academy of Political Science* 9, no. 1: 127–133.

Du Bois, W. E. B. (1906) 2022. "W.E.B. Du Bois (1906), 'L'Ouvrier Negre En Amérique [The Negro Worker in America],' *Revue Économique Internationale*, 3:298–348," translated by Aaron Major. *Critical Sociology*, 1–25. https://doi-org.myaccess.library.utoronto.ca/10.1177/08969205221138011.

Du Bois, W. E. B. 1918. "Close Ranks." *The Crisis* 16, no. 3 (July): 111.

Du Bois, W. E. B. (1920) 2016. *Darkwater: Voices from within the Veil*, introduction by Manning Marable. New York: Verso.

Du Bois, W. E. B. 1926. "Criteria of Negro Art." *The Crisis* 32 (October): 290–297.

Du Bois, W. E. B. (1940) 2007. *Dusk of Dawn: An Essay toward an Autobiography of a Race Concept*. Oxford: Oxford University Press.

Du Bois, W. E. B. 1968. *The Autobiography of W. E. B. DuBois: A Soliloquy on Viewing My Life from the Last Decade of Its First Century*. New York: International Publishers.

Du Bois, W. E. B. 1978. "W. E. B. Du Bois to Herbert Aptheker, January 10, 1956." In *The Correspondence of W. E. B. Du Bois*, vol. 3: *Selections 1944–1963*, edited by Herbert Aptheker, 394–396. Amherst: University of Massachusetts Press.

Du Bois, W. E. B. 1994. *The Souls of Black Folk*. Mineola, NY: Dover.

Du Bois, W. E. B. 1996. "The Talented Tenth." In *The Future of the Race*, edited by Henry Louis Gates and Cornel West, 127–144. New York: Alfred A. Knopf.

Du Bois, W. E. B. 1997. "Worlds of Color: The Negro Mind Reaches Out." In *The New Negro: Voices of the Harlem Renaissance*, edited by Alain Locke, introduction by Arnold Rampersad, 385–415. New York: Touchstone.

Du Bois, W. E. B. 2000. "The Conservation of Races." In *The Idea of Race*, edited by Robert Bernasconi and Tommy L. Lott, 108–118. Indianapolis, IN: Hackett.

Du Bois, W. E. B. 2000. "Sociology Hesitant." *boundary 2* 27, no. 3 (Fall): 37–44.

Du Bois, W. E. B. 2013. "The Development of a People." *Ethics* 123, no. 3 (April): 525–544.

Du Bois, W. E. B. 2015. "The Afro-American" (1894). In *The Problem of the Color Line at the Turn of the Twentieth Century: The Essential Early Essays*, edited by Nahum Dimitri Chandler, 33–50. New York: Fordham University Press.

Du Bois, W. E. B. 2015. "The Present Outlook for the Dark Races of Mankind" (1900). In *The Problem of the Color Line at the Turn of the Twentieth Century: The Essential Early Essays*, edited by Nahum Dimitri Chandler, 111–138. New York: Fordham University Press.

Du Bois, W. E. B. 2015. "The Study of Negro Problems" (1894). In *The Problem of the Color Line at the Turn of the Twentieth Century: The Essential Early Essays*, edited by Nahum Dimitri Chandler, 77–98. New York: Fordham University Press.

DuFord, Rochelle [Nathan DuFord]. 2022. *Solidarity in Conflict: A Democratic Theory*. Stanford: Stanford University Press.

Edwards, Barrington S. 2006. "W. E. B Du Bois between Worlds: Berlin, Empirical Social Research, and the Race Question." *Du Bois Review* 3, no. 2: 395–424.

Ellis, Mark. 1992. "'Closing Ranks' and 'Seeking Honors': W. E. B. Du Bois in World War I." *Journal of American History* 79, no. 1 (June): 96–124.

Elster, Jon. 1995. *The Cement of Society: A Survey of Social Order*. Cambridge: Cambridge University Press.

Engels, Friedrich. 1978. "Socialism: Utopian and Scientific." In *The Marx-Engels Reader*, 2nd edition, edited by Robert C. Tucker, 683–718. New York: W. W. Norton.

Estlund, Davis. 2014. "Utopophobia." *Philosophy & Public Affairs* 42, no. 2 (Spring): 113–134.

Fanon, Frantz. (1952) 2008. *Black Skin, White Masks*, translated by Richard Philcox. New York: Grove Press.

Fanon, Frantz. 1964. *Toward the African Revolution*, translated by Haakon Chevalier. New York: Grove Press.

Fanon, Frantz. 1967. "This Is the Voice of Algeria." In *A Dying Colonialism*, translated by Haakon Chevalier. 69–99. New York: Grove Press.

Fanon, Frantz. 2004. *The Wretched of the Earth*, translated by Richard Philcox. New York: Grove Press.

Fanon, Frantz. 2011. *Œuvres*, edited by Jean Khalfa and Robert Young. Paris: La Découverte.

Forman, James, Jr. 2017. *Locking Up Our Own: Crime and Punishment in Black America*. New York: Farrar, Straus and Giroux.

Forst, Rainer. 2014. *Justification and Critique: Towards a Critical Theory of Politics*, translated by Ciaran Cronin. New York: Polity Press.

Forst, Rainer. 2017. *Normativity and Power: Analyzing Social Orders of Justification*, translated by Ciaran Cronin. New York: Oxford University Press.

Foucault, Michel. 2003. *Society Must Be Defended: Lectures at the Collège de France, 1975–1976*, edited by Mauro Bertani and Alessandro Fontana, translated by David Macey. New York: Picador.

Francis, Megan Ming. 2014. *Civil Rights and the Making of the Modern American State*. Cambridge: Cambridge University Press.

Fraser, Ian. 1998. *Hegel and Marx: The Concept of Need*. Edinburgh: Edinburgh University Press.

Fraser, Nancy, and Rahel Jaeggi. 2018. *Capitalism: A Conversation*. Cambridge, UK: Polity Press.

Fricker, Miranda. 2007. *Epistemic Injustice: Power and the Ethics of Knowing*. New York: Oxford University Press.

Fukuyama, Francis. 1995. *Trust: The Social Virtues and the Creation of Prosperity*. New York: Free Press.

Garvey, Marcus. 2004. *Selected Writings and Speeches of Marcus Garvey*, edited by Bob Blaisdell. Mineola, NY: Dover.
Garvey, Marcus. 2014. *Philosophy and Opinions of Marcus Garvey*. Vols. 1 and 2, edited by Amy Jacques-Garvey. Mansfield Centre, CT: Martino.
Garvey, Marcus. 2014. "Capitalism and the State." In *Philosophy and Opinions of Marcus Garvey*. Vol. 2, edited by Amy Jacques-Garvey. Mansfield Centre, CT: Martino. 72–74.
Garvey, Marcus. 2014. "The Negro, Communism, and His Friend." In *Philosophy and Opinions of Marcus Garvey*. Vol. 2., edited by Amy Jacques-Garvey Mansfield Centre, CT: Martino. 69–72.
Garvey, Marcus. 2020. *Message to the People: The Course of African Philosophy*. Mineola, NY: Dover.
Gaus, Gerald F. 2006. "Hayek on the Evolution of Society and Mind." In *The Cambridge Companion to Hayek*, edited by Edward Feser. 232–259. Cambridge: Cambridge University Press.
Gay, Peter. 1969. *The Enlightenment: An Interpretation*. Vol. 2: *The Science of Freedom*. New York: Alfred A. Knopf.
Geoghehan, Vincent. 2004. "Ideology and Utopia." *Journal of Political Ideologies* 9, no. 2: 123–138.
Geras, Norman. 1971. "Essence and Appearance: Aspects of Fetishism in Marx's *Capital*." *New Left Review* 65: 69–85.
Getachew, Adom. 2019. *Worldmaking after Empire: The Rise and Fall of Self-Determination*. Princeton, NJ: Princeton University Press.
Gilmore, Glenda Elizabeth. 2008. *Defying Dixie: The Radical Roots of Civil Rights, 1919–1950*. New York: W. W. Norton.
Gilmore, Ruth Wilson. 2022. "Race and Globalization." In *Abolition Geography: Essays toward Liberation*, edited by Brenna Bhandar and Alberto Toscano. 107–132. New York: Verso.
Gilroy, Paul. 1993. *The Black Atlantic: Modernity and Double-Consciousness*. Cambridge, MA: Harvard University Press.
Gilroy, Paul. 2000. *Against Race: Imagining Political Culture beyond the Color Line*. Cambridge, MA: The Belknap Press of Harvard University Press.
Gilroy, Paul. 2000. "Black Fascism." *Transition* (Kampala, Uganda) 9, no. 1: 70–91.
Givens, Jarvis R. 2021. *Fugitive Pedagogy: Carter G. Woodson and the Art of Black Teaching*. Cambridge, MA: Harvard University Press.
Gooding-Williams, Robert. 1987. "Philosophy of History and Social Critique in *The Souls of Black Folk*." *Sur les Sciences Sociales* 26 (March): 99–114.
Gooding-Williams, Robert. 1996. "Outlaw, Appiah, and Du Bois's 'The Conservation of Races.'" In *W. E. B. Du Bois on Race and Culture*, edited by Bernard W. Bell, Emily R. Grosholz, and James B. Stewart, 15–37. New York: Routledge.
Gooding-Williams, Robert. 2009. *In the Shadow of Du Bois: Afro-modern Political Thought in America*. Cambridge, MA: Harvard University Press.
Gourevitch, Alex. 2015. *From Slavery to the Cooperative Commonwealth: Labor and Republican Liberty in the Nineteenth Century*. New York: Cambridge University Press.
Gramsci, Antonio. 1992. *Selections from the Prison Notebooks*, edited and translated by Quintin Hoare and Geoffrey Nowell Smith. New York: International Publishers.

Gregory, Steven. 2002. "The 'Paradoxes' of Misplaced Concreteness: Thinking through the State." *Political Power and Social Theory* 15: 289–300. https://doi.org/10.1016/S0198-8719(02)80029-1.

Guess, Raymond. 1989. *The Idea of a Critical Theory: Habermas and the Frankfurt School*. Cambridge: Cambridge University Press.

Habermas, Jürgen. 1969–1970. "Ernst Bloch—A Marxist Romantic." *Salmagundi*, nos. 10–11 (Fall–Spring): 311–325.

Habermas, Jürgen. 1975. *Legitimation Crisis*. Translated by Thomas McCarthy. Boston: Beacon Press.

Hägglund, Martin. 2020. *This Life: Secular Faith and Spiritual Freedom*. New York: Anchor Books.

Hahn, Steven. 2009. *The Political Worlds of Slavery and Freedom*. Cambridge, MA: Harvard University Press.

Hamann, Byron Ellsworth. 2016. "How to Chronologize with a Hammer, or, The Myth of Homogenous, Empty Time." *HAU: Journal of Ethnographic Theory* 6, no. 1: 261–292.

Hanses, Mathias. 2019. "Cicero Crosses the Color Line: *Pro Archia Poeta* and W. E. B. Du Bois's *The Souls of Black Folk*." *International Journal of the Classical Tradition* 26, no. 1: 10–26.

Hargreaves Heap, Shaun P. 2011. "The Magic of the Market." *International Review of Economics* 58, no. 1: 105–115. https://doi.org/10.1007/s12232-011-0116-y.

Harootunian, Harry. 2017. *Marx after Marx: History and Time in the Expansion of Capitalism*. New York: Columbia University Press.

Harris, Kimberly Ann. 2019. "W. E. B. Du Bois's 'Conservation of Races': A Metaphilosophical Text." *Metaphilosophy* 50, no. 5: 670–687.

Hartman, Saidiya. 2019. *Wayward Lives, Beautiful Experiments: Intimate Histories of Riotous Black Girls, Troublesome Women, and Queer Radicals*. New York: W. W. Norton.

Hartsock, Nancy. 1983. "The Feminist Standpoint: Developing the Ground for a Specifically Feminist Historical Materialism." In *Discovering Reality: Feminist Perspectives on Epistemology, Metaphysics, Methodology, and the Philosophy of Science*, edited by Sandra Harding and Merrill Hintikka, 283–310. Dordrecht: D. Reidel.

Haslanger, Sally. 2013. *Resisting Reality: Social Construction and Social Critique*. Oxford: Oxford University Press.

Haslanger, Sally. 2017. "Culture and Critique." *Proceedings of the Aristotelian Society Supplementary* 91: 149–173.

Haslanger, Sally. 2017. "Racism, Ideology, and Social Movements." *Res Philosophica* 94, no. 1: 1–22. https://doi.org/10.11612/resphil.1547.

Hayek, F. A. 2007. *The Road to Serfdom*, edited by Bruce Caldwell. Chicago: University of Chicago Press.

Hayek, F. A. 2011. *The Constitution of Liberty*. Chicago: University of Chicago Press.

Hayek, F. A. 2018. *Studies on the Abuse and Decline of Reason*. Chicago: University of Chicago Press.

Heath, Joseph. 2000. "Ideology, Irrationality and Collectively Self-Defeating Behavior." *Constellations* 7, no. 3: 363–371.

Hegel, G. W. F. 1977. *Hegel's Phenomenology of Spirit*, translated by A. V. Miller. New York: Oxford University Press.

Hegel, G. W. F. 1991. *The Encyclopedia Logic (with the Zusätze)*, translated by T. F. Geraets, W. A. Suchting, and H. S. Harris. Indianapolis, IN: Hackett.
Hegel, G. W. F. 1991. *Hegel: Elements of the Philosophy of Right*, edited by Allen Wood. Translated by H. B. Nisbet. Cambridge: Cambridge University Press.
Heidegger, Martin. [1927] 2010. *Being and Time*, translated by Joan Stambuagh, revised by Dennis J. Schimdt. Albany: State University of New York Press.
Herder, Johann Gottfried. [1787] 1968. *Reflections on the Philosophy of History of Mankind*. Edited by Frank E. Manuel. Chicago: University of Chicago Press.
Hill, Latoya, and Samantha Artiga. 2023. "What Is Driving Widening Racial Disparities in Life Expectancy?" KFF, May 23. https://www.kff.org/racial-equity-and-health-policy/issue-brief/what-is-driving-widening-racial-disparities-in-life-expectancy/.
Hindriks, Frank. 2022. "Institutions and Their Strength." *Economics and Philosophy* 38, no. 3: 354–371. https://doi.org/10.1017/S0266267121000195.
Hirst, Paul. 1979. *On Law and Ideology*. London: Macmillan Press.
Hodges, Bert H., and Reuben M. Baron. 1992. "Values as Constraints on Affordances: Perceiving and Acting Properly." *Journal for the Theory of Social Behavior* 22, no. 3: 263–294.
Hoffman, Frederick L. 1896. *Race Traits and the Tendencies of the American Negro*. New York: American Economic Association.
Honneth, Axel. 2009. *Pathologies of Reason*, translated by James Hebbeler. New York: Columbia University Press.
Honneth, Axel. 2014. *Freedom's Right: The Social Foundations of Democratic Life*, translated by Joseph Ganahl. New York: Columbia University Press.
Horkheimer, Max. 1993. "Materialism and Morality." In *Between Philosophy and Social Science: Selected Early Writings*, translated by G. Frederick Hunter, Matthew S. Kramer, and John Torpey. 15–48. Cambridge. MA: MIT Press.
Hudson, Wayne. 1982. *The Marxist Philosophy of Ernst Bloch*. London: Macmillan.
Husserl, Edmund. [1900] 1970. *Logical Investigations*, translated by J. N. Findlay. London: Routledge and Kegan Paul.
Isaac, Jeffrey C. 1987. "Beyond the Three Faces of Power: A Realist Critique." *Polity* 20, no. 1: 4–31. https://doi.org/10.2307/3234935.
Iton, Richard. 2008. *In Search of the Black Fantastic: Politics and Popular Culture in the Post–Civil Rights Era*. Oxford: Oxford University Press.
Jaeggi, Rahel. 2009. "Was ist eine (gute) Institution?" In *Sozialphilosophie und Kritik*, edited by Rainer Forst, Martin Hartmann, Rahel Jaeggi, and Martin Saar, 528–544. Frankfurt: Suhrkamp.
Jaeggi, Rahel. 2016. "What (If Anything) Is Wrong with Capitalism? Dysfunctionality, Exploitation and Alienation: Three Approaches to the Critique of Capitalism." *Southern Journal of Philosophy* 54, Spindel Suppl.: 44–65.
Jaeggi, Rahel. 2018. *Critique of Forms of Life*, translated by Ciaran Cronin. Cambridge, MA: The Belknap Press of Harvard University Press.
Jagmohan, Desmond. 2020. "Between Race and Nation: Marcus Garvey and the Politics of Self-Determination." *Political Theory* 48, no. 3: 271–302.
James, Joy. 1997. *Transcending the Talented Tenth: Black Leaders and American Intellectuals*. New York: Routledge.
Jameson, Fredric. 1982. "Progress versus Utopia: Or, Can We Imagine the Future?" *Science Fiction Studies* 9, no. 2 (July): 147–158.

Jameson, Fredric. 1988. "Cognitive Mapping." In *Marxism and the Interpretation of Culture*, edited by Cary Nelson and Lawrence Grossberg, 347–356. Urbana: University of Illinois Press.
Jeffers, Chike. 2013. "The Cultural Theory of Race: Yet Another Look at Du Bois's 'The Conservation of Races.'" *Ethics* 123, no. 3: 403–426. https://doi.org/10.1086/669566.
Jendrysik, Mark Stephen. 2020. *Utopia*. Cambridge, UK: Polity Press.
Johnson, Cedric. 2007. *Race Revolutionaries to Race Leaders: Black Power and the Making of African American Politics*. Minneapolis: University of Minnesota Press.
Johnson, Cedric. 2022. *The Panthers Can't Save Us Now: Debating Left Politics and Black Lives Matter*. London: Verso.
Jonas, Hans. 1984. *The Imperative of Responsibility: In Search of an Ethics for the Technological Age*, translated by Hans Jonas and David Herr. Chicago: University of Chicago Press.
Judy, R. A. 2015. "Lohengrin's Swan and the Style of Interiority in 'Of the Coming of John.'" *CR* (East Lansing, MI) 15, no. 2: 211–258.
Kelley, Robin D. G. 2022. *Freedom Dreams: The Black Radical Imagination*. Boston: Beacon Press.
Kennedy, Duncan. 2002. "The Critique of Rights in Critical Legal Studies." In *Left Legalism/Left Critique*, edited by Wendy Brown and Janet Halley, 178–228. Durham, NC: Duke University Press.
Kinney, David, and Liam Kofi Bright. 2023. "Risk Aversion and Elite-Group Ignorance." *Philosophy and Phenomenological Research* 106, no. 1: 35–57. https://doi.org/10.1111/phpr.12837.
Koselleck, Reinhart. 1985. *Futures Past: On the Semantics of Historical Time*, translated by Keith Tribe. Cambridge, MA: MIT Press.
Koselleck, Reinhart. 2018. *Sediments of Time: On Possible Histories*, translated by Sean Franzel and Stefan Ludwig-Hoffmann. Stanford: Stanford University Press.
Kramer, Sina. 2019. *Excluded Within: The (Un)Intelligibility of Radical Political Actors*. New York: Oxford University Press.
Landes, David S. 2000. *Revolution in Time: Clocks and the Making of the Modern World*, revised and enlarged edition. Cambridge, MA: Harvard University Press.
Laurence, Ben. 2021. *Agents of Change: Political Philosophy in Practice*. Cambridge, MA: Harvard University Press.
Laurence, Ben. 2023. "Justice in Theory and Practice: Debates about Utopianism and Political Action." *Philosophy Compass* 18, no. 11: 1–12. https://doi.org/10.1111/phc3.12945.
Lebowitz, Michael A. 2003. *Beyond Capital: Marx's Political Economy of the Working Class*. 2nd edition. New York: Palgrave Macmillan.
Lebron, Christopher J. 2013. *The Color of Our Shame: Race and Justice in Our Time*. New York: Oxford University Press.
Lemke, Sieglinde. 2000. "Berlin and Boundaries: *Sollen* versus *Geschehen*." *boundary 2* 27, no. 3 (Fall): 45–78.
Leopold, David. 2016. "On Marxian Utopophobia." *Journal of the History of Philosophy* 54, no. 1 (January): 111–134.
Levitas, Ruth. 2013. *Utopia as Method: The Imaginary Reconstitution of Society*. New York: Palgrave Macmillan.

Lewis, Oscar. 1998. "The Culture of Poverty." *Society* 35, no. 2: 7–9.
Lewis, W. Arthur. 1985. *Racial Conflict and Economic Development*. Cambridge, MA: Harvard University Press.
Lloyd, Vincent W. 2016. *Black Natural Law*. New York: Oxford University Press.
López, Ian Haney. 2006. *White by Law: The Legal Construction of Race*. New York: New York University Press.
Losurdo, Domenico. 2021. *Nietzsche, the Aristocratic Rebel: Intellectual Biography and Critical Balance-Sheet*, translated by Gregor Benton, introduction by Harrison Fluss. Chicago: Haymarket Books.
Lukács, Georg. 1971. *History and Class-Consciousness*, translated by Rodney Livingston. Cambridge, MA: MIT Press.
Lukes, Steven. 1982. "Can a Marxist Believe in Human Rights?" *Praxis International* 4: 81–92.
Lyons, David. 2013. "The Social Dimension of Rights." *Journal of Social Philosophy* 44, no. 1: 43–50. https://doi.org/10.1111/josp.12010.
MacIntyre, Alasdair. 1977. "Epistemological Crises, Dramatic Narrative and the Philosophy of Science." *The Monist* 60, no. 4 (October): 453–472.
MacIntyre, Alasdair. 1990. "The Privatization of the Good: An Inaugural Lecture." *Review of Politics* 52, no. 3: 344–361.
Macpherson, C. B. 1962. *The Political Theory of Possessive Individualism: Hobbes to Locke*. Oxford: Oxford University Press.
Maher, Chauncey. 2012. *The Pittsburgh School of Philosophy: Sellars, McDowell, Brandom*. New York: Routledge.
Major, Aaron. 2023. "Race, Labor and Postbellum Capitalism in Du Bois's 'The Negro Worker in America.'" *Critical Sociology* 49, no. 3: 383–393.
Mannheim, Karl. 2015. *Ideology and Utopia: An Introduction to the Sociology of Knowledge*. Mansfield Centre, CT: Martino.
Mao, Douglas. 2020. *Inventions of Nemesis: Utopia, Indignation, and Justice*. Princeton, NJ: Princeton University Press.
Marable, Manning. 2016. *W. E. B. Du Bois: Black Radical Democrat*. London: Routledge.
Marriott, David. 2018. *Whither Fanon? Studies in the Blackness of Being*. Stanford: Stanford University Press.
Marx, Karl. 1978. "For a Ruthless Criticism of Everything Existing (Marx to Arnold Ruge)." In *The Marx-Engels Reader*, 2nd edition, edited by Robert C. Tucker. 12–16. New York: W. W. Norton.
Marx, Karl. 1978. "On the Jewish Question." In *The Marx-Engels Reader*, edited by Robert Tucker, 26–53. New York: Norton.
Marx, Karl. 1990. *Capital: A Critique of Political Economy*. Vol. 1, translated by Ben Fowkes, introduction by Ernest Mandel. New York: Penguin Classics.
Marx, Karl. 1993. *Grundrisse: Foundations of the Critique of Political Economy*, translated by Martin Nicolaus. London: Penguin Books.
Marx, Karl, and Friedrich Engels. (1848) 1998. *The Communist Manifesto*. New York: Monthly Review Press.
Marx, Karl, and Friedrich Engels. 1976. *The German Ideology*, edited by James S. Allen, Philip S. Foner, Dirk J. Struik, and William W. Weinstone. In *Collected Works*. Vol. 5. New York: International Publishers. 19–453.

Marx, Karl, and Frederick Engels. 1976. *Theses on Feuerbach*, edited by James S. Allen, Philip S. Foner, Dirk J. Struik, and William W. Weinstone. In *Collected Works*. Vol. 5. New York: International Publishers. 3–6.

Mau, Søren. 2023. *Mute Compulsion: A Marxist Theory of the Economic Power of Capital*. London: Verso.

McCarthy, Michael. 2016. "Alternatives: Silent Compulsions: Capitalist Markets and Race." *Studies in Political Economy*, 97, no. 2: 195–205.

McCarthy, Thomas. 2009. *Race, Empire, and the Idea of Human Development*. Cambridge: Cambridge University Press.

McGary, Howard. 1999. *Race and Social Justice*. Malden, MA: Blackwell.

Medina, José. 2013. *The Epistemology of Resistance: Gender and Racial Oppression, Epistemic Injustice, and Resistant Imaginations*. New York: Oxford University Press.

Medina, José. 2017. "Epistemic Injustice and Epistemologies of Ignorance." In *The Routledge Companion to Philosophy of Race*, edited by Paul Taylor, Linda Alcoff, and Luvell Anderson, 247–260. New York: Routledge.

Medina, José. 2013. "Color Blindness, Meta-ignorance, and the Racial Imagination." *Critical Philosophy of Race* 1, no. 1: 38–67. https://doi.org/10.5325/critphilrace.1.1.0038.

Menke, Christoph. 2020. *Critique of Rights*. Cambridge, UK: Polity Press.

Mennozi, Filippo. 2020. "Inheriting Marx: Daniel Bensäid, Ernst Bloch and the Discordance of Time." *Historical Materialism* 28, no. 1: 147–182.

Merleau-Ponty, Maurice. [1945] 2012. *Phenomenology of Perception*, translated by Donald A. Landes. London: Routledge.

Merrill, David. 1998. "Hegel's System of Needs: The Elementary Relations of Economic Justice." *Hegel Bulletin* 19, nos. 1–2: 51–72.

Merton, Robert King. 1968. *Social Theory and Social Structure*. Enlarged edition. New York: Free Press.

Mészáros, István. 1989. *The Power of Ideology*. Hemel Hempstead: Harvester Wheatsheaf.

Mészáros, István. 2022. *Beyond Leviathan: Critique of the State*, edited by John Bellamy Foster. New York: Monthly Review Press.

Miles, Kevin Thomas. 2000. "Haunting Music in *The Souls of Black Folk*." *boundary 2* 27, no. 3 (Fall): 199–214.

Mills, Charles W. 1986. "The Concept of Ideology in the Thought of Marx and Engels." *Owl of Minerva* 17, no. 2: 244–245.

Mills, Charles W. 1997. *The Racial Contract*. Ithaca, NY: Cornell University Press.

Mills, Charles W. 1998. *Blackness Visible: Essays on Philosophy and Race*. Ithaca, NY: Cornell University Press.

Mills, Charles. 2010. *Radical Theory, Caribbean Reality: Race, Class and Social Domination*. Kingston: University of West Indies Press.

Mills, Charles W. 2015. "Global White Ignorance." In *Routledge International Handbook of Ignorance Studies*, edited by Matthias Gross and Linsey McGoey, 217–247. Abingdon: Routledge.

Mills, Charles W. 2015. "Racial Rights and Wrongs: A Critique of Derrick Darby." *Radical Philosophy Review* 18, no. 1: 11–30.

Mills, Charles W. 2017. *Black Rights/White Wrongs: The Critique of Racial Liberalism*. New York: Oxford University Press.

Mills, Charles W. 2020. "The Chronopolitics of Racial Time." *Time & Society* 29, no. 2: 297–317.
Milstein, Brian. 2015. "Thinking Politically about Crisis: A Pragmatist Perspective." *European Journal of Political Theory* 14, no. 2: 141–160.
Moak, Daniel. 2021. "Thurgood Marshall: The Legacy and Limits of Equality under the Law." In *African American Political Thought*, edited by Melvin L. Rogers and Jack Turner, 386–412. Chicago: University of Chicago Press. https://doi.org/10.7208/9780226726076-018.
Moir, Cat. 2019. *Ernst Bloch's Speculative Materialism: Ontology, Epistemology, Politics*. Leiden: Brill.
More, Thomas. 2016. *Utopia*, 3rd edition, edited by George M. Logan, translated by Robert M. Adams. Cambridge: Cambridge University Press.
Morfino, Vittorio. 2017. "On Non-contemporaneity: Marx, Bloch, Althusser." In *The Government of Time: Theories of Plural Temporality in the Marxist Tradition*, edited by Vittorio Morfino and Peter D. Thomas, 117–148. Chicago: Haymarket Books.
Morris, Aldon D. 1986. *The Origins of the Civil Rights Movement: Black Communities Organizing for Change*. New York: Free Press.
Morris, Aldon D. 2015. *The Scholar Denied: W. E. B. Du Bois and the Birth of Modern Sociology*. Oakland: University of California Press.
Morrison, Toni. 1975. "A Humanist View." Portland State University's Oregon Public Speakers Collection, May 30. https://www.mackenzian.com/wp-content/uploads/2014/07/Transcript_PortlandState_TMorrison.pdf.
Moses, Wilson Jeremiah. 2004. *Creative Conflict in African American Thought: Frederick Douglass, Alexander Crummell, Booker T. Washington, W. E. B. Du Bois, and Marcus Garvey*. Cambridge: Cambridge University Press.
Mouffe, Chantal. 2005. *On the Political*. New York: Routledge.
Muhammed, Khalil Gibran. 2010. *The Condemnation of Blackness: Race, Crime, and the Making of Modern Urban America*. Cambridge, MA: Harvard University Press.
Mumford, Lewis. 2010. *Technics and Civilization*. Chicago: University of Chicago Press.
Negt, Oskar. 1976. "The Non-synchronous Heritage and the Problem of Propaganda." *New German Critique*, no. 9 (Autumn): 46–70.
Neocleous, Mark. 1998. "Policing the System of Needs: Hegel, Political Economy, and the Police of the Market." *History of European Ideas* 24, no. 1: 43–58.
Neuhouser, Frederick. 2018. "Marx and Hegel on the Value of 'Bourgeois' Ideals." In *Reassessing Marx's Social and Political Philosophy*, edited by Jan Kandiyali, 149–162. New York: Routledge.
Neuhouser, Frederick. 2022. *Diagnosing Social Pathology: Rousseau, Hegel, Marx, and Durkheim*. Cambridge: Cambridge University Press.
Ng, Karen. 2015. "Ideology Critique from Hegel and Marx to Critical Theory." *Constellations* 22, no. 3: 393–404.
Ng, Karen. 2021. "Humanism: A Defense." *Philosophical Topics* 49, no. 1: 145–164. https://doi.org/10.5840/philtopics20214919.
Omi, Michael, and Howard Winant. 2015. *Racial Formation in the United States*. 3rd edition. New York: Routledge.

Outlaw, Lucius. 1996. "'Conserve' Races?" In *W. E. B. Du Bois on Race and Culture*, edited by Bernard W. Bell, Emily R. Grosholz, and James B. Stewart, 15–37. New York: Routledge.

Paris, William Michael. 2019. "Gender and Technology in Frantz Fanon: Confrontations of the Clinical and Political." *Philosophy Compass* 14, no. 9: 1–10. https://doi.org/10.1111/phc3.12616.

Paris, William Michael. 2019. "'One Does Not Write for Slaves': Wynter, Sartre, and the Poetic Phenomenology of Invention." *Journal of Speculative Philosophy* 33, no. 3: 407–421.

Patterson, Orlando. 2018. *Slavery and Social Death: A Comparative Study*. Cambridge, MA: Harvard University Press.

Pettit, Philip. 1997. *Republicanism: A Theory of Freedom and Government*. Oxford: Oxford University Press.

Pettit, Philip. 2023. *The State*. Princeton, NJ: Princeton University Press.

Pew Research Center. 2022. "Public Trust in Government: 1958–2021." June 6. https://www.pewresearch.org/politics/2021/05/17/public-trust-in-government-1958-2021/.

Pierson, Paul. 2000. "Increasing Returns, Path Dependence, and the Study of Politics." *American Political Science Review* 94, no. 2: 251–267. https://doi.org/10.2307/2586011.

Pierson, Paul. 2000. "Not Just What, but When: Timing and Sequence in Political Processes." *Studies in American Political Development* 14, no. 1: 72–92. https://doi.org/10.1017/S0898588X00003011.

Pinkard, Terry. 2017. *Does History Make Sense? Hegel on the Historical Shapes of Justice*. Cambridge, MA: Harvard University Press.

Pinkard, Terry. 2012. *Hegel's Naturalism: Mind, Nature, and the Final Ends of Life*. New York: Oxford University Press.

Pinkney, Alphonso. 1976. *Red, Black, and Green: Black Nationalism in the United States*. Cambridge: Cambridge University Press.

Plato. 2003. *The Republic*, edited by G. R. F. Ferrari, translated by Tom Griffith. Cambridge: Cambridge University Press.

Polanyi, Michael. 2009. *The Tacit Dimension*, foreword by Amartya Sen. Chicago: University of Chicago Press.

Popper, Karl. 2013. *The Open Society and Its Enemies*, introduction by Alan Ryan. Princeton, NJ: Princeton University Press.

Postone, Moishe. 1993. *Time, Labor, and Social Domination: A Reinterpretation of Marx's Critical Theory*. Cambridge: Cambridge University Press.

Purnell, Derecka. 2021. *Becoming Abolitionists: Police, Protests, and the Pursuit of Freedom*. New York: Astra House.

Rampersad, Arnold. 1990. *The Art and Imagination of W. E. B. Du Bois*. New York: Schocken Books.

Rancière, Jacques. 1999. *Disagreement: Politics and Philosophy*, translated by Julie Rose. Minneapolis: University of Minnesota Press.

Randolph, A. Philip. 1996. "The Negro in Politics." In *African American Political Thought, 1890–1930*, edited by Cary D. Wintz, 245–253. New York: Routledge.

Rawls, John. 1993. *Political Liberalism*. New York: Columbia University Press.

Rawls, John. 2001. *Justice as Fairness: A Restatement*, edited by Erin Kelly. Cambridge, MA: The Belknap Press of Harvard University Press.

BIBLIOGRAPHY 243

Redecker, Eva von. 2021. *Praxis and Revolution: A Theory of Social Transformation*, translated by Lucy Duggan. New York: Columbia University Press.

Reed, Adolph L., Jr. 1997. *W. E. B. Du Bois and American Political Thought: Fabianism and the Color Line*. Oxford: Oxford University Press.

Reed, Touré F. 2020. *Toward Freedom: The Case against Race Reductionism*. New York: Verso.

Reed, Touré F. 2022. "Review of *Pittsburgh and the Urban League Movement: A Century of Social Service and Activism*." *Journal of American History* 109, no. 2: 453–454. https://doi.org/10.1093/jahist/jaac296.

Rehmann, Jan. 2013. *Theories of Ideology: The Powers of Alienation and Subjection*. Chicago: Haymarket Books.

Reis-Dennis, Samuel, and Vida Yao. 2021. "I *Love* Women: An Explicit Explanation of Implicit Bias Test Results." *Synthese* 199, nos. 5–6: 13861–13882. https://doi.org/10.1007/s11229-021-03401-3.

Restifo, Salvatore J., Vincent J. Roscigno, and Zhenchao Qian. 2013. "Segmented Assimilation, Split Labor Markets, and Racial/Ethnic Inequality: The Case of Early-Twentieth-Century New York." *American Sociological Review* 78, no. 5: 897–924.

Rezsoházy, Rudolf. 1972. "The Concept of Social Time: Its Role in Development." *International Social Science Journal* 24, no. 1: 26–36.

Ricœur, Paul. 1986. *Lectures on Ideology and Utopia*, edited by George H. Taylor. New York: Columbia University Press.

Ripstein, Arthur. 1987. "Commodity Fetishism." *Canadian Journal of Philosophy* 17, no. 4 (December): 733–748.

Ripstein, Arthur. 2009. *Force and Freedom: Kant's Legal and Political Philosophy*. Cambridge, MA: Harvard University Press.

Roberts, William Clare. 2016. *Marx's Inferno: The Political Theory of Capital*. Princeton, NJ: Princeton University Press.

Robin, Corey. 2019. *The Enigma of Clarence Thomas*. New York: Metropolitan Books.

Robinson, Dean E. 2001. *Black Nationalism in American Politics and Thought*. Cambridge: Cambridge University Press.

Rogers, Melvin L. 2015. "David Walker and the Political Power of the Appeal." *Political Theory* 43, no. 2: 208–233. https://doi.org/10.1177/0090591714523623.

Rogers, Melvin L. 2020. "Race, Domination, and Republicanism." In *Difference without Domination*, edited by Danielle S. Allen and Rohini Somanathan, 59–90. Chicago: University of Chicago Press. https://doi.org/10.7208/9780226681368-003.

Rosen, Michael. 1996. *On Voluntary Servitude: False Consciousness and the Theory of Ideology*. Cambridge, UK: Polity Press.

Rousseau, Jean-Jacques. 2011. *Basic Political Writings*, 2nd edition, translated by Donald A. Cress, introduction by David Wootton. Indianapolis, IN: Hackett.

Sankaran, Kirun. 2019. "What's New in the New Ideology Critique?" *Philosophical Studies* 177, no. 5: 1441–1462.

Sartre, Jean-Paul. 2021. "Existentialism Is a Humanism." In *Existentialism Is a Humanism*, translated by Carol Macomber, 17–72. New Haven, CT: Yale University Press. https://doi.org/10.12987/9780300242539-003.

Sartre, Jean-Paul. (1943) 1983. *Being and Nothingness: An Essay in Phenomenological Ontology*, translated by Hazel Barnes. New York: Washington Square Press.

Sawyer, Michael E. 2020. *Black Minded: The Political Philosophy of Malcolm X.* London: Pluto Press.

Schiller, Friedrich. 1993. "Letters upon the Aesthetic Education of Man." In *Essays*, edited by Walter Hinderer and Daniel O. Dahlstrom, translated by Elizabeth M. Wilkinson and L. A. Willoughby. New York: Continuum. 86–179.

Schmidt, Alfred. 1971. *The Concept of Nature in Marx*, translated by Ben Fowkes. London: NLB.

Schmitt, Carl. 2007. *The Concept of the Political*, translated by George Schwab. Chicago: University of Chicago Press.

Sciabarra, Chris Matthew. 1995. *Marx, Hayek, and Utopia.* Albany: State University of New York Press.

Scott, David. 2004. *Conscripts of Modernity: The Tragedy of Colonial Enlightenment.* Durham, NC: Duke University Press.

Scott, James C. 2020. *Seeing Like a State: How Certain Schemes to Improve the Human Condition Have Failed.* New Haven, CT: Yale University Press.

Searle, John. 1996. *The Construction of Social Reality.* London: Penguin.

Searle, John. 2008. *Freedom and Neurobiology: Reflections on Free Will, Language, and Political Power.* New York: Columbia University Press.

Searle, John. 2010. *Making the Social World: The Structure of Human Civilization.* New York: Oxford University Press.

Sellars, Wilfrid. 1997. *Empiricism and the Philosophy of Mind.* Cambridge, MA: Harvard University Press.

Sewell, William H. 2005. *Logics of History: Social Theory and Social Transformation.* Chicago: University of Chicago Press.

Shaw, Stephanie. 2013. *W. E. B. Du Bois and* The Souls of Black Folk. Chapel Hill: University of North Carolina Press.

Sheth, Falguni. 2009. *Toward a Political Philosophy of Race.* New York: SUNY Press.

Shelby, Tommie. 2003. "Ideology, Racism, and Critical Social Theory." *Philosophical Forum* 34, no. 2 (Summer): 153–188.

Shelby, Tommie. 2005. *We Who Are Dark: The Philosophical Foundations of Black Solidarity.* Cambridge, MA: The Belknap Press of Harvard University Press.

Shelby, Tommie. 2013. "Racial Realities and Corrective Justice: A Reply to Charles Mills." *Critical Philosophy of Race* 1, no. 2: 145–162.

Shelby, Tommie. 2014. "Racism, Moralism, and Social Criticism." *Du Bois Review* 11, no. 1: 57–74. https://doi.org/10.1017/S1742058X14000010.

Shelby, Tommie. 2016. *Dark Ghettos: Injustice, Dissent, and Reform.* Cambridge, MA: The Belknap Press of Harvard University Press.

Shelby, Tommie. 2022. *The Idea of Prison Abolition.* Princeton, NJ: Princeton University Press.

Shklar, Judith. 1967. "The Political Theory of Utopia: From Melancholy to Nostalgia." In *Utopias and Utopian Thought*, edited by Frank E. Manuel, 101–116. Boston: Beacon Press.

Shklar, Judith. 2020. *After Utopia: The Decline of Political Faith.* Princeton, NJ: Princeton University Press.

Shoikhedbrod, Igor. 2019. *Revisiting Marx's Critique of Liberalism: Rethinking Justice, Legality and Rights.* Cham: Palgrave Macmillan.

Skinner, Quentin. 2008. "Freedom as the Absence of Arbitrary Power." In *Republicanism and Political Theory*, edited by Cécile Laborde and John W. Maynor. Oxford: Blackwell. 83–102.

Smith, Justin E. H. 2015. *Nature, Human Nature, and Human Difference: Race in Early Modern Philosophy*. Princeton, NJ: Princeton University Press.

Smith, Mark H. 1997. *Mastered by the Clock: Time, Slavery, and Freedom in the American South*. Chapel Hill: University of North Carolina Press.

Smith, Tony. 2017. *Beyond Liberal Egalitarianism: Marx and Normative Social Theory in the Twenty-First Century*. Leiden: Brill.

Soon, Valerie. 2019. "Implicit Bias and Social Schema: A Transactive Memory Approach." *Philosophical Studies* 177, no. 7: 1857–1877.

Soon, Valerie. 2021. "Social Structural Explanation." *Philosophy Compass* 16, no. 10: 1–12. https://doi.org/10.1111.phc3.12782.

Soper, Kate. 1981. *On Human Needs: Open and Closed Theories in a Marxist Perspective*. Sussex: Harvester Press.

Sorokin, Pitirim, and Robert K. Merton. 1937. "Social Time: A Methodological and Functional Analysis." *American Journal of Sociology* 42, no. 5 (March): 615–629.

Sowell, Thomas. October 12, 1981. "Culture—Not Discrimination—Decides Who Gets Ahead: A Conversation with Thomas Sowell." *U.S. News & World Report*.

Spillers, Hortense. 1977. "Ellison's 'Usable Past': Toward a Theory of Myth." *Interpretations* 9, no. 1: 53–69.

Sterelny, Kim. 2010. "Minds: Extended or Scaffolded?" *Phenomenology and the Cognitive Sciences* 9, no. 4: 465–481.

Swain, Dan. 2019. *None So Fit to Break the Chains: Marx's Ethics of Self-Emancipation*. Boston: Brill.

Swidler, Ann. 2000. "What Anchors Cultural Practices." In *The Practice Turn in Contemporary Theory*, edited by Theodore R. Schatzki, Karin Knorr Cetina, and Eike von Savigny. 83–102. New York: Routledge. https://doi.org/10.4324/9780203977453-13.

Sypnowich, Christine. 1990. *The Socialist Concept of Law*. Oxford: Oxford University Press.

Táíwò, Olúfemi. 2018. "The Empire Has No Clothes." *Disputio* 10, no. 51 (December): 305–330.

Táíwò, Olúfemi. 2020. "Identity Politics and Elite Capture." *Boston Review*. https://bostonreview.net/race/olufemi-o-taiwo-identity-politics-and-elite-capture.

Taylor, Keeanga-Yamahtta. 2021. *Race for Profit: How Banks and the Real Estate Industry Undermined Black Ownership*. Chapel Hill: University of North Carolina Press.

Taylor, Paul C. 2011. "William Edward Burghardt Du Bois." In *The Wiley-Blackwell Companion to Major Social Theorists*, edited by George Ritzer and Jeffrey Stepnisky. 426–447. Oxford: Wiley-Blackwell.

Taylor, Paul. 2016. *Black Is Beautiful: A Philosophy of Black Aesthetics*. Malden, MA: Wiley-Blackwell.

Therborn, Göran. 1999. *The Ideology of Power and the Power of Ideology*. London: Verso Classics.

Thompson, E. P. 2018. "Time, Work-Discipline, Industrial-Capitalism." In *Class: The Anthology*, edited by Stanley Aronowitz and Michael J. Roberts, 27–41. Hoboken, NJ: John Wiley & Sons.

Thompson, Janna. 2001. "Historical Injustice and Reparation: Justifying Claims of Descendants." *Ethics* 112 (October): 114–135.

Thompson, Mark Christian. 2007. *Black Fascisms: African American Literature and Culture between the Wars*. Charlottesville: University of Virginia Press.

Thompson, Peter. 2013. "Introduction: The Privatization of Hope and the Crisis of Negation." In *The Privatization of Hope: Ernst Bloch and the Future of Utopia*, edited by Peter Thompson and Slavoj Žižek, 1–21. Durham, NC: Duke University Press.

Thompson, Peter. 2015. "Ernst Bloch, *Ungleichzeitigkeit*, and the Philosophy of Being and Time." *New German Critique* 42, no. 2 (August): 49–64.

Tombazos, Stavros. 2014. *Time in Marx: The Categories of Time in Marx's Capital*. Chicago: Haymarket Books.

Toole, Briana. 2019. "From Standpoint Epistemology to Epistemic Oppression." *Hypatia* 34, no. 4: 598–618.

Ture, Kwame, and Charles V. Hamilton. (1967) 1992. *Black Power: Politics of Liberation in America*. New York: Vintage.

Waldron, Jeremy. 1992. "Superseding Historic Injustice." *Ethics* 103 (October): 4–28.

Warner, Michael. 2002. "Publics and Counterpublics." *Public Culture* 14, no. 1: 49–90. https://doi.org/10.1215/08992363-14-1-49.

Warren, Calvin L. 2015. "Black Nihilism and the Politics of Hope." *CR* (East Lansing, MI) 15, no. 1: 215–248. https://doi.org/10.14321/crnewcentrevi.15.1.0215.

Wartenberg, Thomas E. 1988. "The Situated Conception of Social Power." *Social Theory and Practice* 14, no. 3: 317–343. https://doi.org/10.5840/soctheorpract19 8814314.

Wartenberg, Thomas E. 1990. *The Forms of Power: From Domination to Transformation*. Philadelphia: Temple University Press.

Weeks, Kathi. 2011. *The Problem with Work: Feminism, Marxism, Antiwork Politics, and Postwork Imaginaries*. Durham, NC: Duke University Press.

Wegner, Phillip E. 2002. *Imaginary Communities: Utopia, the Nation, and the Spatial Histories of Modernity*. Berkeley: University of California Press.

West, Cornel. 1999. *The Cornel West Reader*. New York: Basic Civitas Books.

White, E. F. 2002. "Africa on My Mind: Gender, Counter Discourse, and African American Nationalism." In *Is It Nation Time? Contemporary Essays on Black Power and Black Nationalism*, edited by Eddie S. Glaude Jr, 130–156. Chicago: University of Chicago Press.

Whitehead, A. N. (1925) 1953. *Science and the Modern World*. New York: Free Press.

Wilderson, Frank B. 2003. "Gramsci's Black Marx: Whither the Slave in Civil Society?" *Social Identities* 9, no. 2: 225–240. https://doi.org/10.1080/13504630 32000101579.

Wilderson, Frank B. 2010. *Red, White and Black: Cinema and the Structure of U.S. Antagonisms*. Durham, NC: Duke University Press.

Wilkerson, Isabel. 2020. *Caste: The Origins of Our Discontents*. New York: Random House.

Williams, Robert W. 2018. "A Democracy of Differences: Knowledge and the Unknowable in Du Bois's Theory of Democratic Governance." In *A Political Companion to W. E. B. Du Bois*, edited by Nick Bromell, 181–204. Lexington: University of Kentucky Press.

Wills, Vanessa. 2018. "What Could It Mean to Say, 'Capitalism Causes Sexism and Racism?'" *Philosophical Topics* 46, no. 2: 229–246.

Withun, David. 2022. *Co-workers in the Kingdom of Culture: Classics and Cosmopolitanism in the Thought of W. E. B. Du Bois*. New York: Oxford University Press.
Wood, Allen W. 1972. "The Marxian Critique of Justice." *Philosophy & Public Affairs* 1, no. 3 (Spring): 244-282.
Wood, Ellen Meiksins. 1995. *Democracy against Capitalism: Renewing Historical Materialism*. Cambridge: Cambridge University Press.
Woodson, Carter G. (1933) 1990. *The Mis-Education of the Negro*. Trenton: Africa World Press.
Wright, Erik Olin. 2010. *Envisioning Real Utopias*. New York: Verso.
Wynter, Sylvia. 1994. "'No Humans Involved': An Open Letter to My Colleagues." *Forum N.H.I.: Knowledge for the 21st Century* 1, no. 1 (Fall): 42-74.
Wynter, Sylvia. 1996. "Is Development a Purely Empirical Concept, or also Teleological? A Perspective from 'We the Underdeveloped.'" In *Prospects for Recovery and Sustainable Development in Africa*, edited by Aguibou Y. Yansané, 299-316. Westport, CT: Greenwood Press.
Wynter, Sylvia. 2003. "Unsettling the Coloniality of Being/Power/Truth/Freedom: Towards the Human, after Man, Its Overrepresentation—An Argument." *CR* (East Lansing, MI) 3, no. 3: 257-337. https://doi.org/10.1353/ncr.2004.0015.
Wynter, Sylvia. 2006. "On How We Mistook the Map for the Territory, and Reimprisoned Ourselves in Our Unbearable Wrongness of Being, of *Désêtre*." In *Not Only the Master's Tools: African American Studies in Theory and Practice*, edited by Lewis R. Gordon and Jane Anna Gordon, 107-170. New York: Routledge.
Yancy, George. 2017. *Black Bodies, White Gazes: The Continuing Significance of Race in America*. 2nd edition. New York: Rowman & Littlefield.
Yokum, Nicole. 2022. "A Call for Psycho-affective Change: Fanon, Feminism, and White Negrophobic Femininity." *Philosophy & Social Criticism* 50, no. 2: 1-26.
Zamalin, Alex. 2019. *Black Utopia: The History of an Idea from Black Nationalism to Afrofuturism*. New York: Columbia University Press.
Zamir, Shamoon. 1995. *Dark Voices: W. E. B. Du Bois and American Thought, 1888-1903*. Chicago: University of Chicago Press.
Zamir, Shamoon. 2008. "*The Souls of Black Folk*: Thought and Afterthought." In *The Cambridge Companion to W. E. B. Du Bois*, edited by Shamoon Zamir, 7-36. New York: Cambridge University Press.
Zipes, Jack. 1997. "Traces of Hope: The Non-synchronicity of Ernst Bloch." In *Not-Yet: Reconsidering Ernst Bloch*, edited by Jamie Owen Daniel and Tom Moylan, 1-15. New York: Verso.
Žižek, Slavoj. 2008. *The Sublime Object of Ideology*. New York: Verso.

Index

For the benefit of digital users, indexed terms that span two pages (e.g., 52–53) may, on occasion, appear on only one of those pages.

action, in problem solving, 74–75
Adam, Barbara, 17
Adorno, Theodor, 71–72
Al-Saji, Alia, 151–52
anagnorisis, 76, 77–78, 79–80, 87, 89–90, 95
anchoring practices, 19–22, 113–19, 124–27, 143–44, 201–2, 206–7
Anders, Günther, 161–62
Anderson, Benedict, 103, 111–12
Atheism in Christianity (Bloch), 62
awareness model of consciousness, 24–42, 50, 53–55

belief formations, 23–24
Benhabib, Seyla, 36–38
Benjamin, Walter, 170–71
Bernasconi, Robert, 69–70
binding powers, 121–22
black body philosophy, 136–43
Black Mindedness, 137
black nationalism
  anchoring practices and, 113–19, 124–27, 143–44
  binding powers, 121–22
  black body philosophy, 136–43
  civil rights and, 134
  Delany, Martin and, 102–3, 113–30
  Garvey, Marcus and, 10, 19–20, 102–3, 128, 130–43
  introduction to, 98–103
  non-synchronicity of, 99, 101, 111–13, 143
  original identity and, 119–20, 124–25
  political wrongs and, 126–30
  racial domination and, 100–1, 105–6, 109, 112, 127–30, 144
  racial injustice and, 98–103
  racism and, 98–99, 112–13, 118–19, 124, 126–27, 128, 139
  rights externalism and, 119–26
  as social disease, 126–27
  social space and time, 103–13
  space of reasons and, 102–3, 106–11, 113, 115–16, 119, 120–21, 125–26, 131–32, 135–36, 138–39, 143–44
  struggle for autonomy and, 143–44
  Universal Intelligence, 139–40
  utopia and, 10, 19–20
  voting and, 115–16
black power
  Boggs on, 178–93, 196–97, 201–2, 205–6, 208, 210
  capitalist power and, 187–89, 190–93, 198–99, 207, 217
  as ethnic ideology, 214
  introduction to, 21
  racial domination and, 176, 179, 184–85, 198–99, 224
  as revolutionary ideology, 214
  self-emancipation of, 3–4, 183, 190–91, 208–16, 220–24
  white power and, 177–78, 187–93, 198–99, 207, 217
black salvation, 78–84
Black Skin, White Masks (Fanon), 149–51, 153–54, 159–60, 172–73

Bloch, Ernst, 2, 19, 45–49, 58–59, 145, 176
Boggs, Grace Lee, 193–94
Boggs, James, 21, 152, 176–218. *See also* black power

capitalist power, 187–89, 190–93, 198–99, 207, 217
Celikates, Robin, 24–25
Chance, Du Bois on, 65–69, 70–71, 74, 93–96
Chandler, Nahum, 76
civil rights
  black nationalism and, 134
  Boggs on, 177–79, 184–89, 192, 194–96, 198–208, 210–15
  racial fetishism and, 145
civil society, 177, 184–86, 189–90, 195–96, 202, 210–11, 217
Civil War (US), 78–79, 81–82, 114–15, 124–25
clock time, 12–16
cognitive dependence, 180
cognitive distortion, 20–21, 28–29, 85–87
Colleti, Lucio, 181–82
colonial glueing, 151–52
colonialization of language, 154–60
The Color of Our Shame (Lebron), 118
commodity fetishism, 20–21, 165–66, 219
consciousness and racial justice
  awareness model of consciousness, 24–42, 50, 53–55
  crisis consciousness, 18–19, 26–28, 36–42, 43–45, 47–48, 50–52, 145–46, 209–10, 223–24
  introduction to, 23–28
  normative expectations in, 25–26, 38–45, 47–48, 50–55
  racism and, 30–31, 41, 52–53
  utopian consciousness, 18–19, 26–28, 43–52, 55–56, 71–72, 133–34, 145–48, 167, 209–10, 219–22, 223–24, 225–27
  utopias of, 52–55
consciousness-raising, 23, 39–40
conservatism, 27–28, 32–35, 43–44, 49, 130, 180–81, 183, 194
COVID-19 pandemic, 18–19, 50, 52–53

crisis consciousness, 18–19, 26–28, 36–42, 43–45, 47–48, 50–52, 145–46, 209–10, 223–24. *See also* consciousness and racial justice
critical theory of utopia, 4–11, 16–17, 55, 59, 96–97, 145–46, 161–62, 217, 222–23, 226–27

Darby, Derrick, 122–23
Dawson, Michael, 135
Delany, Martin, 10, 19–20, 102–3, 113–19
distributive justice, 40
Douglass, Frederick, 108–9n.26, 109–11
Du Bois, W. E. B., 19, 56. *See also The Souls of black Folk* (Du Bois)

economic disempowerment, 193–99
egalitarian time, 13–14, 21
emancipation
  psychic, 220–21
  self-emancipation, 3–4, 183, 190–91, 208–16, 220–24
  social, 179, 221, 222–23, 225–26
Engels, Friedrich, 3–4, 44–45
Enlightenment, 13–14, 32–33, 80
epistemic practices, 26–27, 29, 48–49, 94–95, 149–51, 167, 222, 223–24
ethnic ideology, 214

false consciousness, 23–24. *See also* consciousness and racial justice
Fanon, Frantz, 20–21, 145–75. *See also* racial fetishism
Floyd, George, 41, 52–53
forms of life
  constraints on, 28–32
  crisis consciousness and, 36–42
  culture and, 46
  introduction to, 12–18
  not-yet form of life, 43–52
  radical critiques of, 41–42
Forst, Rainer, 21, 153–54, 177, 189–90
freedom
  inhibition of, 16
  racial fetishism and, 149–54, 160–68
  self-emancipation and, 3–4, 183, 190–91, 208–16, 220–24

INDEX 251

social, 7–8, 48–49, 71–72, 112–13, 124, 126–27, 145, 148, 153–54, 161–62, 176, 177–78, 181–82, 197–99, 219
social unfreedoms, 123–24, 145, 175
universal, 215–16
French Revolution, 43–44, 214
future expectations, 50–52, 224–27

Garvey, Amy Jacques, 133
Garvey, Marcus, 10, 19–20, 102–3, 128, 130–43
Gilmore, Ruth Wilson, 4–5, 98–100
Gramsci, Antonio, 53

Habermas, Jürgen, 45
Hägglund, Martin, 16
Hahn, Steven, 141
Hamilton, Charles V., 178–79, 184–85
Hayek, F. A., 8–9, 27–28, 31–33, 48–49
Hayekian social theory, 33–36
Hegel, G. W. F., 66–67, 90
Heinrich, Michael, 165–66
Herder, Gottfried von, 75
Hoffman, Frederick L., 69

ideal-as-idealized-model, 1–2
incarceration, 4–5

Jaeggi, Rahel, 13, 40–41, 47–48, 74, 113–14
Jim Crow segregation, 9–10
justification narratives, 9–10, 109–10, 129, 140, 143, 144, 185–86, 189–90, 227
justifying beings, 153–54

Kant, Immanuel, 66–68
kingdom of culture, 58–59, 61–62, 65, 75, 80, 82, 92, 96
Koselleck, Reinhart, 50, 224–25

Lebron, Christopher J., 118–19, 127
Lenin, Vladimir, 181, 208–9
Levitas, Ruth, 3
liberalism, 8–9, 10–11, 13–14, 27–28, 76–77, 87–89, 102, 144, 179–80, 188–89, 212–15
lived crisis, 36–37

lived experience, 122–23, 145–48, 150–51, 152, 159–60, 173–74

Macpherson, C. B., 185–86
Maher, Chauncey, 107
Malcolm X, 137
Mao, Douglas, 10–11
Marx, Karl, 13, 20–21, 23–24, 187–88, 210–11, 219
materialism, 13–14, 82–84, 159–60, 210–11
Merton, Robert K., 16–17
Miles, Kevin Thomas, 89–90
Mills, Charles, 1–2, 13–14, 28–29
Milstein, Brian, 37–38
mirage and the real in utopianism, 95–97
Morrison, Toni, 4–5
Mumford, Lewis, 12
music of black folk, 85–95

natural time, 14–15
Negro problem, 68–69, 72–74, 78–79
Ng, Karen, 160–61
non-synchronicity, 19–20, 58–62, 64, 68–70, 80, 85–97, 99, 101, 111–13, 143, 174, 176, 194–95, 219, 223–25. *See also Ungleichzeitigkeit* (non-synchronicity)
normative expectations, 25–26, 38–45, 47–48, 50–55, 59–60, 154–55, 181, 186–87, 198, 201, 203, 213–17, 222, 224–26
not-yet form of life, 43–52
noumenal power, 189–90

objective crisis, 36, 37–38
original identity, 119–20, 124–25

Parks, Rosa, 134
Patterson, Orlando, 99–100
perfect justice, 7–8
petit-negre example, 156–59
Pinkard, Terry, 53–54
Plato, 57, 82–84
political injustice, 99
political philosophy, 1–2, 3–4, 119–20
political wrongs, 126–30
Popper, Karl, 8–9

possessive individualism, 185–86
power over, 14–15, 20–21, 26–27, 98–99, 108–9, 110–11, 121, 188–90, 195–96, 206–7, 216
practical dependence, 182–83, 198–99
practical distortion, 86–87, 177–78
pragmatic reform, 35
premature death, 4–5, 98–100
primitivism, 13–14, 92–93, 112–13
problem-space, 111–12
propaganda, 3–4, 139
psychic emancipation, 220–21

racial domination
  black nationalism and, 100–1, 105–6, 109, 112, 127–30, 144
  black power and, 176, 179, 184–85, 198–99, 224
  consciousness and racial justice, 28–29, 34–35, 56
  introduction to, 1–2, 3, 4–10, 14–15, 18–22
  racial fetishism and, 147–48, 163
racial fetishism (Fanon)
  Boggs on, 199–208
  civil rights and, 145
  cognitive and practical pathologies of, 174–75, 176–77
  colonialization of language, 154–60
  defined, 16, 20–21
  Du Bois on, 62, 86–87
  economic disempowerment and, 193–99
  freedom and, 149–54, 160–68
  intersubjectivity and, 154–60
  introduction to, 145–48
  racial domination and, 147–48, 163
  racial justice and, 168–74
  racism and, 148–52, 153–54, 157–60, 162–67, 170–71, 174–75
  reparations and, 168–74
  social action and, 160–68
  social reality and, 160–61, 165
  utopian consciousness and, 145–48, 167
  zone of non-being, 20–21, 170
racial injustice
  black nationalism and, 98–103
  capitalist power and, 187–89, 190–93, 198–99, 207, 217
  overview of, 18–22
  social domination and, 4–18, 98–99, 181–82, 205–6
  social theory and, 1–2, 4, 11, 18–21
racialization, 16, 58, 63–65, 88, 102–3, 143–44, 151–52, 164–65
racial justice
  black power and, 178–93
  Boggs on civil rights, 177–79, 184–89, 192, 194–96, 198–208, 210–15
  civil society and, 177, 184–86, 189–90, 195–96, 202, 210–11, 217
  racial fetishism and, 168–74
  social freedom and, 176, 177–78, 181–82, 197–99
  utopia and, 1–2, 5–7, 9–10, 15–16, 18–22, 52–55
  See also consciousness and racial justice
racism
  black nationalism and, 98–99, 112–13, 118–19, 124, 126–27, 128, 139
  consciousness and racial justice, 30–31, 41, 52–53
  defined, 4–5, 98–99
  Du Bois on, 62, 68–69, 71–74, 77–78, 82, 88, 92–94
  Fanon on, 148–52, 153–54, 157–60, 162–67, 170–71, 174–75
  as psychological flaw, 164
radical consciousness, 23, 39–40. *See also* consciousness and racial justice
Redecker, Eva von, 93
reparations, 168–74
Republic (Plato), 57
revolutionary ideology, 214
Rezsoházy, Rudolf, 6–7
Ricoeur, Paul, 9–10
rights externalism, 119–26
Robinson, Dean E., 112
Rogers, Melvin L., 100, 104–5, 123–24, 127
Ruge, Arnold, 65
ruling element, 114–15, 116–17, 120–21
Russian Revolution, 181, 214

Sartre, Jean-Paul, 226–27
Sawyer, Michael E., 137

INDEX 253

Scott, David, 111–12
self-determination, 12, 16–17, 96, 102, 121–22, 132–34, 150–51, 192–93, 213–14
self-emancipation, 3–4, 183, 190–91, 208–16, 220–24
Shaler, Nathan, 69–70
shared public, 106
Shaw, Stephanie, 91–92
Shklar, Judith, 8–9
Smith, Mark, 14–16
Smith, Mark H., 5–6
social disease, 126–27
social domination, 4–18, 98–99, 181–82, 205–6
social emancipation, 179, 221, 222–23, 225–26
social freedom, 7–8, 48–49, 71–72, 112–13, 124, 126–27, 145, 148, 153–54, 161–62, 176, 177–78, 181–82, 197–99, 219
social injustice, 99
social reality, 1–2, 24–25, 46–47, 66–67, 70–71, 89–90, 96–97, 160–61, 165, 176
social space and time, 103–13
social theory, 1–2, 4, 11, 18–21, 33–36, 37–38
social time, 4–5, 12–18, 34–35, 40–41, 48–49, 51–52, 60–61, 105–6, 170, 173–74, 175, 191–92, 198, 222–23
social unfreedoms, 123–24, 145, 175
Sorokin, Pitirim A., 16–17
The Souls of black Folk (Du Bois)
  anagnorisis, 76, 77–78, 79–80, 87, 89–90, 95
  black salvation, 78–84
  Chance and, 65–69, 70–71, 74, 93–96
  educational utopianism, 71–78
  introduction to, 57–64
  kingdom of culture, 58–59, 61–62, 65, 75, 80, 82, 92, 96
  mirage and the real, 95–97
  Negro problem, 68–69, 72–74, 78–79
  racism and, 62, 68–69, 71–74, 77–78, 82, 88, 92–94
  social reality and, 70–71, 89–90, 96–97

Talented Tenth, 19, 64, 78–97, 226–27
  utopianism of, 57–78, 82–83, 85–97
space of reasons
  black nationalism and, 102–3, 106–11, 113, 115–16, 119, 120–21, 125–26, 131–32, 135–36, 138–39, 143–44
  Boggs on, 176, 186–87, 198, 204, 208
  Fanon on, 150–51, 173–75
  introduction to, 19–20, 219
State and Revolution (Lenin), 181, 208–9
subjection-qualification, 190, 192, 208
Swain, Dan, 3
systemic crisis, 36–37
systemic racism, 30–31, 41, 52–53

Talented Tenth, 19, 64, 78–97, 226–27
temporally out of joint, 18–19, 58–59, 78, 98–99, 227
Therborn, Göran, 190, 209–10
Thompson, Mark Christian, 137–38
true self-consciousness, 76, 81
Ture, Kwame, 178–79, 184–85, 215

Ungleichzeitigkeit (non-synchronicity), 19–20, 58–59, 145, 176. *See also* non-synchronicity
United Negro Improvement Association, 102
universal freedom, 215–16
Universal Intelligence, 139–40
utopian consciousness, 18–19, 26–28, 43–52, 55–56, 71–72, 133–34, 145–48, 167, 209–10, 219–22, 223–24, 225–27. *See also* consciousness and racial justice
utopian temporality, 170, 172, 173–74, 176, 227
utopia/utopianism
  black nationalism and, 10, 19–20
  critical theory of, 4–11, 16–17, 55, 59, 96–97, 145–46, 161–62, 217, 222–23, 226–27
  as historical tendency, 1–4
  mirage and the real in, 95–97
  racial domination and, 1–2, 3, 4–6, 14–15, 18–22
  racial justice and, 1–2, 5–7, 9–10, 15–16, 18–22, 52–55

utopia/utopianism (*cont.*)
 social domination and, 4–11
 social relations and, 1–2, 3, 9–11, 18–21
 in *The Souls of black Folk* (Du Bois), 57–78, 82–83, 85–97

voting and black nationalism, 115–16

Washington, Booker T., 86, 131

Weeks, Kathi, 35, 226–27
welfare rights, 180–81
white power, 177–78, 187–93, 198–99, 207, 217
Wood, Ellen Meiksins, 180
Wynter, Sylvia, 220–22

Žižek, Slavoj, 153
zone of non-being, 20–21, 170